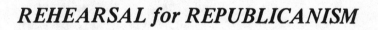

REHEARSAL for REPUBLICANISM

Kennikat Press
National University Publications
Series in Political Science

JOHN MAYFIELD

REHEARSAL
for
REPUBLICANISM

Free Soil
and the
Politics of Antislavery

National University Publications
KENNIKAT PRESS // 1980
Port Washington, N.Y. // London

for Carol

Manufactured in the United States of America

Published by
Kennikat Press Corp.
Port Washington, N.Y. / London

Library of Congress Cataloging in Publication Data

Mayfield, John, 1945-
  Rehearsal for Republicanism.

  (National university publications)
  Includes bibliographical references and index.
  1. United States–Politics and government–1849-
1861. 2. Free-Soil Party. 3. Slavery in the United
States–Anti-slavery movements. I. Title.
E415.7.M26   320.9'73'06   79-23903
ISBN 0-8046-9253-X

CONTENTS

	INTRODUCTION	3
1.	*THE BARNBURNERS*	8
2.	*THE CONSCIENCE WHIGS*	34
3.	*THE LIBERTY PARTY*	60
4.	*THE WILMOT PROVISO*	80
5.	*1848*	101
6.	*COALITIONS AND DIVISIONS*	126
7.	*COMPROMISE AND DISSENT*	148
8.	*"THE WORK IS TO BE DONE OVER"*	167
	EPILOGUE	184
	STATISTICAL APPENDIX AND MAPS	191
	NOTES	203
	INDEX	219

ACKNOWLEDGMENTS

No historian works alone. In preparing this work I have often been helped by people I know and people I have never met. The footnotes indicate some of my intellectual debts; these acknowledgments tell of my personal ones. For their aid to a wary and harried traveler, I thank the staffs of the many libraries and historical societies which I visited throughout the North. They were more than patient in giving me a place to work and materials to work with. As good typists, Ms. Dorothy Leathers and Ms. Natalie Schick of the University of Kentucky put up with far more deadlines than they should have, and always managed to meet them. Professors Michael Baer and William Baldwin of the same institution helped me with the complexities of statistical analysis and computer programing. Professors Lance Banning, Eric Christianson, and Robert Seager II, all of the University of Kentucky, were kind but thorough critics at various stages of the manuscript.

I owe special debts to James P. Shenton of Columbia, who first encouraged me to study antislavery as an ideological movement, and to Milton Cummings of Johns Hopkins, who helped clarify my thinking on the role of ideology in politics. Ronald G. Walters, also of Johns Hopkins, offered suggestions and criticisms that were unfailingly on the mark. Professor David Herbert Donald of Harvard University was immensely helpful to me during the early stages of my work, and has been warmly generous with his support ever since.

The mistakes, however, are mine.

ABOUT THE AUTHOR

John Mayfield is Director of Special Programs and Interdisciplinary Studies at the University of Kentucky. He developed an early interest in reform movements and their ideologies, and continued to pursue this topic at Johns Hopkins University, where he received his Ph.D. Dr. Mayfield has held several fellowships including one from the Ford Foundation. He is coauthor of the forthcoming second edition of *The New Nation, 1800-1845.*

INTRODUCTION

SHORTLY before the election of 1848 Horace Greeley, editor of the Whig New York *Tribune,* penned a long letter to a young friend in Indiana. Greeley had reluctantly concluded to remain a Whig that year, although he did not like the party candidate, Zachary Taylor, nor did he favor his party's position of compromise with the South concerning slavery. He would vote for Taylor only because—if the Whig party failed—"some good men I love would be crushed beneath its ruins." Still, he liked the principles of the Free Soilers, "the only live party around us. It ought to triumph, but God works out his ends by other instruments than majorities. Wherefore it will fail, but fail gloriously." In another part of the North the abolitionist William Lloyd Garrison saw Free Soil in similar terms. "I long to see the day," Garrison wrote, "when the great issue with the Slave Power, of the immediate dissolution of the Union, will be made by all the free States; for then the conflict will be a short and decisive one, and liberty will triumph. The free soil party inevitably leads to it, and hence I hail it as the beginning of the end."[1]

Greeley was a party man; Garrison never voted. Yet the observations of each were based on the same point. Both recognized that the two-party system of Whigs and Democrats could not survive a prolonged debate over the issue of slavery. Before 1848 American politics had been based on a delicate, intersectional alliance of diverse interests and conflicting desires which gathered themselves into two loose organizations that scrupulously avoided any topic likely to polarize voters along moral or sectional lines. The system had worked well, for it encouraged compromise in an age of continental and economic expansion. As national organizations, however, the parties were

3

poorly served by issues that were simultaneously moral and sectional. George W. Julian, another abolitionist, seized upon this point when surveying the wreckage of the party system in the early 1850s. Southerners, he concluded, "saw clearly that what slavery needed was two pretty evenly divided parties, pitted against each other upon economic issues . . . ; and they were justly alarmed at the prospect of a new movement, basing its action upon moral grounds." The "new movement" of which Julian wrote was Republicanism, yet its appearance as a major party could not have taken place had the two-party system not already broken down. Perhaps the collapse would have occurred inevitably, but it was hastened by the rise during the 1840s of Free Soil.[2]

Much of this study of Free Soil is narrative, based on the assumption that one cannot understand how or why a third party appears without knowing something of the personalities, platforms, and politicking which goes into the formation of any political movement. The narrative, however, is organized around two related themes which are common to any political reform. The first concerns the ideology of Free Soil. Contrary to what some historians and political scientists say, Americans are quite capable of basing their political action on ideals. American parties exist, to some, as no more than mass machines, organized simply to obtain office and dispense power, devoid of any ideological context. In recent years, however, historians have rediscovered the role of ideology in American life, applying it to topics as diverse as the Revolution, education, and economic enterprise. Eric Foner's study of Republicanism, for example, unfolds a rich and persuasive ideology which permeated the antebellum north. Since Republicans borrowed freely from Free Soilers, it seems only logical to examine the latter movement for its ideals. Ideology was vital to Free Soil, its very life blood.[3]

A definition of the term may be in order. "Ideology," as used here, does not refer to the sort of structured, logical articulation of beliefs that is properly the sphere of the philosopher or trained political theorist. The term suggests, rather, the complex pattern of values, attitudes, preconceptions, and even prejudices that are part of every person's special cultural heritage. Free Soil had its share of intellectuals and theoreticians, some of whom made significant contributions to the evolution of an antislavery ideology. On another level, however, were the journalists, speechmakers, and letter writers who were not intellectuals in any formal sense, but who were able to articulate their feelings and opinions concerning the threat of slavery. That these opinions were often vague and sometimes contradictory did not neutralize their impact upon sympathetic voters. The silent thousands who vote for any reform presumably do so because that reform speaks to their concerns. It is reasonable to assume that they were familiar with the ideological stance of their leaders, and that the positions taken by the leadership made sense. Ideology of this sort may in fact be one good way of peering into the mind of the ordinary voter.[4]

The ideology of Free Soil was not monolithic. Free Soilers came from many backgrounds and possessed many interpretations of what the good society should be, yet the threat of an expanding slave empire threatened each, in his own way, and formed the basis for a common movement. The first chapters of this study, then, trace the ideologies of three groups which were prominent in Free Soil: Conscience Whigs in Massachusetts and Ohio; Radical Democrats in New York; and Liberty men. The last are a special group, since they had already formed a political party opposed to slavery. Their hatred of slavery was total, so much of the discussion of their beliefs concerns their internal debate over the question of tactics. How could one best organize to defeat the political power of slavery? The first two groups, on the other hand, were directly descended from the major parties. They were not representative of those parties, nor were they divorced completely from them. Each drew upon the ideology of its parent organization, and each constructed an attack on slavery within this broader context. All three factions disagreed on several essential points, but merged their protest under the banner of the Wilmot Proviso—the simple plan to end slavery by confining it to the South.

The second theme within the narrative deals with political action. Ideology, however persuasive, does not stand alone. It is shaped, modified, supported, and undermined by its political context. Free Soilers matured during the age of the second party system and thus inherited certain organizational forms, constitutional and electoral limitations, and types of leadership and voter recruitment which both helped and hampered them. In certain respects, then, Free Soilers were no different from Whigs or Democrats. They existed as a genuinely national party only in years in which the presidency was at stake. Otherwise, Free Soil began and lived in the states. Again, the three factions examined here provide different examples of how a peculiar political climate affects the growth and death of reform. Conscience Whigs in Massachusetts operated in a political world that was dominated by Whigs. Radical Democrats in New York, on the other hand, voiced their protest almost completely within the parameters of the Democratic party. In Ohio Free Soil was a delicate combination of men sympathetic to three parties—Whig, Democratic, and Liberty—and emerged in a state where the two-party rivalry was intense. In each state political stresses merged with ideology, and vice versa, to propel dissidents into the formation of a new party.

To implement their ideology, Free Soilers realized that they must have political power. Securing and maintaining office is a need common to all parties, but it is especially pressing to reform movements, where lack of numbers must be offset by a skillful manipulation of the everyday game of politics. There were those Free Soilers who thought sincerely that the party could exist solely as a national movement. In this they were overconfident of the appeal of ideology in winning the affections of mass numbers of voters. Most Free Soilers recognized that a successful movement must build state and local bases of power to sustain the party from one presidential election to the next. For them the major question after 1848 was easy to state, hard to resolve: should Free Soilers remain independent, or should they form coalitions with one or the other of the major parties in an attempt to secure office?

Here Free Soilers discovered that—just as politics affects ideology—ideology affects politics. All Free Soilers had once been members of another party, and the memory of that party—whichever one it was—lingered after 1848. These old inclinations were present whenever Free Soilers met to discuss the problem of forming coalitions. What began as an issue of tactical expediency soon became one of fundamental beliefs as each faction attempted to impose its preferences on the others. The predictable result was a series of bitter internal fights which left Free Soilers divided and disheartened. In time those who favored coalitions found themselves outcast, and Free Soil fell into the hands of men who—using the ill feeling left by the debates—kept the party independent and small.

It is tempting, of course, to praise one faction and damn the other. Some have held the independents in high esteem for their moral courage and refusal to compromise. Others have seen the coalitionists as realists who knew that politics is a game of power as well as principles. Both positions have their merits and shortcomings. There is a fine line between courage and stubbornness, and an equally fine line between compromise and surrender. It is hoped that both viewpoints have been treated fairly here.

Whatever the ultimate causes of the death of Free Soil, the movement counted several successes. Confronted by an electorate that was not accustomed to discussing slavery and by a party system that was unwilling to take a forthright stand on the issue, Free Soilers

proved that ideology could be a major force in American politics. *Thesis*
They developed an attack on slavery that was rich enough and varied
enough to provide the raw materials for the ideology of Republicanism. And, by disrupting the normal course of the two-party
system, they helped make it possible for a larger, more powerful
assault on slavery to take form.

CHAPTER ONE

THE BARNBURNERS

THE opinion most widely held is that John Tyler was among the most inept politicians ever to occupy the White House. Thrown into the presidency by the accident of William Henry Harrison's death, a Democrat living amid a nest of Whigs, obstinate, sour, and snobbish as only a Virginia aristocrat could be, Tyler succeeded in making few political friends and countless enemies. Yet he was, despite his faults, a man of vision and ambition. Ambition, in that he desperately wanted a second term as president. Vision, in that he saw clearly the westward drive of American expansionism and the promise of a United States that would extend unbroken from the Atlantic to the Pacific. Each of these traits found expression—late in Tyler's term— in a single issue, the annexation of the Republic of Texas. Tyler's relentless pursuit of Texas won him little support in his quest for another term, but it did make Texas the primary issue in the campaign of 1844.[1]

Annexation was more than a presidential dream. The acquisition of Texas had many supporters in the North, where it was linked to the addition of the Oregon Territory and the fulfillment of a continental empire. Texas was also popular in the South; there, however, it took on an added urgency. For the South Texas was more than a luxury. It was a matter of defense and survival. As the eastern South languished amid worn-out soils and economic depression, many southerners— like Tyler—had become convinced that the Cotton Kingdom must expand or face extinction. Southern entrepreneurs needed the fresh lands west of the Mississippi for their slaves and their cotton, and

Texas, vast and empty, seemed ideal. Moreover, if the United States did not absorb Texas, Britain might. This posed a threat no southerner could ignore, for Britain had abolished slavery in 1833 and was now courting Texas with promises of trade and money. Should the British gain a foothold in the Southwest, southern slaveholders faced the unsettling prospect of a free republic on the Gulf Coast.

The presidential election of 1844 was crucial to the fulfillment of these desires. Whig or Democrat, southerners needed and demanded an executive who would move quickly to annex Texas—with slavery. Tyler was so massively unpopular that few seriously considered him as a candidate; yet in the spring of that year, as the nominating conventions drew near, no other prominent contender had emerged who was both capable of winning and committed to annexation. Those who could in fact win—Martin Van Buren of the Democrats and Henry Clay of the Whigs—were uncertainties in the southern mind. So a southern strategy emerged: stall the major candidates, bind up the conventions, and wait patiently until the proper man could be found. Whether this tactic was the product of careful political planning or simply a natural posture, it had the effect of generating a crisis in the second American party system and a rebellion among those in the North who, for whatever reasons, saw Texas as a threat.

Among the most unlikely groups to have opposed annexation were the loyal partisans of Martin Van Buren. They traveled under various names. Some called them Barnburners, after the legendary and overzealous Dutch farmer who burned his barn to rid it of rats. Neither Van Buren nor his supporters much liked the title, since it suggested they were unrealistic, perhaps a bit daft. They preferred to be called Radical Democrats, because they conceived of themselves as the true heirs of Jeffersonian republicanism—the best and surest defenders of a proud tradition. They combined this idealism with a tough professionalism that made them consummate politicians. Radicals were hardworking, incredibly patient, and generally successful. In their home state of New York they excited both fanatical loyalty and respectful fear.[2]

Their leaders bore yet another name, the Albany Regency. Van Buren was its unquestioned head—the saloonkeeper's son who had clawed his way expertly from the tavern to the White House. His ablest lieutenant was Silas Wright from the St. Lawrence, a quiet man with an enormous influence that he never quite wanted. Following Wright were William L. Marcy, who became governor of New York in

1834, Azariah C. Flagg, the state comptroller, and Benjamin F. Butler, Jackson's attorney general. As time passed, the Regency attracted younger men, among them Preston King, Wright's exuberant and erratic protégé from the St. Lawrence, and two lawyers from New York City—Samuel J. Tilden and John A. Dix. There was also the President's promising, if temperamental, son John. Among them they built a party machine during the 1820s and 1830s that was a model of efficiency and energy. "I do not believe that a stronger political combination ever existed at any state capital, or even at the national capital," wrote Thurlow Weed, their staunchest opponent. "They were men of great ability, great industry, indomitable courage, and strict personal integrity. Their influence and power for nearly twenty years was almost as potential in national as in state politics."[3]

Van Buren's presidency should have been the high point of the Radicals' prestige and power. Instead, it was four long years of frustration—years spent in an ineffectual attempt to lift the nation from a grinding depression, and years spent watching the opposition consolidate as Whigs. In 1840 the inevitable happened as Van Buren saw his chance for a second term evaporate. Yet Harrison's death and Tyler's disastrous presidency offered hope for 1844. As the campaign approached, the Regency formed a virtual shadow cabinet, confidently awaiting the call back to Washington.[4]

By the spring of 1844, however, Radicals sensed a growing unrest within their party at the prospect of another Van Buren candidacy. Democrats were desperately anxious to regain the White House, and some—among them old friends—suggested that Van Buren was not the man to lead the party to victory. Their reasons were simple: Van Buren had lost popularity as President; he bore the mark of a loser. Beyond this was the unsettling question of Texas. Southern Democrats, especially John C. Calhoun, were properly chary of trusting Van Buren with annexation. Van Buren as President had quietly set Texas aside. There was no guarantee that he would not do so again. During February and March both these arguments against Van Buren merged and became, instead of discreet suggestions, ultimatums.[5]

Radicals conveniently ignored the fact that Van Buren was indeed a weak candidate and concentrated on their southern opposition. In their view of the situation, the nomination and their power in the party were slipping away at the urging of a small group. Texas had been unwisely and prematurely injected into the campaign; Texas was the fetish of southerners; all those southerners were slaveholders. The specter of a conspiracy began to take hold in the Radical mind—a conspiracy of slaveholders to use Texas to deny them a restoration.

The swiftness and thoroughness with which that specter took hold during 1844 suggested that it had roots going deep in the Radicals' perception of their world. Radicals had, in a sense, been conditioned by their own ideology to see such things.

"Whatever weaknesses I may be subject to—and doubtless they are numerous—dogmatism, I am very sure, is not one of them."[6] Van Buren was technically correct; neither he nor any of the Radicals had a well-formed, articulated ideology. What they did have was a world view, a set of preconceptions, values, and attitudes that opened their eyes to some things and closed them to others. For them certain symbols or events took on meanings quite different from those perceived by others. They interpreted the world around them as their attitudes led them to interpret it. Perhaps what is equally important, their world view caused them to look for what was not—on close inspection—real as well as what was. The line between the two was not always sharp. Hence in a given situation Radicals took the facts available to them, narrowed those facts to a pertinent few, and then interpreted them in light of convictions that were more felt than spoken. No other segment of Free Soil was less intellectual or more dogmatic.

As Radicals were quick to admit, they were the nineteenth-century heirs of a world view that could be traced directly back to the Jeffersonian republicans. The Jeffersonian tradition was complex and many-sided; even to call it "Jeffersonian" is too narrow, for that label ignores many of its most articulate spokesmen such as John Taylor of Caroline or James Madison. Still, inspired by the writings of classical writers such as Polybius and Cicero and English political theorists such as James Harrington and Lord Bolingbroke, Jeffersonians developed a theory of government that was at once both conservative and radical. At the heart of their republicanism lay an emphasis on the virtue of the independent citizen.[7]

Virtue, as the English Whigs defined it, meant an absolute independence of the responsible citizen from the pressures, patronage, and influence of others and a capacity to place the public welfare above private needs. It could, and should, be exercised by any class or estate, be it monarch, aristocrat, or commoner. As the Jeffersonians interpreted it, however, virtue was most firmly seated in one particular class. "The small landholders are the most precious part of a state," Jefferson assured Madison. They were independent because they earned their livelihood from the soil, by their own efforts and by the grace of nature and God. Hence the small landholders were the surest defenders of natural rights and the repositories of virtue, which Jefferson defined as the ability to see the "utility" behind laws, their usefulness and practicability in promoting the public good. Although yeoman farmers might occasionally be led astray, their inherent virtue and utilitarianism would ultimately bring them back to first principles. "In general," Jefferson advised John Adams, "they will elect the really good and wise."[8]

Jefferson's preoccupation with true leadership stemmed from these convictions. He was eager to redefine the meaning of aristocrat. To him the aristocrat was not ordained by birth or special privilege, but grew to his station through the exercise of superior talent and wisdom. Again he returned to the small landholder for his source. "There is a natural aristocracy among men," he announced in the same letter to Adams. "The grounds of this are virtue and talents. There is also an artificial aristocracy, founded on wealth and birth, without either virtue or talents." To insure the ascendancy of the natural aristocrat, it was necessary to divide power as equally as possible among the people to keep it from slipping into the hands of a few. On this John Taylor, who identified the farmer as the only source of virtue, was explicit. "Where power is not an exclusive, but a general interest, agriculture can employ its own energies for the attainment of its own happiness."[9]

To this optimistic assessment of the promise of republicanism, Jeffersonians added a portion of fear. Virtue was the supreme good, yet it struggled daily with corruption. Again borrowing from Harrington and the country Whigs, Jeffersonians argued that any ruling group was prone to abuse its powers in the quest for personal gain. The court of George III had proved to be corruptive of the rights of Englishmen, and that conviction had prompted the revolutionary generation to the defense of their own rights. Artificial aristocracies, with privileges and power to tempt them, could be easily duped. So, alas, could democracies.

The sources of corruption were readily identified. Anything that tended to concentrate power, create a class of dependents, and thus upset the natural equality of a republican society eroded liberty. The resulting inequality could be either social or political, or both. Great disparities in the division of wealth led to an impoverished class dependent upon the rich. The rich, in turn, could use the offices of government to reinforce their own status. Artificial aristocracies were the worst offenders in a democracy, for they assumed powers and privileges by which the virtuous citizen could be manipulated and ultimately enslaved. There were ample means of doing this. Persons who by influence or wealth governed for life or for long periods would in time come to confuse the public good with their own self-interest. They would turn themselves into courtiers, dependent upon the favor of the executive rather than the will of the people. Similarly, once possessed of administrative power, they were prone to attempt to take over the very means of forming the law itself. Where the government could change laws of its own accord, it further removed itself from any responsibility to the people. "An *elective despotism* was not the government we fought for," argued Jefferson. Finally, and most insidiously, artificial aristocracies, by manipulating the finances of the country, would make the plain republican their economic slave. Money begat power, and power begat money. Banks, taxes, or levies of any sort created an elite that did not sweat in the fields and factories yet grew powerful in their idleness. Society, argued Taylor "is thus unavoidably thrown into two divisions. One containing all those who pay, and the other those who receive contributions, required either for public use, or to foster private avarice or ambition."[10]

To prevent corruption from setting in, it was necessary to set strict limits upon power. The means of patronage must be limited. Rotation in office would preclude the emergence of a "court." Legislative tyranny must be resisted by constant reference to the popular will. Control of the nation's finances must be placed in the hands of the people, whose healthy competitiveness and practical wisdom would prevent it from being abused by a clique. Finally, and most importantly, the common republican must be ever watchful. Men might form a plan or clique for the best of reasons and still be unable to resist the temptations of power. This was natural and unavoidable; but it was corruptive nonetheless. "Human nature is the same on every side of the Atlantic," Jefferson had declared, "and will be alike influenced by the same causes. The time to guard against corruption and tyranny, is before they shall have gotten hold on us. It is better to keep the wolf out of the fold, than to trust to drawing his teeth and talons after he shall have entered."[11]

These concepts were the nucleus of Jeffersonian thought, although they did not exhaust the range and scope of eighteenth-century republican ideology. Jefferson's fear of the cities, his love for the French, as well as Taylor's singleminded devotion to agriculture, for example, did not survive the transition into the nineteenth century. Jefferson's own presidency succeeded in lowering the national debt but left the national bank largely intact. His use of patronage, moreover, set standards which later presidents studiously followed. Yet the adoration of republican virtue and the fear of corruption persisted, and by the 1830s Barnburners had transformed the core of republicanism, had added to it, and had made it their own.

The clearest expression of the Barnburner world view appeared in the *United States Magazine and Democratic Review* in its premier issue of October, 1837. In two articles on the "Democratic Principle" and the Panic, the editor, John L. O'Sullivan, attempted to define republicanism and vindicate it from "the charges daily brought against it," a task which the Panic and Van Buren's endangered presidency had made necessary. Working closely with loyal Radicals such as Bryant and Theodore Sedgwick, Jr., O'Sullivan formulated a theory of democratic rule that closely paralleled Jeffersonianism.[12]

The heart of every republic was its workingmen. "We have an abiding confidence in the virtue, intelligence, and full capacity for self-government, of the great mass of our people—our industrious, honest, manly, intelligent millions of freemen," O'Sullivan announced. This great mass was not limited to the small landholders, but included the urban workers and artisans who tended the business of an expanding, entrepreneurial country and who formed a vital part of the Democratic party. This shift in the Jeffersonian emphasis did not, however, destroy the basic tenet that independent citizens—whatever their occupation—were the surest defenders of democracy. The collective virtue of society proceeded from the individual virtue of its members. This paralleled the law of nature, which achieved its harmony from the constant interplay of its parts. As the Creator had instilled laws of "free competition and association" in nature, all overseen by a guiding benevolence, so did republics. "Afford but the single nucleus of a system of administration of justice between man and man, and, under the sure operation of this principle, the floating atoms will distribute and combine themselves, as we see in the beautiful natural process of crystallization, into a . . . perfect and harmonious result." Republics, then, far from tending to anarchy, were inherently stable.[13]

But virtue, as ever, was under attack, this time under the sophism of minority rights. Translated, the defense of minority rights was in reality an attempt to perpetuate the same artificial aristocracy deplored by Jefferson. Aristocrats, arguing that their "more enlightened wisdom" and their possession of property gave them a "stake in the community," naturally concluded that the "popular opinion and will must not be trusted with the supreme and absolute direction of the general interests." This, according to the Barnburners, was dangerous nonsense. As Jefferson had pointed out, mistakes in the popular will might sometimes occur, but in general the masses would perceive their own best interests. Moreover, the dissemination of knowledge through education and the press had refuted any claim that the wealthy were more intelligent. Finally, majorities by their very nature could never live off the minority. The reverse was true, for minorities used the labor of the ordinary man to surround themselves with "wealth, splendor, and power" and to perpetuate "those artificial social distinctions which violate the natural equality of rights of the human race."[14]

They did so through government. "Understood as a central consolidated power, managing and directing the various general interests of the society," the editor explained, "all government is evil, and the parent of evil." Again, the problem was the corrupting temptations of power. "No human depositories can with safety, be trusted with the power of legislation upon the general interests of society so as to operate directly or indirectly on the industry and property of the community," O'Sullivan pointed out. "Such power must be perpetually liable to the most pernicious abuse, from the natural imperfection . . . of all human legislation, exposed constantly to the pressure of partial interests." Similar warnings came from the pen of William Leggett, who wrote for the New York *Evening Post.* "All acts of partial legislation are undemocratic," Leggett stated. "They are subversive of the equal rights of men; are calculated to create artificial inequality in human condition; . . . and, in their final operation to build up a peaceful aristocracy."[15]

It was the holy mission, then, of the Radical Democrats to simplify government and to purge it of all vestiges of corruption. Amid the burgeoning entrepreneurialism of Jacksonian America, the most likely means by which corruption could work its influence, and aristocracy take root, lay in the manipulation of money. Radicals praised Jackson's war on the Second United States Bank and explained the Panic that followed as the result of the Bank's misdeeds. The *Democratic Review* argued that the entire crisis was brought on by the attempts of a financial aristocracy to secure their influence by linking the power of money with the power of government. By issuing credit banks enslaved even the smallest retail merchant; commercial men became their "dupes." The American equivalent of an English "court" was the result. "The entire business community . . . became thus dependent, as it were, for its life-blood, on these institutions. They stood in the perpetual relation of applicants for, and dispensers of, 'accommodation.' " To liberate the ordinary republican from this manipulation, it was necessary to remove the government, once and for all, from the direction of financial policy. It was also necessary for the people to remain vigilant watchmen against any future effort to abuse power. The people, Leggett wrote (in terms borrowed almost intact from the Jeffersonians) "cannot be too jealous of the exercise of unnecessary powers by the state government. The nearer they kept all power to their own hands, and the more entirely under their own eyes, the more secure are they in their freedom and equal rights."[16]

But how, exactly, were the people to retain their power? Jefferson's prescription had been both vague and complex, involving rotation in office, limited government, and the protection of the small landholder from the poison of cities and their mobs of dependent laborers. To offset Jefferson's fear of mob rule, Barnburners turned to the organized political party. Here they made their most radical break with the teachings of their mentor.

In the decade following the War of 1812, Van Buren carefully constructed what was at that time the most efficient, systematic, and tightly run state party in the nation. He did so from both expediency and conviction. The initial impulse came from the need to remove DeWitt Clinton as governor and as leader of the New York Democratic party. Clinton had long used his power of appointment to staff governmental offices, and he did so from a firm belief that only the "best men"—certainly not saloonkeeper's sons—should rule. The Bucktails, as Van Buren's group was then called, chafed under Clinton's patriarchal rule, yet there was little they could do to oust him, for he held his office by nomination of the party caucus.

Patient as always, Van Buren used the caucus itself to remove his enemy. Publicly he swore fealty to the caucus and praised it as the voice of the people. Privately he worked to undermine Clinton's strength. By 1820 he had succeeded in persuading many of his party that their allegiance lay first with the caucus and only second with the man. Thus, when he had finally gathered enough votes to overturn Clinton's majority, he defended his action by proclaiming simply that the people had spoken. Later, when the caucus system had succumbed to the convention, he supported the latter's nominees on the same ground.[17]

This was more than brilliant politics, however. It rested on an entirely new concept of parties. Van Buren and the men who followed him had been raised amid party strife. They had worked their way into positions of influence by supporting their party completely and unquestioningly. As a result, they lacked the fear of parties which haunted Jefferson's generation. Washington had warned of the "baneful influence" of party competition in his farewell address—believing, as did most of his peers, that parties were merely factions writ large. Factionalism ran counter to the eighteenth-century notion of an enlightened leadership that labored to bring about a republican consensus. The idea that parties were essential to the democratic process was unthinkable. Yet it was precisely this idea that defined Van Buren's attitude toward them. "Political parties," he wrote, "are inseparable from free governments."[18]

At first glance parties—with their discipline and patronage—might appear to conflict with the Jeffersonian tradition. In fact, they modernized it. To begin, they provided the essential forum in which public issues could be debated. Enos Throop, who replaced Van Buren as governor in 1829, stated the matter concisely: "Organized parties watch and scan each other's doings"; through them "the public mind is instructed by ample discussions of public measures, and acts of violence are restrained by the convictions of the people, that the prevailing measures are the results of enlightened reason." Thus parties were a check on the anarchistic tendencies inherent in a democracy.[19]

By exposing conflicts to public scrutiny parties held corruption in check. The tendency to do evil as well as good was merely part of human nature, and some effective barrier to the selfish graspings of mortal man was needed. Parties were an effective remedy. They were, according to Throop, the "vigilant watchman, over the conduct of those in power." By exposing the acts and designs of leaders to the popular eye, parties provided the people with yet another restraint on the abuse of power. "Doubtless excesses frequently attend them and produce many evils, but not so many as are prevented by the maintenance of their organization and vigilance," Van Buren concluded. "This disposition to abuse power, so deeply planted in the human heart, can by no other means be more effectually checked."[20]

Parties became, in effect, the agents by which Jefferson's independent citizens could control government, and the expression of their control was the popular will. All branches of government, wrote O'Sullivan, "should be dependent with equal directness and promptness on the influence of public opinion; the popular will would be equally the animating and moving spirit of them all." Public opinion, echoed Throop, "exercising its moral power over the conduct of partizans, applies correctives, through regular party discipline, to such abuses in individual conduct as cannot be reached by the ordinary operation of the laws."[21]

And "regular party discipline," as Throop noted, was essential to the functioning of parties. No one should, with impunity, violate the wishes of his constituents. To do so would be an arrogant slap at the will of the majority. Any man, wrote Jabez Hammond, the Barnburner historian, "elected by a political party, *because* he professes to be a member of that party," and who then changed his opinions, "ought, in such case, to give back the power which has been committed to him by his constituents." This made strict allegiance to the will of the caucus (and later the convention) a moral test. The "sole object of caucussing is to ascertain what is the will of the majority," Hammond concluded. "Unless you intend to carry into effect the wishes of the majority, however contrary to your own, you have no business at a caucus." Coincidentally, this representative accountability helped preserve the Jeffersonian maxim of rotation in office.[22]

Patronage helped enforce the decisions of the majority. Marcy's assertion that "to the victor belong the spoils" may have reeked of Toryism in the eighteenth century, but in the nineteenth it became a means of rewarding the pursuit of republican ideals. Those like Marcy and Van Buren who had patiently and assiduously labored for the success of republican principles deserved the rewards of office. By their virtue and talents they had fulfilled Jefferson's prescription for the natural aristocrat and would move into positions of power accordingly. Moreover, adherence to party principles, backed by patronage, was a sure means for the common man to gain political power. It was a ladder of promotion, but to be effective it had to be grounded in discipline and faithfulness.

But what of the opposition, who pursued the same offices and commanded widespread support? Radicals viewed the existence of an opposing party as natural and even beneficial. The "healthful fluctuations of the will of the people, incident to popular government," according to Throop, insured not only that vital issues would be discussed but also that the republican majority would necessarily stay attuned to the popular will. Whenever they did, the corrective of failure would remind them of their responsibilities.[23]

Of one thing, however, Radicals were convinced. The party of Jefferson and his heirs was the only one based on true republican principles. All others fell into two categories. Either they were factions, "personal parties, whose spirit is overwrought passion, whose object of pursuit is vengeance," or they were coalitions of the misinformed. Followers—as distinct from leaders—of the Whigs "do not rightly understand the questions at issue, in their true popular bearings," O'Sullivan maintained; if the proper foundations of republicanism could be grasped by all, "they would soon be ranged, by the hundreds of thousands, under the broad and bright folds of our democratic banner." To Van Buren this happy event was simply a matter of time. On all the issues that had divided aristocrats from republicans in American history, the people had eventually "decided them in favor of the Republican creed." To pursue republicanism and to champion the Democratic party, then, were one and the same. "In its true character & feelings," he wrote of his party at the end of his career, "it is the only political party which is in harmony with the genius of our Government & the feelings of the great body of the people."[24]

These interpretations of republicanism and partisanship ultimately formed the basis of the Barnburner revolt against the South. During the 1820s and the 1830s Radicals had carried their creed easily and well, fighting the Bank, high tariffs, and federal support of internal improvements with a steady conviction that in doing so they were maintaining virtue and guarding against corruption. They had seldom thought of the South except in terms of another political ally in a holy cause. Yet Texas annexation, and the southern role in it, violated their concepts of republicanism. The campaign of 1844 offended their sense of party.

The dilemma in annexation revolved around a basic conflict in the desires of the North. On the one hand lay an optimistic faith in the correctness and ultimate propriety of American expansion, not only to Texas but to Oregon and the rest of the continent as well. Many assented to Jackson's declaration that annexation would "extend the area of Freedom" and block all further European pretensions in North America. Others simply regarded continental expansion as inevitable. Van Buren's friend and editor of the Washington *Globe,* Francis Preston Blair, Sr., declared that Americans "like all high-spirited industrious Republicans will never have enough while anything is left to their enterprise. The Organ of *Acquisitiveness,*" he added, "is very strongly developed in our people especially the Democracy." It was all part of "our manifest destiny," as O'Sullivan termed it, "to overspread and to possess the whole of the continent which Providence has given us for the . . . great experiment of liberty."[25]

Yet beneath the ebullient optimism lay fears that expansion, especially into the Southwest, was filled with problems that could seriously compromise the "great experiment." Most obvious was the threat of war. Though many Democrats, such as Wright, were ready to see Texas admitted "as soon as it can be done in a proper and constitutional manner, with the free concurrence and consent of Texas," they insisted that annexation must take place "without a violation of sacred Treaty obligations with other powers." The other power was Mexico, which stubbornly refused to yield its claims north of the Rio Grande. Each new Mexican government since 1836 had claimed Texas, despite eight years of failing to regain a single inch of the disputed territory. By 1844 no settlement short of war seemed possible.[26]

It was not the actual violence of war that disturbed Radicals, but its effect upon republicanism. There were different types of war. One fought for defense, where the future of the republic was at stake, was legitimate. But one fought simply for territorial conquest endangered democracy. Such wars were favorite means by which the executive and his advisers could garner power for their personal gain. All states previously annexed to the Union had been created from lands ceded by the states or gained as territories. Texas, being an independent republic, fit neither of those precedents. To annex her would require an expression of majority favor in both the United States and Texas in order to satisfy the demands of republicanism. Yet Tyler had proposed to annex Texas by treaty—a procedure that could be accomplished through the will of very few. This was a usurpation of sovereignty and a violation of the Constitution. "To suppose that the President and the Senate can exercise powers of this kind under the notion that they are incident to sovereignty," the New York *Evening Post* argued, "is to fall into the very difficulty that the constitution was intended to avoid. What becomes of all the limitations imposed upon the central government, if not merely that government, but a portion only . . . can exercise such powers as this?"[27]

Once the evil had been introduced, it would spread. Through the artifice of war, the executive could raise armies, heighten taxes, and create a class of dependents which would surely corrupt virtue. Moreover, it was unlikely that the central power would be satisfied with Texas. A "career of conquest," according to the *Post,* would begin. "That this career, beginning in bad faith, nourished by cupidity, and proceeding in violence, is one calculated to nourish republican virtue . . . it requires no little credulity to believe." The real loser would be the northern workingman. "The hardy sons of the west, misdirected by crafty statesmen," the *Post* continued, "furnish indeed the materials of heroic armies, but with what composure will the industry of the north see debt increased, and taxes levied for southwestern acquisitions?"[28]

That the evils of conquest would fall chiefly on the North suggested that more than executive usurpation concerned the Radicals. Texas, it appeared, was more than the "darling measure" of an ambitious President; it was a pawn in a game of southern expansionism. Tyler was a southerner. So was his chief advisor Calhoun. Most of the clamor for immediate annexation seemed to come from the South, which would gain an enormous political and territorial boost should Texas be admitted. And Texas was almost certain to enter the Union as a slave state. The means of annexation aside, Radicals feared the effects annexing a slave state would have on their republic.[29]

Radicals were not abolitionists. Like most northerners, they shared an indifference bordering on contempt for black rights that proceeded from a deeply ingrained racism. Even as they championed popular rule, they hesitated to endorse political equality for black New Yorkers. In 1821, for example, they succeeded in placing severe property qualifications in a new state constitution. Twenty-five years later, in 1846, Radicals voted overwhelmingly to keep that restriction intact. Articles on black rights were noticeably absent from the state's party newspapers throughout the Jacksonian period. The *Post*'s belated response to the problem was a feeble endorsement of colonization, preferably in Jamaica. "In this country the colored man can aspire to no position, nor even to the comforts of a livelihood, except in the face of difficulties which would make the most disciplined white man falter," the *Post* noted. Only jobs "too menial to invite the competition of white men" were open to him; therefore, he would do well to emigrate to climates where he could "take those primary lessons in civilization, which his race have never yet mastered."[30]

It was the institution of slavery, not the slaves themselves, that worried Radicals. Slavery, by definition, was anti-republican. If the core of republicanism was the working citizen—independent of favors and free from the corrupting temptations of power—then obviously a system of total control and total dependency was intolerable. On one hand, slavery created a class of menials who were powerless to control their own destinies. On the other, it fostered a quasi-aristocracy of slaveholders. Both mocked the democratic experiment. "No man, as an accountable being, has a right to surrender to his fellow man an absolute control over his own actions, relations, and condition in life," declared the Albany *Atlas*; "and that which a man has no right to absolve himself from or divest himself of, no other man has a right to take from him by force or otherwise."[31]

Slavery thus blighted both black and white. Slaves, wrote the *Atlas,* "are men who have no country, no family, no hope, no intellectual light, no emulation in labor, no moral accountability." Clearly, they were unfit for the responsibilities of republicanism. Slaveholders, in turn, would always remain an aristocratic class. Like any form of privilege, slaveholding was perpetual in its temptations. "No class of men ever yet relinquished its superiority over another class as long as it was not inconvenient to hold it," wrote the *Post*. "The possession of slaves gives rank and power, and men will submit to some deduction of pecuniary interest to preserve these."[32]

Radicals were not inclined, however, to meddle with slavery where it existed. Slavery was a creation of state law and was thus protected by the Constitution. As President, Van Buren applied this reasoning to condemn proposals to end slavery in the District of Columbia and to ignore abolitionist appeals for emancipation. "No bill," he stated bluntly, "conflicting with these views can ever receive my constitutional sanction." However, an extension of slavery by the constitutionally dubious annexation of Texas was another matter. "I am willing and I feel bound to support the Slave holding *States* in their right to hold Slaves," wrote Hammond, "but so utterly abhorrent is Slavery to my principles and feelings that I can not in conscience consent to the further *extension* of it."[33]

To extend slavery would indicate a degeneration of America's holy mission to spread republicanism. Foreign nations were watching the United States carefully to gauge the effects of its experiment in democracy. If they saw that America, "the only great Christian civilized slaveholding power," had embarked upon a war to extend an aristocratic institution, then their judgment would be adverse. "Nothing is so likely to excite contempt as when magnificent promises are followed by paltry performances," the *Post* observed. Opposition to annexation, then, was a defensive action against the perversion of destiny. The United States was the only nation "where no opulent aristocracy humbles the laboring class, where property is equally diffused, the only country where man . . . enjoys freedom," the editor continued, and these institutions could flourish only "in their original purity."[34]

The purity of republican institutions, moreover, depended upon natural harmony, a harmony that could be achieved only through the enlightened expression of popular will. "A spirit of harmony . . . is essential to a republican form of government," noted the *Post*. Yet annexation would violate the will of the North, launch the country into wars of aggression, and bring the country under the sway of a southern aristocracy. Do this, the *Post* warned, and "this Union sinks to the level of the cut-throat Republics of South America."[35]

This would be toxic to national unity. The "leading fault" in Tyler's and Calhoun's schemes, wrote the *Morning News,* "is this—that a measure in the broadest sense *national* should have been narrowed down to the grounds of a petty *sectionality* of character." Calhoun's reckless desire to extend slavery had placed a valid need for expansion "on a ground so local that it may almost be called Carolinian." "The worst effect of admitting Texas into the Union," echoed the *Post,* "would be to keep alive a war more formidable than any to which we are exposed from Great Britain or any other foreign power—we mean the dissensions between the northern and southern regions of the Union." The cause of those dissensions, slavery, was gradually dying out—would die quickly, in fact, with the addition of new free states. "But by the admission of Texas it will be reinforced and perpetuated."[36]

Radicals could thus be aggressively expansionist and opposed to annexation at the same time. The nature of the institutions that new states brought with them, not the mere acquisition of territory, was their chief concern. "We are—all the Northern Democracy—friendly to the annexation of Texas and needs must be," Theodore Sedgwick, Jr., wrote in the *Post,* but only if they were "convinced that that measure will *not* have the effect of prolonging the institution of slavery." And yet the administration and the South had chosen to place the question wholly in the opposite light. Sedgwick's opposition, "in the name, not of the North, but of the Nation," centered on the future of republican government itself.[37]

Behind this concern for the Union lay an anxiety for the future of the Democratic party. In truth, there was no clear line between the two. Radicals had no doubts that annexation would disrupt, perhaps destroy, the Democratic party in the North. "I believe the democratic party will fall in every free state except Illinois if [it] can be made responsible for legalizing slavery in the whole of Texas," King warned. Some concession from southern Democrats was absolutely necessary if such a disaster were to be prevented. The *Morning News* adopted a conciliatory stance, urging that Texas be split into two states, one free and one slave. To do so would not erase the affront to republican government, but it would temper northern hostility. And southerners owed a compromise to the North "as a matter of fair and just concession to the Northern sentiment on this subject, which is such as seriously to endanger the Democratic ascendancy in the Free States. . . ."[38]

Privately Radicals had concluded that a confrontation—one based on principle—was inevitable. It would not be wise, Wright advised Van Buren, "to temporize with a matter which may prove so vital to the perpetuity of our institutions." "The truth is," Van Buren wrote, "that the Democrats of this state have suffered so often, & so severely, in their advocacy of Southern men, & Southern measures, as to make them more sensitive in respect to complaints of their conduct from that quarter, than I could wish." Jabez Hammond was more blunt. "More than forty years experience," he stormed, "proves that the more the Northern Democracy yields to the South the more she demands; and Individuals at the North after for years acceding to the wishes of Southern men . . . generally receive from that section of the Country a feeble and reluctant support."[39]

So Van Buren faced a delicate problem as he prepared for the coming convention. He must, by the very nature of two-party politics, be acceptable in all regions of the Union. He must not go against his own inclinations, the advice of his friends, and the sentiments of his supporters. During February and March, 1844, he pondered his dilemma as he prepared a statement on annexation. In April he concluded that, in the interests of party unity, it was best to remain silent on slavery and concentrate instead on the probability of war. On April 21 the statement appeared. The situation in Texas was still too unsettled, he declared, and the involvement of American emigrants still too conspicuous, to permit annexation with honor. A costly war, fought under such questionable circumstances, would humiliate the United States, whoever won. "We have a character among the nations of the earth to maintain," he pleaded. "Could we hope to stand justified in the eyes of mankind for entering into it; more especially if its commencement is to be preceded by the appropriation to our own uses of the territory, the sovereignty of which is in dispute between two nations one of which we are to join in the struggle?" Good republican that he was, Van Buren ended by pledging himself to obey the dictates of Congress and the people on the matter, even if they should insist upon annexation. By coincidence, on the same day that Van Buren's letter appeared, so did one from Henry Clay, the leading Whig candidate, taking substantially the same ground.[40]

Van Buren's letter settled nothing. Most Democrats saw the statement for what it was: an artful dodge and a longwinded evasion of the basic question. Calhoun was predictably outraged; so were more moderate southerners. Radicals had expected that. What they had not expected was the cool reception given both Van Buren's and Clay's letters in the North. Lewis Cass, himself a contender for the nomination, dismissed the entire document as a poor trick. Annexation, he declared, was perfectly proper and necessary regardless of the cost. Furthermore, a large portion of Van Buren's party in New

York gave him only weak support. Calls for Van Buren to step aside increased.

Radicals immediately saw a conspiracy afoot. Annexation, Flagg reasoned, was merely a facade behind which certain southerners and their sympathizers hoped to torpedo a northern candidate. "The people," he complained, "must not be bamboozled out of their expressed desires by cabals at Washington, Richmond, or Albany. The reason assigned for setting Mr. V.B. aside, his Texas letter, renders any yielding, concession or change, wholly inadmissible. Such a policy would be suicidal and give the entire north to Mr. Clay." Flagg was willing to give up Van Buren if the delegates honestly thought he could not win. But, he warned, "if the influence of a cabal is to be thrown into the convention to overrule the fair expression of the people through their representatives, and for the reason that Mr. V.B. has written a frank letter which takes the true ground as the northern democracy believe, the effect of such a proceeding must be disastrous."[41]

Convention day, May 27, came, with noisy delegates crowding into the Odd Fellows Hall on Gay Street in Baltimore. At once the strategy of Van Buren's opponents appeared. Led by Senator Robert John Walker of Mississippi, the opposition clamored for adoption of the two-thirds rule for nomination. The plan was simple: those who were committed to Van Buren on the first roll call could discharge their duty. If Van Buren failed to garner two-thirds on the first try, as expected, the delegates would be free to vote for another man. The Radicals were aware of the scheme and fought it desperately, to no avail. The rule passed, and balloting began.[42]

When it ended, two days later, James K. Polk had been nominated. Van Buren's lieutenants had watched helplessly as their hero's total slipped from a comfortable majority to a meager parity with that of Lewis Cass. They agreed to Polk, Jackson's protégé and a dark horse, only because he was a "*sound* democrat," and not a party to the "compromises and plots" by which Van Buren had been rejected. Although they had successfully persuaded the convention to nominate Wright as vice president, Wright furiously rejected the offer. He would not be a party to annexation, which Polk supported, nor would he insult Van Buren by accepting a consolation prize. George M. Dallas of Pennsylvania was accordingly nominated instead, and the Radicals returned in sorrow to New York.[43]

They did not accept their humiliation at Baltimore easily. To the Radicals the result of the convention was not the rejection of a weak candidate, nor was it the will of the people. It was, rather, evidence of the corruption a slaveholding aristocracy could introduce into democratic politics. This corruption was toxic both to the party and to republicanism. If a party could be undermined by the will of a few, so could republicanism. Four years later, at the height of the Free Soil movement, Hammond identified the convention as a crucial point at which Radicals became convinced that the South was attempting to overthrow democratic politics. Slavery, he observed, "constitutes a common bond of union, of which the free states are destitute." By preying upon the divisions which were natural among free men, the southern aristocracy had succeeded in transferring control of the party from the majority to a minority. They had done so through the skillful use of the two-thirds rule. A convention, Hammond wrote, existed solely for the purpose of ascertaining "who the majority of the party" desired to carry out their will. "Now the two-third rule," he recalled, was "calculated to defeat this great and only object of caucussing, for it vests in the minority the power of controlling the majority." Southerners had blocked Van Buren and had substituted their own man. In the process they had outraged the Radical concept of a unified party working in the interests of republican harmony. "A more effectual means of encouraging faction in a party," Hammond concluded, "could not be devised."[44]

In their despair Radicals never completely understood what had happened at Baltimore. They did not realize that annexation was a valid issue that could not be postponed, nor did they comprehend its popularity in the North. They were impervious to the genuine fears held by Democrats in all sections that Van Buren would lose. They did admit that Polk was a good compromise, but they did not know why. Polk was not the tool of any faction—Radicals recognized that—and therein lay his strength. Van Buren, on the other hand, was too closely identified with a region, and only a portion of that, to win. For Radicals, however, in their blind devotion to the former President, the nomination was a matter of right, popular will, and party principle. Any deviation from their interpretation of the democratic principle was tantamount to treason. Theodore Sedgwick, Sr., summed up their feelings best: "As to Polk and Texas," he stormed, "—I consider this nomination brought about by a rascally fraud—one that would disgrace a well-organized den of thieves."[45]

Van Buren's defeat at Baltimore did more than destroy his influence nationally; it seriously weakened Radical control of the New York party. For most of a decade Radicals had been engaged in a struggle with dissident Democrats in New York—men they labeled Conservatives. Conservatives were in fact moderates who found Radical views on banks and internal improvements restrictive and inflexible. Their fear of corruption and moral decline through debt was not as pronounced as that of the Radicals. While they were unwilling to accept the Whig philosophy of massive internal improvements and strong banks, they could not accede to Radical demands that new canals be created solely from the profits of old ones, or that all corporate stockholders be made personally liable in a bankruptcy. The Panic reinforced their view that looser credit and more state aid were not, by nature, moral sins. Nor did they share the Radicals' visceral suspicion of slavery and annexation.

Yet the Conservatives were a strong faction, well led and popular in several counties and towns throughout the state, especially Oneida, Albany, and New York City. Their best spokesmen were Edwin Croswell of the Albany *Argus,* Henry S. Foster of Oneida, and Daniel S. Dickinson, the lieutenant governor in 1844. Although Marcy remained friendly to the Radicals, he was nonetheless sympathetic to the Conservatives and gradually became identified with them. As the Conservative faction grew in strength, the Radicals began to suspect, unfairly, that another conspiracy was afoot to monopolize state power through office and patronage. Thus a new synonym for Conservative appeared—Hunker. "Hunker, it seems to us," wrote the *Post,* "is properly derived from the verb, *to hanker,* and the Hunker in politics is a hankerer after profit or promotion."[46]

Neither faction enjoyed complete dominance of the party in 1844. Although the Radicals generally controlled the fiscal policies of New York, the Conservatives demanded, and received, many of the state offices, including the governorship, as the price of their cooperation. It was a delicate alliance, of course, for the Radicals detested the Conservative governor William C. Bouck, while the Conservatives only grudgingly accepted Barnburner direction of the banks and canals. The Radicals, however, were clearly potent in one respect. So long as Martin Van Buren remained the most powerful of the Democratic candidates, Conservatives were careful not to let their dissatisfaction spill over into national politics and worked hard to secure Van Buren's renomination.

The selection of Polk, then, presented Radicals with two problems. One was to regain some influence in Washington; the other was to prevent a Conservative takeover of the state. During the summer of 1844 they proposed to solve both by making Silas Wright governor. Wright did not want the job, and the Conservatives did not want

Wright. Radicals countered Wright's personal objections by raising the familiar standard of majority will. If the party wanted him—and he was undoubtedly popular—he had no right to refuse. Wright could not evade this argument, good party man that he was. Responding to the Conservatives, Radicals coldly stated that Polk could never win without New York, and New York could not be secured without Wright. In September they forced the gentle politician through the state convention on the second ballot. Conservatives accepted defeat only because of the real fear of a Whig victory. "The general feeling of the Democracy of the State," summarized the *Morning News,* was "that the great national issue at stake was of an importance too incalculable to permit any risks to be hazarded."[47]

It was apparently a wise strategy. During the campaign both Radicals and Conservatives ignored their differences and worked for unity. Indeed, they ignored almost every issue of consequence. Annexation was studiously avoided. They made little reference to the struggle between landlords and renter-farmers in central New York— the "anti-rent" war that James Fenimore Cooper fictionalized in the Littlepage Manuscripts. They brushed aside the growing evidence of nativism in New York City. And they were quietly contemptuous of the Liberty party. In place of these they tirelessly repeated the ancient party slogans concerning banks and tariffs, guessing that Clay's ambiguous stand on Texas and Wright's popularity would give them victory.

They guessed correctly. In November Polk defeated Clay in New York by 5,000 votes and thus obtained the electoral vote necessary for election. As to whether the 15,000 votes mustered in New York by the Liberty party came from potential Clay voters, the evidence was inconclusive. Wright's majority over his opponent, however, was twice that of Polk over Clay. Instantly a suspicion arose that several of the Radicals had abandoned Polk. O'Sullivan had warned Van Buren of that possibility in late October, and Van Buren had hastened, with unknown effect, to quell it.[48]

Whatever had produced the results, the Radicals were mostly relieved. They had regained control of the state, and they had a fair claim to having won the presidency for Polk. "The principles of your administration," Butler rejoiced to Van Buren, "have at last been vindicated; and the ill-advised & ill-begotten judgment of 1840 rebuked . . . ." For a moment, the bitter trial at Baltimore was forgotten.[49]

It was a brief respite. During 1845 and 1846 a series of blows coming from both Washington and New York shattered the Radicals' illusions that they had retained any semblance of control over the Democratic party. These strikes against their hopes combined to create a sense of near-panic frustration among Barnburners—a frustration which they were conditioned to perceive as the result of a massive conspiracy.

Having worked hard and faithfully to elect Polk, Radicals expected him to reward them with grateful offers of patronage and office in his administration. He did not. Polk was painfully aware of the cacophony of voices clamoring for his attention, and no less aware of the ultimate designs of each. He had voluntarily declined, in advance, a second term, and everyone—southerners, westerners, northerners, moderates, Radicals, and Conservatives—seemed to want cabinet positions as stepping stones for the campaign of 1848. Of all these factions, Barnburners were the most conspicuous. "The truth is," he confided to his diary, "they are looking to the next Presidential election, and nothing could satisfy them unless I were to identify myself with them, and proscribe all other branches of the Democratic party." This Polk would not do. He was a tough, practical, hardworking man who was determined "to be *myself* President of the United States," and not the puppet of Van Buren or anyone else.[50]

But Polk did not wish to offend the Radicals. They had, after all, helped win him the election, and they were too important to be ignored. Accordingly, in late 1844 Polk offered Wright the Treasury Department. Wright naturally refused, but both he and Van Buren were quick to suggest other Barnburners for the job. Confidently they expected Polk to acquiesce.[51]

Polk did precisely what he was not supposed to do. After long weeks of delay, during which his mail overflowed with warnings against the Barnburners, he extended the key cabinet posts to men of other loyalties. Belatedly he offered the War Department to Butler, who refused bluntly and acidly. Less than a week before the inauguration the President-elect turned to Marcy for the job.[52]

The Radicals were furious. From the moment of Marcy's appointment nothing the President did ever quite satisfied them. When he offered them control of federal patronage in New York, they refused. "The manner in which we have been treated by the President . . . ," Van Buren noted, "puts it out of our power . . . to recommend persons to him for office without a sacrifice to self-respect." When Polk naturally offered positions to Conservatives, they felt doubly betrayed. The President's appointment of a Conservative to the prestigious Port of New York stunned them—although Polk in fact had very little choice. In making the choice, Wright informed him, "you took a man identified with the bank interest," one who was "not considered sound" on fiscal policy.[53]

A convergence was taking place in the Radical mind. A group of conspirators had defrauded Van Buren at Baltimore and had thus violated the popular will. Even so, party loyalty had dictated that Radicals support the nominee. The same loyalty had now been affronted by the new President, who seemed to be working in concert with the South and the Conservatives. The logical conclusion was that the original conspiracy, hatched in the South, had spread North. In the Radicals' analysis, the Conservatives had skillfully captured control of the state and the cabinet post. Were not these results, Hammond asked, "in part caused by a plan concocted at Washington in regard to the successor of Mr. Polk, adverse to the views of Mr. Van Buren and Mr. Wright? Did not the far-seeing politicians of the South reason at that time, as they did at the Baltimore Convention?" The South, in short, had already made detailed plans for 1848, and was pursuing its scheme with the help of Hunkers.[54]

The specter of conspiracy raised by the cabinet episode was compounded by events in New York during 1845 and 1846. Barnburners expected Wright's governorship to hold the state secure for them. Instead, they watched in dismay as the Conservatives steadily gained power and thwarted their anticipations. This decline in Radical influence was partly due to the confidence they had misplaced in Polk during the campaign of 1844. They had counted heavily on the President's cooperation; when they did not get it, they were left weakened. The decline was also due to Wright's ineffective leadership as governor. Wright was a highly capable legislator, but a poor executive. He seemed reluctant to use his power to keep the party united; when he did act, it was generally too little, too late.[55]

Three episodes in 1845 fueled the war between Radicals and Conservatives. In January Hunkers allowed John A. Dix to serve the remaining four years of Wright's Senate term. But in a surprise move made possible by precise discipline they chose one of their own, Daniel S. Dickinson, to the other Senate seat for a full six years. The move had all been done accordingly to party rules which Radicals were helpless to overturn. Next Conservatives joined with Whigs in appropriating borrowed money for canal work. Wright was forced to veto. Then the crucial issue of revising the state constitution arose. Radicals wanted to amend the document to prevent exactly the sort of appropriations Wright had so recently turned down. Conservatives objected, and the Barnburners shifted to an uneasy alliance with Whigs, who wanted a new constitution altogether. A convention was called for the summer, 1846, and immediately a violent newspaper war broke out. The Conservative *Argus* offered one slate of candidates; the Radical *Atlas,* another. Horace Greeley of the Whig New York *Tribune* noted the situation with pleasure: "The Hunkers and Barnburners are fighting so savagely" that only a Whig blunder could prevent a Democratic rout.[56]

Increasingly Radicals sensed that some sort of purification was necessary to keep the party true to its heritage. A kind of partisan revolution, separating Tories from Loyalists, was inevitable. "The only course, now, it seems to me," Dix advised Van Buren, "is to carry out the controversy . . . to its true result—a separation of the sound from the unsound elements of the democratic party. We may suffer temporarily—but in the end we must be purified and rise again." O'Sullivan felt the same: "A period has arrived at which the magnitude of the principles involved in the debates of parties, is such as to tend to weaken the cohesion of parties." Party discipline, so essential to republican politics, must be enforced according to strict principles. O'Sullivan predicted an early crisis.[57]

It came in the fall, 1846. While the convention had drawn up a constitution that incorporated most Radical demands, Wright's prospects for reelection had weakened. He had not used his office well. The anti-rent dispute had turned into open war. Two men had died, and too late Wright had sent in the militia. Delighted, the Whigs reaped every outraged voter in the affected counties. Nor had Wright used the patronage effectively to solidify his support within the party. And he had never regained the full confidence of Polk, who was understandably hesitant to become involved in the campaign.[58]

More ominous was the Conservatives' reluctance to give him full support. Throughout the late summer the *Argus* filled its columns with letters from all over the state demanding that Wright step down. In New York City the Radicals were so weak that the *News* collapsed in August for lack of subscribers. While fading in New York City, Wright was incapable of inspiring unity upstate. When the nominating convention met in Syracuse in October, several counties sent two feuding delegations, one Conservative and one Radical. Significantly, the bitterest disputes were over seats from Oneida, where Conservative strength was great, and Albany, where a large defection of Conservative votes in the election could prove disastrous. Overall, the signs were not good. The attitude of the *Argus* faction, Wright concluded, "satisfies me that the ticket is to be opposed to the extent of the ability of these men . . . . The result," he added, "must be very bad."[59]

It was, devastatingly so. Although the new constitution was

adopted by a comfortable margin, Wright lost to the Whig candidate, John Young, by over 10,000 votes, receiving fully 50,000 fewer than his total vote in 1844. Ironically, Wright's running mate, also a Radical, won by 13,000. Livid with rage, the Radicals began combing the returns to discover who constituted the defecting voters. Certainly Wright's unpopularity in the anti-rent district hurt him; the *Atlas* frankly ascribed about 10,000 of his drop to that issue. The simple perseverance of the Whigs, who sensed their opportunity and worked hard to secure it, also cut. But primarily the Barnburners blamed the disaster on the Conservatives. In several counties the returns showed firm support for every Democrat running except Wright, where the vote shifted wholesale to Young. Predictably, Oneida County stood out in this sort of apostasy. Too, rigged ballots, showing Wright as a candidate for senator, not governor, appeared in a few wards in Albany, which cost Wright over 100 votes there. Obviously, the Conservatives had cut Wright from the ticket. "Treachery, proscription, and popular neglect," summarized Dix.[60]

In Albany the *Atlas* boiled for a month, then spewed out its rage for a full week during December. Through thousands of words and dozens of columns of print, the *Atlas* traced in detail the "Causes and Consequences" of the late election. The anti-rent dispute was one reason for Wright's loss. Selfish retribution by those hurt by his veto of the canal bill was another. But these were only secondary causes. When the constitutional convention was called and placed under the sway of the Radicals, the *Atlas* explained, the Conservatives realized that the new document, if wielded by a Radical governor, would be disastrous to their future schemes of speculation. The power of the brokers and bankers would be sapped, as would that of the canal interests. "The final issue was now reached," the *Atlas* concluded, and perfidy resulted. Using trick ballots and split tickets, Conservatives abandoned Wright. "Here, then, we have the causes of the defeat of the democracy . . . traced upon the face of the official canvass. We have said that anti-rentism was *a* cause, and that the local canal feeling was *a* cause, but that Conservative defection was *the* cause. . . ." Almost flippantly the *Argus* admitted that it was so.[61]

By January, 1847, the Barnburners were a broken, bitter faction. In the space of three years all their worst fears about corruption had been confirmed. In their opinion, a cabal had ousted Van Buren, and a formerly trustworthy Polk had fallen under the thumb of the same men. Now Silas Wright had fallen, the victim, they thought, of selfish apostates. Their mood was not improved by the annexation of Texas and the onset of war with Mexico in 1846. Their power in the party was broken, and their principles were cast aside. Crushed, the Radicals searched for a way to force the party back to its true ground.

Almost coincidentally with the Barnburners' collapse a new and explosive issue appeared in Washington. In August, 1846, a young Pennsylvania Democrat, David Wilmot, proposed to exclude slavery from all the territory which the United States expected to gain from Mexico after the war. Although the Wilmot Proviso failed, largely unnoticed at the time, it had potentially great appeal in the North, where slavery was detested and the war unpopular. On January 7, soon after Congress had reassembled, the Proviso was offered again, this time from the hands of the Radical from St. Lawrence, Preston King. Significantly, within a few days the *Atlas* made the Proviso a test of party regularity. The convergence of enemies—southern and northern—was complete in the Radical mind.

CHAPTER TWO

THE CONSCIENCE WHIGS

ANNEXATION was not popular among northern Whigs. Daniel Webster, for example, had declared his opposition to the plan while still a member of Tyler's cabinet, basing his views on the presence of slavery in Texas, the constitutional problems of admitting a foreign nation, and the general need to avoid territorial expansion unless absolutely necessary. "We have a great republic . . . ," he wrote. "Instead of aiming to enlarge its boundaries, let us seek to strengthen its union . . . ." Many of his Whig friends echoed his position. Those who did not go so far as to condemn all expansion were willing to accept Texas only if it were coupled with the acquisition of Oregon, a territory which western Whigs deemed essential to their prosperity and which they wished to secure from the British. Most northern Whigs simply agreed with Clay that annexing Texas would produce an undesirable war and seriously upset the balance of political power in Washington. They were concerned when Clay softened his initial opposition to the plan, and predictably upset when Tyler—with Polk's blessing—succeeded in completing the deal in 1845.[1]

At that point the issue might have died, a political relic of an unsuccessful campaign. Yet the disturbing questions raised by annexation did not evaporate. Texas, whatever its status, was slave territory, and to a large number of northern Whigs slavery threatened essential values and attitudes that made up the core of their political experience. This hostility to slavery was most vocal in a belt which ran from Massachusetts west to the shores of Lake Michigan. Within the belt lay wide diversities of economic pursuits, settlement patterns, and religious persuasions. The underlying link which united them all, however, was a common inheritance of perceptions and ideals which had emerged over the decades from the New England mind.

By 1845 New England had colonized much of western New York, the Western Reserve of Ohio, and the counties of Indiana, Michigan, and Illinois clustered around the southern tip of the Great Lakes. Not all New England traditions had survived the move west. While New England itself had remained religiously conservative—mostly Congregationalist or Unitarian—western Yankees had adopted evangelical Protestantism. Industry was far more developed in Massachusetts than in Ohio. Massachusetts was dominated by one party, the Whig. Western politics was more competitive because the two-party struggle there was intense. Still, certain common bonds linked the two regions. Yankees in both East and West prized education, were disturbed by the cultural pluralism brought on by European immigration, and were receptive to all manner of moral reforms, both those directed at the individual and those pitched to the whole community. They carried this passion for reform into their politics.[2]

The New England influence in Whig politics was the source of what one historian has called the "politics of pietism." The political pietist tended to view all public issues as moral problems for which a moral solution must be found. He was also likely to be socially conservative, intolerant of those who were not born of Anglo-Saxon genes, somewhat elitist—in that he considered those who shared his cultural background to be the "best men"—and eager to stamp his principles upon the whole society. He was intensely concerned over the moral state of individuals, and was convinced that the duty of social institutions lay in protecting the community from moral decay. These attributes, when combined with the zeal of the evangelical, or the assured confidence of the Unitarian, gave his politics a revivalistic, almost desperate, urgency.[3]

The emerging pietist tradition had spawned a variety of political cults and persuasions. Anti-Masonry had been its breeding ground during the 1820s. As they condemned Masonic "conspiracies," bemoaned the influx of Catholic immigrants, and railed against the domination of "King Andrew" Jackson, anti-Masons displayed a moral concern for the fate of American democracy that typified the pietist outlook. In time anti-Masons were joined by pacifists, prohibitionists, nativists, and a host of other reformers, both political and apolitical. Most of these reforms were transitory at best, malicious at worst; one, antislavery, came to dominate the rest.[4]

The Conscience Whig movement against slavery developed within this tradition of political pietism. Its very name suggested the intense concern with moral issues it brought to the antislavery crusade. In general, Conscience Whigs borrowed from their heritage, stressing the responsibilities of virtuous men and the necessity for the entire social order to be erected on moral principles. Their values and attitudes were remarkably consistent from state to state, for all drew upon the same essential concept of the ideal society that characterized the New England mind. They looked forward to a society that was Protestant, entrepreneurial, educated, and culturally homogeneous. The political context within which these values were presented, however, varied as one moved west. As with all reform movements, political needs very often shaped the presentation of ideology. Two states where the movement flourished—Ohio and Massachusetts—reflect this complex interaction between practicality and desire.

On January 29, 1845, hundreds of concerned Bostonians crowded into Faneuil Hall to protest the imminent annexation of Texas. It was a desperate and undoubtedly futile gesture, for Polk was already elected, and the Senate was that day considering various proposals to facilitate admission. The meeting went on nonetheless, with Garrisonian abolitionists occupying the balconies and scores of less vocal, but equally grim, opponents of slavery below. The division between balcony and main floor was suggestive. Garrison and his friends had long been social outcasts; their unqualified hatred of slavery and their demand for immediate emancipation were not well received by most of Boston society. They appeared, rightly or wrongly, to be monolithic in their ideals and aloof. The men on the floor showed no such consistency. On one hand were the representatives of the Whig leadership of Boston, who had brought resolutions from Daniel Webster and the manufacturer Abbott Lawrence—each of whom condemned annexation and prayed for an early, but peaceful, end to slavery. These men were cautious, conservative, and not given to displays of emotion or impetuosity. In their hands rested control of the Whig party machinery.[5]

Between the abolitionists and the conservatives stood a small group of men, most of them young, some of them close friends, to whom Texas and all it implied were anathema. They were a talented and promising group. The most prestigious was Charles Francis Adams, grandson of John and son of John Quincy Adams. Older, and only slightly less well known, was John Gorham Palfrey. Palfrey had led a varied life, being in turn a Unitarian minister, a Harvard professor, an editor of *North American Review,* and, through an inheritance, an owner of slaves, whom he had promptly freed. Samuel Gridley Howe, a noted reformer and head of the Perkins Institute for the Blind, was also prominent, as was a Natick shoe manufacturer, Henry Wilson. The most promising intellectual leader of this amorphous group was Charles Sumner, a tall, idealistic, and eloquent young lawyer who had dined with the literary elite of Europe and who had studied law under Joseph Story of the Supreme Court. Other lawyers were Charles Allen, Stephen C. Phillips, and E. Rockwood Hoar. In January, 1845, these men shared little more than a similar background. All except Wilson had grown up in the genteel traditions of Boston society; all except Adams worshipped Daniel Webster; all, without exception, professed to be thorough Whigs.[6]

The Faneuil Hall meeting brought them together and launched them unexpectedly upon a career of ideological and political rebellion. Beginning as a committee of correspondence to drum up anti-annexation support from other states, the Young Whigs—as they first called themselves—were thrown into a situation where, day by day, they began to work more closely in opposition to a single issue, slavery. Through their efforts they discovered that they held a common set of presumptions and attitudes about the nature of the good society and the evils which threatened it. They also found that they did not fit into the traditional mold of Massachusetts Whig politics. They were much too conservative to use Garrison's tactics of moral persuasion, yet they were considered too radical and too young to be included in the normal process of determining Whig policy. At every turn they found their appeals unheeded and their efforts frustrated. The cautious opposition of the Whig hierarchy fused with their own eagerness for change to give them a sense of common purpose, of shared identity, which would give their movement unity and self-sustaining force. Conscience Whiggery in Massachusetts was an example of the political maturation of a group.

Two incidents during 1845 presaged the sort of opposition the Conscience Whigs would face and helped create their sense of cohesiveness. Soon after the Faneuil Hall meeting the Young Whigs began to notice a discernible decline in anti-annexationism among their party leaders. The Boston *Daily Advertiser,* for instance, gave warm support to the January meeting; once Congress had admitted Texas, however, the paper dropped the subject. This apparent acquiescence was made clear at a banquet on July 4, following a speech in which Sumner pleaded for peace and attacked all war—including, presumably, the threatened one with Mexico. Robert C.

Winthrop, the favorite son of Boston's elite and the heir-apparent to Webster, dismissed the speech with a toast: "Our country, bounded by the St. John's and the Sabine, or however . . . still, *our* country . . . to be defended by all hands." The message was unmistakable. Massachusetts Whigs were not prepared to place their opposition to slavery above the interests of the nation and the party. "In reality," commented Adams, "I infer that [Winthrop] is paddling backwards to what he considers terra firma, attachment to the Union." This was upsetting, for it implied a rejection of what Conscience Whigs considered an essential ethical point.[7]

The second incident followed another anti-Texas meeting on November 4. Texas had not yet been formally admitted, so as a final measure to screw up public opposition the meeting prepared resolutions and commissioned Sumner, Adams, and Palfrey to solicit money and support from the great families of Boston. They were coldly rejected. "I cannot think it good policy to waste our energies in hopeless efforts upon the impossible," wrote Nathan Appleton, a manufacturer; Lawrence agreed. "A majority of our people have decided in favor of annexation," he stated simply. Further opposition was pointless. Beyond these curt replies, it was obvious that other powers in the Whig party were closing their ears to the pleas of the Conscience Whigs. The *Courier,* edited by the usually friendly Joseph Buckingham, treated their meeting with silence. So did the *Advertiser.* Only Webster, who was becoming estranged from the Lawrence faction, maintained good relations with the Conscience group.[8]

A siege mentality began to set in among Conscience Whigs. "This is conclusive of the course of the Whig politicians," Adams noted of the response to the meeting. "Well, we must bear it with dignity—and pursue our course." Yet more frustrations followed. In January tempers flared in the state senate in an incident which gave the group its name. Regular Whigs defeated a series of resolutions condemning the extension of slavery, which prompted an icy rebuttal from Hoar. "It is as much the duty of Massachusetts to pass resolutions in favor of the rights of men as in the interests of cotton," he remarked. Someone call him a "Conscience" Whig—a label the group adopted eagerly. With the spring and the onset of war with Mexico, the Conscience Whigs took another step toward group action. They bought the Boston *Whig,* an ailing daily paper, and settled in for a protracted battle against their three foes: Cotton Whigs, slavery, and public apathy.[9]

While the Conscience Whig movement in Massachusetts sprang from the rebellion of a group, that in Ohio centered on one man and his peculiar political situation. Joshua Reed Giddings was, in 1844, the unquestioned spokesman for antislavery Whigs in Ohio. He had earned his position. Elected to the House in 1838, he had quickly sided with John Quincy Adams to fight the "gag rule," which automatically tabled antislavery petitions and consigned them to legislative purgatory—never debated. Giddings, like Adams, detested the rule for both its tacit defense of slavery and its open attack on free speech. He made these views well known, and by 1842 had so irritated the House that he was censured. He promptly resigned his seat and left for home to win it back.[10]

Such boldness would have earned most congressmen a bitter fight for reelection. Instead, Giddings returned to Washington on the crest of a landslide victory. Giddings was from the Western Reserve, and he knew his supporters well. Settled largely by transplanted New Englanders and emigrants from western New York, the Reserve had long been a home for reforms and reformers. Slavery was massively unpopular there; so were the state's Black Laws, which severely restricted the rights of free blacks. Oberlin College had been established on the Reserve in 1834 as a refuge for abolitionist students from Lane Seminary in Cincinnati. Moreover, recent research has shown that these counties, with their concentration of transplanted Yankees, were particularly susceptible to evangelic revivals, and that those revivals in turn complemented the moral appeal of radical abolitionism.[11]

But Giddings was not popular in southern Ohio. The southern counties contained more transplanted southerners than emigrant Yankees, and received a steady trickle of runaway slaves and free blacks that offended white sensibilities and weakened the opposition to slavery. Giddings's ardent antislavery agitation embarrassed Cincinnati Whigs, who found it necessary to assure their supporters that he did not speak for all of the party. Giddings's district, however, was crucial to Whig prospects on the Reserve, and the Reserve, in turn, was crucial if the Whigs were to carry Ohio. Hence a detente developed. Reserve delegates to the state conventions wisely gave offices and patronage to southern Whigs who, in return, tolerated Giddings and his extreme antislavery. Giddings, meanwhile, was looking to the Senate.[12]

Complicating the quest for Whig unity was the persistent growth of the Liberty party. Liberty men were strong on the Reserve; in every state election since 1840 they had multiplied their numbers. By 1844 they threatened to lure away much of the Whig vote there, and with it the Whig's hopes to clinch the election. They furthermore believed that Henry Clay was a hypocrite who appeared to work against slavery while still retaining slaves of his own. "He is as rotten as a stagnant fish pond, on the subject of Slavery," noted a Liberty leader. "Confound him and all his compromises from first to last." Giddings countered this threat during the campaign of 1844 by reminding voters that a vote for Birney was tantamount to a vote for Polk. He was at least partially successful.[13]

The election, however, brought no respite to the troubles of Ohio Whigs. While Clay carried the state in the national race, Democrats won most of the local offices. Regular Whigs promptly returned to the traditional issues of banks and roads and demanded, as a means of embarrassing Polk, the immediate acquisition of Oregon. "The tide of emigration from the United States, which has commenced tumbling over the Rocky Mountains," was irresistible, announced the Cleveland *Herald*. Polk must secure all Oregon, plus California, to remain a friend to the Old Northwest. In all this expansionist rhetoric Ohio Whigs seemed quietly to forget Texas and slavery.[14]

If Giddings and his followers were aware of this retreat from the slavery issue, they did not show it. Ever since Giddings had won such a thumping popular rebuttal of the vote to censure him, he had enjoyed a privileged position in Ohio; his power on the Reserve was so great that Whig newspapers such as the *Herald* and the Columbus *Ohio State Journal* dared not attack him. For that reason, Giddings remained blissfully aloof to the fact that most of his party, certainly that part outside the Reserve, was gradually abandoning his position.

Giddings was convinced that Whigs needed only to sharpen their opposition to slavery and win over the Liberty party in order to dominate Ohio. For that reason he fostered a series of blistering attacks upon the Liberty men for their vote in 1844. The Ashtabula *Sentinel,* his mouthpiece on the Reserve, bored in on Polk's victory in New York. The Liberty party could have defeated Polk there, the *Sentinel* complained, but they did not. "They have wickedly joined hands with the oppressor—turned recreant to the interests of the down-trodden slave—to the oppressed non-slaveholder of the South— to the freemen of the North . . ." While the *Sentinel* was thus chastising the Liberty men, Giddings himself set out to prove Ohio Whigs could lead the fight against slavery. During 1845 he voted repeatedly to deny Texas admission. The logic, to him, was plain: pull in radical votes from the Liberty party while trusting regular Whigs to stand firm.[15]

But by the end of 1845 the regular Whigs' march away from Giddings's position became increasingly clear. Slowly Giddings's illusions over the sincerity of antislavery among most Ohio Whigs began to pale. When war began with Mexico in May, 1846, he was worried. "It is to be an important crisis to our Country and to our Whigs," he confided to his wife. "Of the slaveholders and the Locofocos I entertain no apprehension, but I greatly fear the cowardice of the Whigs. It is the Curse of our Country and of our party that northern men are too Craven hearted to maintain their own rights." When Polk requested a declaration of war, Giddings's fears were confirmed; only four other Whigs from Ohio—three from the Reserve—voted against it. Only fourteen from the entire nation did so. Clearly Whig antislavery lagged much farther behind Giddings than he had supposed, and clearly Whig antislavery needed much prodding to catch up. In his own way Giddings was confronting the same dilemma that plagued his counterparts in the East: how to convince his party that Texas and slavery were more than questions of expediency, but ones which involved a fundamental crisis in national values.[16]

Like the Barnburners, Conscience Whigs formed their revolt from modes of thought and attitudes common to much of their parent party. Defining those modes of thought, however, is difficult. The Whig world view is elusive. On the surface Whigs appeared to have almost no basic ideals that would separate them from any other major political movement of the age. They began—indeed drew their name—in opposition to Jackson and his perceived usurpation of executive powers. They fought the Democrats tirelessly over specific issues: the desirability of a national bank, a high tariff, and federal aid to internal improvements. Beyond these issues, however, the outlines of their beliefs became vague and muddled. They were every bit as capitalistic and entrepreneurial as Democrats; they simply disagreed on the means to effect economic progress. They were also accomplished politicians. After an initial period of disorientation they combined in 1840 to seek and secure the vote of the common man in an outright mimicry of the tactics of their opponents. They twice elected military heroes of no set party principles because, ostensibly, they could win elections in no other way. They were charged with being conservative aristocrats, yet they appear to have shared most of the values common to all Americans. If they possessed definite values of their own, they cloaked them well.

The thesis is inadequate, for it searches for precise statements of principle that would make the party distinct. Neither major political party of the age had an ideology in a formal sense. Given the diversity of their electorates (divided among sections if nothing else), they could not. The need to present candidates who would be acceptable in all sections led, more than anything else, to the choice of men such as Harrison or Zachary Taylor. Perforce, it also led to the vagueness of principle which characterized each man. In view of the regionalism and localism within the party, this strategy simply made good sense in national elections.

Yet it obscures an underlying unity in Whig thought that did set the party apart from the Democrats. In their own way Whigs championed the common man, the sanctity of republican government, the glories of economic progress, and the inevitability of American expansion— all elements common to the Jacksonian persuasion. In their own way Whigs believed in the necessity of harmony in a democratic society to produce the perfect balance between liberty and order. Yet each of their favored programs, including those that seemed most aristocratic and conservative, reflected their own special interpretation of how harmony could best be achieved.[17]

The concept of harmony, of balance, was central to Whig thought, was what made it distinct. A Barnburner, for example, conceived of republican harmony as the natural offspring of competition among the independent citizenry. In terms that seem almost Darwinian, the extreme Democratic philosophy envisioned a society of competing elements, free of artificial restraints, in which a process of natural selection would ultimately ferret out the bad and leave the good triumphant. The degree to which Democrats espoused this idea varied considerably from region to region according to local need. Western Democrats were, for instance, far more receptive to plans for internal improvements than were their eastern counterparts. Yet almost all agreed with O'Sullivan that the best government was that which governed least.

For Whigs the best government was that which governed most effectively. "The great object of the institution of civil government is the improvement of the condition of those who are parties to the social compact," stated John Quincy Adams in 1825. If government was to fulfill its duties, it was obviously necessary that it be able to act rather than simply to react. To direct, to regulate, to plan—these were essential tasks that government must perform in order to improve the lot of society. Adams's vision of the role of government was vast; it included a national university, the promotion of scientific knowledge, the establishment of an effective foreign policy, and wise regulation of internal affairs of virtually all sorts. Most Whigs narrowed this vision to the economic advantages to be gained from vigorous governmental planning. Clay's American System would have bound each section in reciprocal economic dependency, with the South providing raw materials, the North manufacturing finished goods, and the West feeding all. The tools for achieving economic independence were the familiar Whig programs of protective tariffs, a stable currency, and internal improvements. The expected result was a balanced and prosperous republic.[18]

These aims were to be realized within the context of republicanism. Whigs fully believed that all progress, either political or economic, came from the combined efforts of free men. Railroads, Webster noted, were the logical results not only of technological innovation but of "the spirit and industry of free labor . . . the indomitable history of a free people." To Edward Everett of Massachusetts there was a direct link between economic prosperity and political independence. "It is," he argued, "the spirit of a free country which animates and gives energy to its labor; which puts the mass in action, gives it motive and intensity, makes it inventive, sends it off in new directions." Under despotisms labor was drudgery and its result—stagnation—plain to see. To prove the superiority of democracies, it was only necessary to demonstrate the reverse. "We must preach the great truth of our Declaration of Independence, that all men are created free," announced the Cleveland *Herald,* but to do so "we must build a railroad from the Atlantic to the Pacific, build schools and churches—we must educate all." They were confident they would succeed.[19]

Success, however, depended on how the powers of government and the energies of republicanism were combined. No single man, however capable, could reach utopia alone. It was this ability to think in cooperative terms, to conceive projects on a national scale and develop aggressive plans to carry them out, that set Whigs apart from Democrats. It also gave them the appearance of being conservative when in fact they were anything but. To attain individual republican progress through cooperative action required balance, and balance required order. Whigs had not forsaken competition—they were too capitalistic for that—but they did think that competition could become wasteful if it were not directed to productive efforts. Thus the Whig ideal was to erect a social order that would encourage republicanism, promote the right kind of competition, and spread its benefits among all. In this fusion of system and individual enterprise, of collective activity and republicanism, Whigs anticipated the modernization of industrial America.[20]

Within this intellectual context, Whigs of the Western Reserve and Massachusetts were a special breed. Drawing upon cultural values that were, by 1845, over two hundred years old, they infused traditional Whig attitudes with a moral imperative that formed the core of political pietism. This moral imperative had two parts which, each in its own way, complemented and added to their faith in republicanism and their devotion to social harmony. On one hand lay a belief, old as the Puritans, that each individual was personally accountable for his actions. Puritanism had preached that no man could escape moral responsibility for his sins, and, while the Puritans were gone, the belief had remained. It had been transformed into an optimistic conviction that, through the exercise of self-regulation, mankind could approach perfection. In Boston men as diverse as the Unitarian preacher William Ellery Channing, the abolitionist Garrison, the transcendentalist philosopher Emerson, all reminded their public that the salvation of the world began with each man. No hope for universal redemption could be realized until every indivdual had set his conscience in order. If such a doctrine could be reduced to a rather simplistic anti-institutionalism, it was perfectly fitted to an age in which self-reliance and individual perfectibility seemed attainable goals.[21]

New England culture was much too conservative to accept the prospect of human perfection through self-regulation wholesale, however. So personal accountability was bolstered by a belief that the entire society was responsible for the conduct of its members. A form of moral coercion, of corporate moral responsibility, appeared. As the Puritans had kept a strict eye on the moral health of the community, New Englanders of later years eagerly pursued social reforms of every description and type. At its most ludicrous, corporate moral responsibility produced witchhunts. At its most enlightened, it provided schools, cared for the poor, and ministered to the sick.

The moral imperatives of personal accountability and collective responsibility gave a special meaning to the Whig emphasis on republicanism and regulation. New Englanders always tempered their optimism with doubt. Through education, trade, and self-rule, announced Samuel Bowles of the Springfield *Republican,* "MAN is reformed and revolutionized, and is everywhere adapting himself to the high requirements of freedom." But, Bowles warned, the benefits of progress could be abused. Like its alter ego, liberty, progress could be wasted in frivolous and self-centered pursuits. It would thus become "unintelligent, and therefore debasing and licentious." The educator Horace Mann explained the problem as a natural part of human nature. Each person harbored two selves. One was loving, beneficent, and awake to the moral dictums of God. The other consisted of a "gang of animal appetites, a horde of bandit propensities . . . each one of the whole pack being supremely bent upon its own indulgence, and ready to barter earth and heaven to win it.'' Without some sure form of control individuals would relapse to the state of beasts, and drag society with them. "In a word,'' Mann concluded, ''we must not add to the impulsive, without also adding to the regulating force.''[22]

To the New England mind, then, the ideal society was a delicate combination of opposites. Republican self-rule merged with corporate action to produce a community that was capable of boundless progress. The catalyst which made the ideal possible was an awareness that all progress ultimately rested on moral improvement. And that awareness recognized that no one was born a saint. Thus Whigs could be both conservative and progressive, democrats and elitists, optimists and pessimists—all in perfect consistency—as they worked to produce a balanced harmony of interests. Emerson, for one, recognized their dual nature. "They are the shop-till party,'' he complained of their suffocating conservatism. They were also "the active, enterprising, intelligent, well-meaning, and wealthy party of the people, the real love and strength of the American people.''[23]

Conscience Whigs, too, reacted to the ambivalences in their party. Some, such as Charles Francis Adams, were never entirely comfortable in an organization that seemed to place profit and enterprise above all else. "I do not love the principles of the Whig party,'' he remarked, adding drily, "or rather their want of principles.'' The apparent deification of a wild westerner such as Clay disturbed them. Clay, after all, played poker and drank late into the night—activities that did not coincide with the New England concept of the moral man. Webster was forever in debt, a fact that suggested that personal ambition could be carried to the point where it surpassed personal responsibility. And too often, as in 1840, the party appeared to place the quest for votes above the search for a moral society. Still, the faith and optimism—born of those who were firmly convinced they were right—remained. "Much as I am disturbed by what seems to fill the present,'' Sumner wrote, "I cannot lose my faith in the institutions of my country. I believe they are destined, at no distant date, to exercise a powerful influence over the ancient establishment of Europe.''[24]

When Conscience Whigs turned their eyes south, then, they experienced a twofold shock. In all its essential aspects the South represented a society gone out of control. Slavery—the peculiar institution that dominated all the rest—was incompatible with republicanism and self-regulation. It was, to be sure, an effective means of social control, but this control did not produce harmony. Instead, it threw society out of balance and defeated the very purpose for which it ostensibly existed. In the process slavery gave free reign to the worst instincts of human nature—the "animal appetites" so feared by Horace Mann—and retarded progress. Most damaging, it mocked the moral imperative.

The effect upon the slave was obvious. Under the absolute domination of the master, the slave had neither motive nor opportunity to exercise his capacity for self-control. While freemen toiled happily, gauging their rewards according to their personal initiative, slaves moped along, "indolent and wasteful, because without any better excitement than fear; stupid, because forbidden to learn." Without the inducement of personal progress, Palfrey maintained, the slave was trapped, unable to raise himself and certainly incapable of perfection. Free him, introduce "a new element of personal interest, and an intelligent hopeful purpose," and his self-esteem and hence his capacity for moral improvement would soar. Without that, he wallowed in a "brute life," no better than a serf.[25]

Apart from the plight of the individual black, the very existence of such a class eroded the moral foundations of social control in a republican society. No Conscience Whig ever argued that the members of a free society were absolutely equal. Their concept of natural harmony had strong elements of paternalism, for it assumed that the gifted and powerful would aid the weak. "Obviously, men are not born equal in physical strength, or in mental capacities . . .," wrote Sumner. "Diversity or inequality, in these respects, is the law of creation. From this difference springs divine harmony." It was no less true, however, that moral equality was a birthright of all. All societies were stratified, but those that used physical or intellectual inequalities as the basis for a civil caste system automatically ran against the will of God. Having ignored a moral imperative to treat each citizen as a child of the Creator, such societies risked destruction. Sumner argued his point before a state court considering a case of school desegregation. "We abjure all inequality before the law, but here is an inequality which touches not an individual, but a race. We revolt at the relation of caste; but here is a caste which is established under a constitution, declaring that all men are born equal." To Sumner the contradiction in terms was painfully, and perilously, obvious.[26]

Racial attitudes of the Conscience Whigs developed from this context. Admitting, with Summer, "that there is a distinction between the Ethiopian and Caucasian races," that the two were not equal, Conscience Whigs were still disturbed by the absurdity of erecting a caste system within a republic. Both North and South were guilty of perverting a basic tenet of republicanism through racism. J.A. Giddings, Joshua's son, was irate that Ohio prohibited blacks from voting. "It makes the color of a man's skin, the test of right to the privileges of citizenship," Giddings wrote. "No matter if he possesses a mind and talents that makes him the equal of HENRY CLAY or DANIEL WEBSTER, with ten times their moral honesty, yet if he happens to have any African blood in his veins he is excluded from the ballot box and from all political association with those that govern him . . ." And, Giddings concluded, "this is wrong. It is a violation of the fundamental principles of our government. It is an outrage upon a large and valuable class of our people."[27]

Giddings used the same argument to brush aside fears of miscegenation. Given the natural inequality of men, the very idea of race mixing was ludicrous, for neither race would be attracted to the other. Those who fretted over such things missed the essential point: that racism undermined the moral basis of a society. Misled by the "principle of *caste,*" they foolishly worried over the false issue of "*contamination of their blood with that of the negroes.*" "No consideration of the *rights* of the respective races, of their mental or moral improvement, or of the high duties devolving upon those most highly favored by Providence, can be brought to bear upon the dignified intellect"—Giddings was in a splendid fury—"of these beasts in human shape."[28]

There was a subtle casuistry in this argument. The younger Giddings seemed to be saying that, for the good of the republic, the races must be treated equally—when in fact blacks were generally inferior to whites. But if blacks were inferior, and if all societies were stratified, why not admit the fact and continue to treat them as such, even as slaves? One writer, Henry Wilson, perceived the question and attempted to deflect it by contending that—given their present status—blacks were incapable of moral equality with whites. And the moral issue was, again, paramount.

Addressing his remarks to a conservative friend in Maine, Wilson noted that most northerners opposed slavery for its degrading effect upon the white race. This Wilson could not accept. "The reason why I and those with which I act," he explained, "oppose Slavery, is because it is WRONG—a violation of Heaven's laws, a violence done to humanity, a libel upon our character as a nation professing universal freedom, but guilty of the 'vilest oppression the sun ever saw.'" The greatest curse of slavery, to Wilson, was in forcing the slave "to toil beneath the bloody lash through a life greatly abbreviated by the severity of the unpaid tasks and the moral and social deprivations, necessarily a part of this stupendous legalized system of injustice and oppression."[29]

Comparing the white and black races directly, Wilson argued that it was true that blacks in Africa were guilty of outrageous crimes and brutality, particularly in their religious rites. Moreover, he admitted that he thought that Western culture was far advanced over African and thus implied a greater capacity on the part of whites for progress. But, he pointed out, even though the whites were supposedly civilized and Christian, their "thirst for power and endless domain" belied their claim for superiority. They bought and sold slaves, they warred upon each other, all in the name of *"God, Mammon, Avarice."* "The practices of the 'two races,' " he concluded, *"differ but little in kind,* though enacted under widely different circumstances, and presenting quite a different aspect at first sight . . ." Thus moral degeneracy did not adhere to a color line. It could be accentuated, however, by the depravity of slavery. "How much improvement do you expect in any race, during two hundred years, whose country during all that time is invaded by a foreign, *mercenary* race . . . Pray, what improvement has any country ever been known to make in learning and the arts of civilized life during an invasion? Is Mexico growing wiser and better by the present invasion of her soil by us?"[30]

Wilson's remarks were revealing. He never explicitly said that whites and blacks were equal. His argument that whites could be as uncivilized as tribal Africans proved nothing; it did not talk of the equal abilities of blacks and whites for self-improvement, only their equal ability for war. He did, of course, imply that blacks deserved the same chance, the same rights, as did whites, but his argument here was directed more toward ending the brutalizing institution of slavery than to placing whites and blacks on an equal plane. In the end he was left in a position that closely resembled that of the Barnburners: he was violently agitated over slavery; he was unsure as to what would happen to blacks after emancipation.

The surest ground, then, for attacking slavery was its effect upon the whole society, white and black, individual and collective. "The chain of slavery is of necessity a double chain," wrote Stephen C. Phillips, "and . . . will be found to bind as closely across the hands of the master as around the neck of the slave." Slavery violated the sense of regulated power that Whigs praised so loudly in their economic plans and that pervaded their concept of the entire society. By providing unlimited authority of one class over another, slavery opened the door to all manner of abuses. This upset the natural harmony of a regulated society. While the rights of the slave were abrogated, the slaveholder was left to slip into "such idleness and gross indulgences as the forced labor at [his] command may admit." In short, the condition of the South fulfilled Jefferson's observation—which the Conscience Whigs were fond of pointing out— that slavery warped the democratic ideal by allowing "the most unremitting despotism on the one part, and degrading submissions on the other."[31]

Robbed of his incentive for self-regulation, the slaveholder would certainly lapse into moral degeneracy. Work, for example, was an excellent companion to moral development, for it taught habits of thrift, responsibility, and personal accountability. Where work was associated with a degraded caste, however, idleness became the ideal and moral corruption the result. "White males at the South, as a mass, do not labor," complained the Ashtabula *Sentinel*. "Their business is law, medicine, theology, politics, and slave driving, mingled with the idle habits of gambling, horse racing, cock fighting, and sporting." The ultimate effect was "to drive all industrious mechanics into regions of free labor, where they are not contaminated by contact with slavery, which degrades them." Those who remained were incapable of self-support, became more idle and more vicious as time passed. "When slavery dies, as die it must," the *Sentinel* asked, "what is to become of this slough of the accursed system?"[32]

The effects of all this upon social progress were plain. In Kentucky, for example, Phillips observed that "the progressive increase of slavery" had wasted the economy of that state and had stifled the industry of its citizens, while immediately to the north Ohio, "with no advantage but that which makes the difference between a Free and a Slave State," flourished. Ohio offered "enterprise attracting and accumulating capital and investing it in every form of improvement"—good Whig activities—"education diffusing intelligence, Industry crowned with plenty, science erecting its observatory, and the arts reviving in their classic glory." Kentucky offered none of these, only slaves in chains and masters idling away in sleepy dissipation.[33]

All these degrading aspects of slavery might have been tolerable if they had affected only the South. Barnburners, for instance, disliked slavery but were willing to leave the institution alone as long as it did not adversely affect politics in New York. The case was different with the Conscience Whigs. Taught to think in broad national terms, the younger Whigs viewed slavery as "a sure prognostic of National degeneracy and disgrace." Its extension proclaimed American democracy a fraud, arrested progress, and threw the active social order out of balance. While Europe moved toward democracy, slavery held the United States back. Extending slavery, Adams wrote, was a "backward step of liberty in the new hemisphere . . . The settled policy of the United States is to be defiance of the world . . . And the free States are to be crippled in their commerce and drained of their wealth, to sustain this new crusade in support of the new democratic principle, now proclaimed in America, that all men are *not* born free and equal." Giddings too was disgusted. Even the monarch in Tunisia had curbed slavery, he noted, and remarked: "This Barbarian Prince has gone entirely ahead of this nation in civilization and refinement."[34]

These regressive effects of slavery were intolerable to the political pietist, who pursued his crusade with religious fervor directed primarily at restoring the country to its former role as the first modern democratic republic. A "great struggle was to be made," announced Adams, "to maintain the original purposes of the Constitution, against the perversion of it to the protection of an aristocracy." If the extension of slavery could be stopped, Palfrey wrote:

then would a triumph be won for liberty and righteousness . . . . Then would the civilized and Christian world ring with applauses to a nation, at whose threatened abandonment of the principles, that had raised it to honor, it is now gazing with consternation and amazement. Then would be manifested a principle of permanency in our institutions, and a character in our people, which would make the good and wise throughout the earth devoutly thank God and take courage.

Henry Wilson put it simply: "We must restore our government to its original and pristine purity."[35]

But it was obvious that slavery would not die quickly or soon. Until it did, and until the blot of slavery could be erased entirely from the national character, the Conscience Whigs worked to confine its power, to make it strictly local in its influence, and to dissociate it from the free states completely. The path for their efforts was clear: they must see that the free states had no part in extending slavery through acts of the national government, and they must resist all wars waged to protect slavery. "Have not the free states as clear and undisputable a right to be entirely exempt from the expense and from what they deem to be the guilt and disgrace of Slavery," Giddings asked Calhoun, "as the Slave States have to continue and enjoy that institution?" The annexation of Texas plainly violated that right, for admitting new states required an act of Congress, which made all states partners in the crime. "God forbid that the voters and voices of Northern freemen should help to bind anew the fetters of the slave!" cried Sumner in one of his more strident moments. And he brought the guilt progressively closer to home. "God forbid that the lash of the slave dealer should descend by any sanction of New England! God forbid that the blood which spurts from the lacerated, quivering flesh of the slave should soil the white garments of Massachusetts!"[36]

Presented as an abstract set of ideals, these attitudes toward slavery were readily accepted by New England Whigs or those on the Western Reserve. Incorporating them into a statement of party principles, however, met stiff resistance. Conscience Whigs in Massachusetts faced problems that were especially severe. By 1845 Massachusetts lagged behind other states in the modernizaton of its party system. At a time when the state was emerging as an industrial and urban power with few, if any, equals its politics remained locked in the traditions of an earlier age. The political power of a few families was immense. The Appletons, Lawrences, and Winthrops were more than "gentlemen of property"; they also possessed the key element of deferential elites, "standing." Taking their influence from wealth, family, commercial or industrial leadership, or any combination of the three, these families wielded political power with unassuming ease, as had the Adamses or Otises before them. Early in the century Jefferson had observed a "traditionary reverence for certain families, which has rendered the offices of government nearly hereditary" in Massachusetts. Time had modified the picture only slightly.[37]

This situation was largely due to tradition, yet other factors supported it. Political power in Massachusetts focused primarily on the town, not the larger and more diverse county. With over three hundred townships spread over a small area, most political or governmental business was transacted within a personal, almost familial, framework. Of all the other states only Kentucky, with its numberless small counties, divided power so minutely. While this division may have encouraged democratic participation in local affairs, its effect on state politics was precisely the reverse. There Boston—with its disproportionately large representation and immense wealth—was clearly dominant. Those who ruled Boston, then, possessed remarkable influence over the rest of the state. And those who ruled Boston were few. Throughout the first half of the nineteenth century, much of Massachusetts political development involved a longstanding power struggle between the established power of the metropolis and its elite and the rising demands of the countryside and its townships. Even after the Civil War it remained unclear who had won.[38]

Augmenting the influence of Boston's upper class was the general absence of vigorous two-party competition. Boston Whigs reigned supreme over a field that offered only weak resistance. Twice—and no more—between 1830 and 1850 were the Democrats able to win the yearly contest for governor. At no time did they elect a senator. Never did they carry the state for a Democratic president. Although the Democrats consistently made up 40 percent of the electorate, they were able to win only when the Whigs were divided. Reduced to the status of a permanent minority, Democrats neglected their party machinery and instead concentrated on securing and manipulating federal partonage. Hawthorne drafted *The Scarlet Letter* at federal expense in the Salem custom house. George Bancroft sat in the cabinet, but never in the state capitol. Marcus Morton and David Henshaw feuded incessantly over the division of presidential spoils, but only Morton, who was not the more powerful of the two, ever became governor.[39]

Reinforcing all this was the New England world view itself. In a society that praised order, stability, and social control, any change in policy had to move through carefully delineated channels of power. Conscience Whigs were of course aware of this; they even applauded it. "Our movement is conservative," Sumner declared at the meeting on November 4. Adams agreed. It was not proper, not natural, for ad hoc meetings to demand change, no matter how worthy the cause. "The tendency of such assemblages is to extreme violence, which defeats its own end . . .," he wrote. "If the people really feel the necessity of exerting themselves, they may do it most effectually by concentrating in the regular and customary forms."[40]

The regular and customary forms involved, of course, the great families of Boston. Men such as Winthrop or Lawrence were more than mere local overlords. They were persons of national prominence, with close ties to all regions of the country through their economic or political positions. Moreover, they were among the stoutest defenders of order and stability. They believed in change and innovation (the Lawrences, for example, were pioneers in corporate management), but they also believed that change must be slow, developmental, and ordered. These attitudes characterized their view of the slavery issue. If the moral and political stewardship of the community rested with the elite, then the task of leading the battle against slavery fell to their hands. Any sudden or extreme change of policy—as embodied in their party principles—would surely upset the delicate political balance within the nation. That could produce only ill, for it would exacerbate sectional tensions. Slavery, therefore, must be attacked gradually, with a proper respect for southern society and a keen eye on the welfare of New England textile mills. Thus the urgency with which Conscience Whigs voiced their demands appeared, to the elite, radical and unsettling. They would have none of it.

The cautious power of the Whig leadership frustrated Conscience Whigs immensely. Not wishing to seem radical, they did not want to see their cause die of neglect. Convinced that the mass of voters supported them, Conscience Whigs could not utter a word without appearing impertinent or disrespectful. The fact that many Cotton Whigs privately agreed with the views of the Conscience faction only made matters worse. Conscience Whigs could never understand why the leadership, having gone part way down the path of antislavery, could not go further. The "thin, colorless antislavery" of Winthrop and Lawrence was infuriating.[41]

Thus the developing clash between the two groups became increasingly acrimonious and almost self-defeating. Sumner, for example, often led in attacking the complacency of Cotton Whigs such as Winthrop. Yet when he did so he grieved over his action because he had long respected and deferred to the man. Whenever Winthrop replied in kind, as he was bound to do, Sumner sulked mightily. Only after many such battles and defeats did the Conscience Whigs begin to set aside their respect for authority and for the whole structure of deference among Bostonians. When they did so, they immediately began to cut themselves off from the Whig party.

Giddings's problems in Ohio were quite different. There was, to begin, no elite to be persuaded, no traditions of deference to be overcome. Ohio was a far more typical political arena than Massachusetts. It mixed regional divisions with vigorous two-party competition in a state that was, compared to Massachusetts, geographically large and culturally heterogeneous. Thus, while Giddings enjoyed considerable support in his home territory, he always faced the resistance of Whigs in southern Ohio. An unqualified opposition to slavery was feasible on the Western Reserve; not so farther south. One solution to this political conundrum would have been conciliation. For the sake of party unity Giddings could have softened his attacks on slavery. Yet neither Giddings nor his supporters were inclined to do so. Instead, as the crisis deepened, Giddings began to adopt a harder line on slavery in an attempt to preempt the appeal of the Liberty party and to fuse their support with his own. Given the impossibility of convincing Whigs in southern Ohio to adopt a strong stand against slavery, and given the moral urgency with which Giddings approached his task, his course was logical.

Whatever political climate the Conscience Whigs worked in, the onset of war in May, 1846, produced a crisis. War was a statement of national policy, and war fought to defend slave territory (obtained by questionable means) in a sense committed the United States to the perpetuation of human bondage. "Its prosecution," warned Giddings, "will be but an increase of our national guilt." Resistance was of course inescapable, and the articulation of that protest provided the catalyst for the organization of the Conscience Whig movement.[42]

As the war began, Giddings prepared once more to stamp his opinions upon the Whig party. Annexation, he reasoned, had been palatable to moderate Whigs because it involved no violence; war, on the other hand, might produce the shock needed to pull them into a firm stand against slavery. There were signs that this change had already begun. The war was unpopular on the Reserve, and Thomas Corwin, the Whig senator from Ohio, had publicly expressed his disgust at the hostilities. Giddings concluded that a radical statement against the violence might crystallize the opposition.

In June he released a long polemic which declared the Union dissolved and the war unconstitutional. The simple act of annexation had severed the Union, he declared, by admitting a foreign nation. A cruel trick had been played upon the North "by the votes of southern slaveholding members of Congress, and northern men who were servilely subject to Southern dictation." Now these same conspirators had called upon the North "to go to the Rio Grande, meet the dangers of war and pestilence, in order to defend the slavery of Texas." "No such moral or political obligation rests upon us," he countered. The people of Ohio and the North had authorized no one "to subject us to dishonorable deaths in defence of Texian slavery." In light of the conspiracy, therefore, "our Union of 1787 has been entirely dissolved."[43]

Giddings in fact believed no such thing. The argument was a political ploy by which he hoped to accomplish two things. First, it was a warning that the time for compromises with the South had ceased. If the Constitution could be bent and betrayed by a small group of slaveholders, the only recourse was to "depend upon our own resistance, for the prevention of this nefarious conspiracy against

Northern freedom." Second, he was taking a calculated risk. Giddings had advocated a position so extreme that only the Liberty party could seriously endorse it. Yet moderate Whigs would be compelled to deal with it, and in doing so might settle for a compromise that would still be an improvement over their earlier vacillations concerning slavery.[44]

Giddings judged wrongly. Moderate Whigs, on and off the Reserve, were appalled by his statement, which conjured up unpleasant memories of the Hartford convention of 1815. The Cleveland *Herald* observed coolly: "We think it the better part of wisdom . . . to bear the ills we have, than to fly and bid welcome to those which would immediately come with the dissolution of these States." Giddings's good friend Albert Gallatin Riddle cautioned that such an opinion, released in an election year, was explosive. "Those who are trying to succeed you," he warned, "are attempting to Strongly use it against you."[45]

His political life suddenly at stake, Giddings turned to the only course left—cooperation with the Liberty party. Yet even that proved unfeasible. Regular Whigs such as Senator Thomas Corwin were "not for such an union," since it would offend those in southern Ohio. And Liberty men such as Salmon P. Chase of Cincinnati could not tolerate the idea of joining the Whig ranks. "Liberty men," he observed, "cannot be mustered *there*." Left without the protection of a formal alliance, Giddings was forced to walk a delicate line between Whigs and Liberty men.[46]

He did so skillfully. Edward Wade, a prominent leader of the Liberty party in Ohio, described Giddings's tactics bitterly. Giddings, wrote Wade, could say "to the Pro Slavery portion of his party, 'take me or the Liberty men will succeed,' and to the Anti Slavery Whigs, 'we the Whig party are the real & true Liberty party, take me or Loco Focoism will triumph." Giddings was not quite that unscrupulous, but Wade's analysis was essentially correct. Giddings's strongest tactic in retaining his support was to play upon the intense party rivalry between Democrats and Whigs. "Whig biggotry," as Wade called it, combined with moral appeals against the war, kept Giddings's coalition together. He won handily in November.[47]

Yet he grew despondent at the course of the Whigs. The party had not given him the kind of spontaneous support he had wanted, and when Congress convened in December he noted a marked deterioration of Whig opposition to the war. "There is a concerted effort to lead the public mind to the support of this . . . miserable war," he wrote to Horace Greeley. "I hope you may look ahead and see where that policy is to lead." Giddings noted that David Wilmot had introduced a proposal to exclude slavery from conquered Mexican territories. The Proviso would no doubt fail, in which case the war "will be admitted as a war of *Conquest to Extend Slavery,* and our Whigs voting to pay out the public treasure for that purpose." In that event, antislavery Whigs and compromisers "must come to a separation."[48]

"There is a tendency to the dissolution of existing parties," Adams noted in July, 1846, "but what shape they will take I cannot see." Like all Conscience Whigs, Adams devoutly believed that the moral purity of their cause would arouse widespread, if latent, support. Yet, like anyone acquainted with the realities of party politics in Massachusetts, he knew that the invisible power of the Whig elite would seek to temper any spontaneous movement against slavery. The subscription list of the *Whig* bore silent testimony to the difficulty of fielding an antislavery crusade. Circulation had shot up at first, but as 1846 wore on the list of new subscribers dwindled. Still, Adams and his friends believed that there was enough antislavery sentiment in the state to pull the party away from compromise with the South, especially over the war. While Adams talked of dissolution, Conscience Whigs continued to work through the traditional channels of the regular party.[49]

Those channels were fast closing, however. The first test came over Winthrop's endorsement of the war bill. In May Polk had asked for money and arms for the war, cleverly prefacing his request with the statement that hostilities had begun by the act of Mexico. A congressman who disapproved of the war but who did not want to see his own troops slaughtered for lack of ammunition was forced to vote for both or neither. While seven representatives from Massachusetts chose not to approve the bill, Winthrop did. Although he considered Polk's preamble a lie, he felt obligated to supply the troops. "When the Condition of things was so critical," he observed, "I could not allow the insertion of a false fact to prevent my being found on the side of the National Defense." Privately he added that he did not want to be "mixed up with a few third party men."[50]

Conscience Whigs struck hard at Winthrop's vote. "Either the preamble to the War bill tells the truth, or it tells what is not," exclaimed the *Whig.* Winthrop, confronted by a moral dilemma, had given in to a lie, setting his name "in perpetual attestation to a falsehood." Sumner was more graphic. Regardless of the congressman's personal character, he wrote, Winthrop had sanctioned "unquestionably the most wicked act, in our history." In the process he had disgraced the state and the party and had consigned innocent men to death. "Blood! Blood!" he raged, "is on the hands of the representative from Boston."[51]

This was too much. Mudslinging was not a gentlemen's game, and in the paternalistic atmosphere of Boston politics Sumner's attack echoed like the screamings of a demented child. (Sumner himself immediately regretted it.) It offended the Whig emphasis on order and stability. If one man or one faction were allowed to strike at one of the most respected pillars of society with impunity, then the entire social structure was in peril. Quietly the doors of the Whig party began to swing shut to the Conscience group. "The course taken by the Whig . . . ," declared the editor of the Boston *Atlas*, "is perfectly inexcusable and outrageous." Winthrop, deeply hurt, ended all relations with Sumner. "Your habitual indulgence in strains of extravagant thought & exaggerated expressions . . . ," he explained, "has, perhaps, impaired your discrimination in the employment of language." But he was in no mood to forgive. "My hand is not at the service of any one, who has denounced it . . . as being stained with blood."[52]

In another state Winthrop's reaction would have been but one episode in the game of politics. In Boston, however, with its quasi-deferential political structure and one-party domination, it spelled trouble for any group seeking influence in the highest party councils. The Conscience Whigs were at best a faction. They held no real leverage in the making of party decisions and as a result relied upon the good will of the party hierarchy to make their case known. By going outside the party structure—in fact, by offending it—they were attempting to change the rules by which politics was governed in Massachusetts. Established political leaders naturally would not allow such an eventuality without a long and arduous fight.

Increasingly aware of these facts, the Conscience Whigs attempted one more time to commit the party to an unequivocal stand against the war and slavery, this time by popular mandate. Fortunately, their campaign through the *Whig* had produced some tangible results, for at the state convention in September, 1846, they could count on several delegates from the rural areas to identify the war squarely with the slavery issue. Moreover, Cotton Whigs, alarmed by the controversy, thought it "politic" to allow the Conscience faction a certain number of seats. What was needed was a firm platform to rally the antislavery forces.[53]

Meeting in Adams's office, Sumner, Palfrey, and Phillips drew up a resolution that directly labeled slavery as the root cause of all the troubles plaguing the Union and the party. All previous issues—banks and tariffs—had been absorbed into the conflict between the free and the slave states, the resolution stated. "The political power of Slavery, entrenched behind the pillars of the Constitution, and now grasping the purse and wielding the sword of the Union, is the most formidable antagonist which the Whigs . . . are now compelled to encounter." It was incumbent upon Massachusetts Whigs, therefore, to cease all compromises with the South. "This will make a platform for us to stand upon," Adams remarked, "but we shall also be compelled to a difference with the party. Well, this must be hasarded too. We are on a deep sea and there is no going backward."[54]

As usual, however, the Whig leadership frustrated their plans. Calmly allowing the Conscience group to present their case, the Cotton Whigs quietly introduced a far milder resolution that condemned slavery as "a great, moral, political, and social evil" and which promised to support "all constitutional and proper means" to curtail it. The move worked well. Where the specific, strongly worded motion of the Conscience Whigs subordinated all other party issues to the slavery question, the vague, hazy one of the party leaders simply condemned the institution in terms that anyone in Boston could support. After a brief debate the delegates adopted the Cotton plank and adjourned.[55]

Stunned, the Conscience Whigs watched their efforts of the past months apparently collapse. Confused and disheartened, they decided to run Sumner as an independent against Winthrop. It was a serious blunder. The *Atlas* quickly labeled the Conscience Whigs as political interlopers, greedy young men who wanted only office, not principles. "We brand this conduct as deceptive, insincere, and hypocritical. If they have ever been members of the Whig Party, we publicly denounce them as deserters from its ranks, and traitors to the true political faith." Sensitive to the charge of opportunism, Sumner withdrew, and Samuel Gridley Howe took his place. In the election Winthrop crushed both Howe and the Democratic contender. At the same time Palfrey, who had hoped to win the seat from Middlesex County, was forced into a runoff because no candidate there won the prescribed majority. "This is all of it very bad," Adams confessed.[56]

The results of the convention and of the election drove one fact home to the Conscience Whigs: so long as they relied solely on appeals to conscience, so long as they lacked a strong base of political power and had no means of clear, effective organization, they would remain helpless to check the influence of the conservative, regular party

organizations. Since neither regular Whigs nor regular Democrats would have them, the old idea of a third party, broader and more inclusive than the Liberty, began to take on new importance. By January, 1847, they noted that some Democrats were beginning to rally behind the Wilmot Proviso, which had been introduced in August; a new party, constructed on the principle of opposition to slave extension, seemed possible. Accordingly, both Adams and Sumner began to probe the sentiments of other antislavery Whigs. Foremost in their minds was the election of 1848. "We have been reflecting here upon the propriety of a declaration, *in advance,*" Adams wrote to Giddings, "that the crisis is such we can no longer trust a slaveholder at the head of the government. Do you think the time has come for it?" Sumner was more direct. "There is a breaking up of both parties," he wrote. "The Northern wing of the Democracy is breaking off from its slaveholding allies, and so is the Northern wing of the Whigs." Of one thing he was certain: slavery "has at last got into our politics. It will enter the next Presidential election in 1848."[57]

CHAPTER THREE

THE LIBERTY PARTY

THE situation of the Liberty party in 1844 was, by definition, different from that of the Barnburners or the Conscience Whigs. Barnburners were a potent, well-disciplined, and well-led faction of a major party. They had traditionally assumed an important role in governing national affairs, and part of their rage was fueled by the conviction that their status was in decline. Conscience Whigs were weak and youthful in Massachusetts, strong and established in Ohio—but like the Barnburners anxious to act within the framework of their traditional party organizations. By contrast, the Liberty party stood apart. It was the unwelcome child of the second American party system, the third party. Having renounced both Whigs and Democrats, having done so for the sake of a particular and upsetting cause, Liberty men labored under the most hostile of political environments. To make matters worse, their efforts were not producing the results they had anticipated when, in 1840, they had formed their organization.

The Liberty party had begun in 1840 as an outgrowth of the American and Foreign Anti-Slavery Society. The latter organization appeared in the wake of an acrimonious split between the followers of William Lloyd Garrison and his critics in the American Anti-Slavery Society. The immediate cause of the division was over the question of women's rights—which Garrison advocated and which he successfully introduced into the practices of the AASS. Most historians, however, have concluded that the split ran much deeper. Garrison was the perfect radical. He championed a variety of reforms (some thought, indiscriminately) including abolition, pacifism, and feminism, all within a framework of "non-resistance." Non-resistance was essentially a form of anarchism. It denounced human government as hopelessly corrupt and evil, and posited instead the government of God on earth. Only in a spirit of brotherly love, not political manipulation, could mankind hope to achieve perfection. The tactics of the non-resistant, then, were distinctly apolitical: to teach, to disturb, to elevate the public conscience were the proper activities of the agitator. Political action, grounded as it was in a corrupt system, was itself corrupting.[1]

Those who criticized this philosophy were a diverse and numerous lot. Lewis and Arthur Tappan of New York were wealthy business-men who disliked Garrison's radicalism, particularly his insistence on women's rights. So did James G. Birney of Michigan, an ex-slaveholder who twice ran as the Liberty party's candidate for president. More complex was Gerrit Smith of upstate New York. Smith was absurdly rich, intimate with Garrison, yet convinced that political action was just and feasible. He ran as the party's first candidate for governor in New York. Gamaliel Bailey, editor of the Cincinnati *Philanthropist,* was an eager convert to abolitionist politics, and the party's best journalist. Finally, Theodore Dwight Weld, as influential as Garrison but without the latter's flair for publicity, was crucial in directing abolitionists to political action by helping Giddings battle the gag rule in 1838 and 1839. He never, however, participated actively in the Liberty party.[2]

All found Garrison's ideas either misdirected or naive. Birney, for example, could not accept the proposition that human government was inherently evil or that political action was debasing. Civil government, he explained, was "a blessing," and the franchise a sacred trust. Thus every form of struggle against slavery, including politics, was legitimate. "We cannot be innocent," Birney concluded, "if we neglect the power it confers." Moreover, Garrison's concept of Christian anarchism offered no realistic alternative in combatting an institution that was itself organized and political. Garrison's plan "of navigating our poor, misguided ship," commented one observer, "is to renounce helm, ropes, compass, anchor, all, jump overboard and scream!" A far better and more effective tool was a political party devoted entirely to the cause of emancipation.[3]

One might conclude that Garrison and his critics stood poles apart; in reality, they shared many basic assumptions, and these as-sumptions, in turn, gave the Liberty party its special nature. The

Liberty party was the political expression of an evangelical tradition that stressed the inner laws of morality above devotional adherence to forms. Both Garrisonians and Liberty men assumed that every person possessed an innate ability to comprehend God's moral laws and to act accordingly. The rules of right conduct came not from established institutions or traditions—however worthy—but from within. Garrison carried this concept so far that he became an anti-sabbatarian. Every day, not just Sunday, was holy.

Yet man was also prone to corruption. Blinded to the true nature of moral law or simply ignorant of its meaning, men erected institutions that degraded and debased both those who led them and those who served them. Such institutions were inherently sinful and could not be explained away by appeals to tradition or custom. Thus the eighteenth-century concept of gradual reform gave way to a more urgent demand that society renounce its evil ways immediately— exactly as the dying thief might repent of his sins.

Slavery was such a sin. By holding other men in bondage slaveholders had attempted to interpose their own temporal authority between God and the slave. This was theft of the soul. "He who robs his fellow man of this," Weld charged, "tramples upon right, subverts justice, outrages humanity, unsettles the foundations of human safety, and sacrilegiously assumes the prerogative of God." The only way to rid society of this monstrosity, then, was through an immediate, unqualified act of repentance. To do otherwise would perpetuate a crime. Immediate emancipation was "nothing more or less . . . than immediate repentance, applied to this particular sin."[4]

Of course, no abolitionist seriously believed that 300,000 southerners would emancipate their slaves in a single, instantaneous act. They did not, in fact, believe that slaveholders had any desire to do so. They were convinced, however, that an aroused public could bring such pressure upon the South that ultimately the slaveholder would have no other choice. Again, this conviction proceeded from their concept of moral law. It resided within each heart; if awakened, it would produce the kind of outrage necessary to uplift and reform even the most hardened criminal. In short, men sank to the lowest level of degeneracy allowed them. If that level were raised, they would have to rise with it.[5]

The abolitionist, then, was a teacher. Whether Garrisonian or not, the role of the agitator was to instruct the unenlightened concerning the true meaning of righteousness. There was in this attitude a marriage of the intuitive and the rational, which could be seen in the types of appeals the abolitionist made. On one hand, he could be devastatingly effective in playing upon the emotional. The abolitionist painted lurid scenes of the barbarities of slavery, pointing to lacerated flesh, motherless infants, shortened lives. On the other hand, he could be deftly analytical, showing that slavery was not profitable, not in accord with biblical teachings, contrary to the letter of the Declaration of Independence. Both approaches were valid, for each attempted to awaken the moral sense through a form of education.

The major difference between Garrison and the Liberty men concerned the means, not the intent, of abolitionist action. While Garrison condemned all human institutions, government as well as slavery, as corrupt, political abolitionists were more sanguine. They were also, presumably, more pragmatic. Non-resistance was fine as a form of moral coercion, but since government was a divine gift it, too, should be brought to bear in the battle against evil. All methods of protest, short of violence, were legitimate. The split with Garrison was inevitable in a movement that by 1840 had reached the point of diversification. Abolitionism had grown so large that it needed other outlets for expression.[6]

Since the ideological basis for the Liberty party was so similar to that of the non-resistants, the tactics and organizational form of the party were radically different from either of the major parties. The Liberty party was primarily an educational institution, with a declared purpose of instructing voters in their moral duty. The aim of Liberty men, wrote one editor, lay "in the moral influence we exert, and in the moral and reformatory character we give to the enterprize." Accordingly, the party avoided the traditional role of being all things to all people. It did not speak to economic issues, nor did it promise the rewards of office to its patrons. Instead, it focused on the one issue of slavery; all others were irrelevant, because they did not involve great moral questions. "The people would contrive some way to live," wrote Zebina Eastman of the Chicago *Western Citizen,* whether they had a bank, a high tariff, or neither. It was time, he added, for voters to consider "Whether there are not greater ideas and principles on which we can now unite." Lewis Tappan was more succinct. The Liberty party, "in order to accomplish much, must be a one issue party." The issue was slavery. In this respect the Liberty party was an extreme example of the politics of pietism, and for this reason Liberty men generally felt most comfortable with antislavery Whigs who thought in similar terms.[7]

Yet Liberty men were reluctant to form coalitions with the Whigs or anyone else. Behind their concept of the party as an educational aid lay a deep mistrust of the very existence of parties. Believing, as they did, in the moral duty of the individual, political abolitionists were alarmed by the nature of organized parties in the Jacksonian era. Both Whigs and Democrats depended upon machine-like systemization and regularity to insure voter loyalty. This subordination of the individual to an institution was precisely the kind of debasement that allowed southerners to defend slavery without reference to personal sin. Slavery, wrote one abolitionist, denied the black his humanity, ranked him not among *"sentient beings,* but among things." In strikingly similar terms an abolitionist in New Hampshire condemned parties. Those who regimented themselves to the call of party were "not men by themselves, but a portion—a toe or finger or a fragment of dead flesh, without any individual soul—of the party to which they belong."[8]

Garrison, of course, agreed. Party politics corrupted all who participated, he argued. The temptations of power, sharpened by compromise and deceit, were incompatible with the duties of the agitator-teacher. Yet Garrison took this logic in one direction; Liberty men, in another. The latter countered Garrison's doubts by promising that their organization would be different. The focus on the single issue of slavery was as much an expression of desire to remain pure as it was an ideological necessity to awaken the public. They had little hope that they would actually win, but they did foresee the day when the logic and righteousness of their position would become irresistible to an enlightened electorate—and hence, to the men who led them. "Our Motto should be, *'form alliances with no political party, but enstamp our principles upon all!* '" Against this policy of political regeneration by moral example, Garrison's withdrawal appeared self-defeating.[9]

According to Garrison, however, it was the Liberty party, not he, that was doomed to defeat. Garrison possessed a tough, shrewd political sense that neither his critics nor most historians have granted him. He never underestimated the value of political action. Quite the reverse. "I have always expected, I still expect, to see abolition at the ballot box," he noted in 1839. He supported abolitionists who used their votes as barter in elections. Where campaigns were close, abolitionists could wring concessions from one of the regular parties without becoming directly involved in politics. This course seemed to him to be the best way to reap the fruits of politics without being ripped apart by the thorns. A separate antislavery party, however, could succeed only if it adopted wholesale the tactics of the opposition. It would have to form coalitions, make concessions, and dilute the purity of its moral message in order to win. In doing so abolitionists would cease to be abolitionists and would become partisans. Garrison was entirely willing that others—not devoted to immediate emancipation—should form antislavery parties. These he would encourage. But for an abolitionist to do so meant either compromise or humiliating defeat, or both.[10]

Liberty men never quite understood Garrison's analysis. From the start of their movement, however, they experienced precisely the kinds of pressures and ambiguities he had predicted. Suspicious of parties, they did not behave as a party. Their candidate, Birney, was a poor and unexciting campaigner by design. He did not wish to appear actually to want the presidency, but used the stump as a lectern for moral instruction. The party avoided all issues not involving slavery in an effort to remain pure and in so doing presented itself as radical or irrelevant to most voters. A few Liberty men were more flexible. In certain states, particularly in the West, they attempted to form coalitions with Whigs. But these efforts were sporadic, largely unsuccessful, and frowned upon by the party leadership. Thus the course of the Liberty party from 1840 to 1844 presented a curious spectacle: composed of men who did not believe in parties, guided by principles that precluded compromise, avoiding systematic organizations and campaigns in order to maintain its moral mission, it attempted to change the course of party politics.

The results were disheartening. During the campaign of 1844, when the Texas issue had injected slavery deep into political debate, Liberty men found themselves unable to capitalize on their fortune. In drafting a platform, for example, they attempted to walk the narrow line between purity and compromise and succeeded in only blurring their identity. They condemned slavery as a great moral evil. They denounced slaveholders as a "privileged aristocracy" growing powerful on the backs of the disfranchised. They contended that the evil influence of slavery had introduced "the grossest form and most revolting manifestation of Despotism" into a nation that was supposed to be a democracy. They promised to rescue the federal government "from the grasp of the slave power."[11]

But as to how the rescue would take place the platform was vague. In drafting their resolutions Liberty men realized that, as politicians, they must obtain votes. They could not allow themselves to be identified in the public mind with Garrison's anarchism. The result was a platform demanding that slavery be kept "strictly local," under the protection of the state governments only. That being the case, the federal government must dissociate itself from supporting slavery either directly or indirectly. It must renounce all measures "continuing or favoring slavery in the District of Columbia, in the Territory of Florida, or on the high seas." It must not extend its protection into the territories. There was no mention in the platform of direct abolition, nor was there hint that Congress should interfere with slavery in the states. On only one point did the party advocate oppositive action against slavery: the fugitive law should be treated as "utterly null and void."

This was not enough to make the party distinct. Clay's initial letter opposing annexation was sufficient to reassure most antislavery Whigs that their own party was an adequate safeguard against slavery. Even Bailey grudgingly admitted that Clay's letter was "highly honorable." Webster undercut their appeal further by proposing to do away with the problems of Texas and slavery entirely simply by adding no more territory to the United States. Liberty men heartily endorsed the notion. "I know no good reason why we should desire to have Texas united to us," Birney declared. Such a move proceeded from a "wild, bucanneer spirit of adventure" which was "at war with all solid improvement and true civilization." Unfortunately for the Liberty party, Webster commanded far more respect than Birney among antislavery Whigs. Moreover, he already held enormous political power.[12]

The outcome was predictable. Party loyalty and fear of the annexationist Polk kept most Whigs true to their organization in 1844. Party loyalty and outright hostility to the Liberty men sufficed for the Democrats. In a campaign for the presidency the Liberty party mustered a scant 5,000 votes more than they had polled in the state elections of 1843. That gave them a total of about 60,000 supporters—hardly a ripple in an aggregate vote of over 2,600,000. The only tangible result Liberty men could point to was the vote in New York. There it appeared that the party had drained off just enough support from Clay to give the state and the electoral college to Polk. It was a pyrrhic victory, for an outspoken annexationist was now president.

The results of the election sharply divided Liberty men and exposed yet another type of abolitionist—a type which had not been prominent in the formative years of the 1830s. Originating primarily in the West, particularly Ohio, the new breed accepted both the desirability and legitimacy of parties. They were fearless of coalitions, although not all their attempts to fashion them had been satisfactory. They did not wish to see the Liberty party remain a small, one-issue organization. Their design was for a broader, more comprehensive coalition which would speak to the major issues of the day, expose the corrupting influence of the slave power, and convince the electorate that only by voting against slavery would they serve their own best interests. The emphasis on the role of the Liberty party as a teacher of moral principles would remain; but would take on new meaning. All this disturbed the party's leaders. The Ohio Liberty party, Birney confided to his diary, "wishes to be considered purely a *political* one." Such a course he considered "injurious to the whole cause."[13]

The leader of the Ohio coalitionists was Salmon P. Chase. Only thirty-six years old in 1844, Chase had emerged as one of the leading lawyers in Cincinnati and one of the best-known Liberty leaders in the West. He was a man of paradoxes. Tall and massive, with a seemingly inexhaustible energy that allowed him to travel all night and work all day, he wrote in a delicate, small script that was almost feminine. He was ambitious to a point that caused others to distrust him, but he was also an intensely religious man who worried constantly about the state of his soul and the purity of his motives. Each day he tried to memorize some scripture, including the entire 119th Psalm, repeating the verses while soaking in his bathtub. He speculated in both real estate and philosophy. By day he bought and sold large chunks of Cincinnati; by night he read widely in Tocqueville, Cobbett, and Carlyle. He was a formidable lawyer and legal theorist, a lofty idealist, and after 1836 a confirmed abolitionist. He also possessed a shrewd, tough political sense.[14]

That sense led him, shortly after the election of 1840, to search for a means of deepening Liberty support. Chase had not voted for Birney in 1840; he had preferred William Henry Harrison, the Whig, as one who might be convinced to take some initial steps toward eliminating slavery. When Harrison died, Chase left the Whig party and turned to the new Liberty movement. What few fears he had of the corrupting influence of parties soon disappeared, and by 1842 he was actively pressing Liberty men to admit the need for a broader coalition based, if need be, on cooperation with one of the major parties. In this way he hoped gradually to bend the federal government toward antislavery.

These ideas were heartily approved by Gamaliel Bailey of the Cincinnati *Philanthropist,* and the two soon became close friends and the two strongest Liberty leaders in southern Ohio. In many ways they were ideal champions for a coalition movement. Both were articulate and persuasive, with strong antislavery credentials. They had entered the movement late enough to escape any identification with Garrison. And they were from Ohio, where the call for political action was loudest and where Giddings's attempts to capture the Liberty party forced them to seek broader support.[15]

Chase favored a coalition with the Democrats. He was, despite his vote for Harrison, closer to the Democrats in ideological matters than to the Whigs. He generally argued for a strict interpretation of the powers of Congress, and he believed the Democratic emphasis on individual rights could be used to destroy slavery. "I think that the political views of the Democrats are, in the main, sound," he wrote, "and the chief fault I have to accuse them of, is that they do not carry out their principles in reference to the subject of slavery." That Democrats did not extend their doctrine of "Equal rights and equal privileges for all men" to blacks, he imputed to "ignorance of the proper application of these principles to Slavery." Bailey was far less sanguine in his hopes for the Democrats, but he also rejected a coalition with the Whigs.[16]

Before Chase could build a coalition, he had to dump Birney as the head of the Liberty party. Bailey endorsed the effort. Chase feared that Birney's appeal was too confined to the East to be of use to the party in the West. "Some dissatisfaction," he remarked to Giddings in 1842, "is felt here in the west with the nominations of the National Convention at New York, because that convention is regarded rather as a meeting of the National Antislavery Society than as a Convention of the Liberty Party." The reason was plain; Birney was too radical an abolitionist to attract a broad following. "It is vain to expect the West to support Mr. Birney," he informed Tappan. "He can command no support out of the ranks of abolitionists strictly so called." Birney, moreover, was not generally known, and Chase preferred a prominent figure such as John Quincy Adams of Massachusetts or William Henry Seward of New York, neither of whom was an outspoken abolitionist. Bailey concurred: "I have no doubts, as to your entire fitness for the presidential chair . . . ," he wrote Birney. "But I have had doubts as to your being the most eligible candidate. You have always appeared in the character of a Moralist, a reformer, rather than a Politician or Statesman."[17]

Accordingly, Chase and Bailey began working immediately after the election of 1844 to preclude Birney's renomination in 1848. Bailey began by urging that no nominations be made for at least two and preferably three years, while Chase scribbled off letters to friends in and out of the party, urging a coalition of antislavery men of all parties. By April, 1845, he had worked up a call for a great "Southern and Western Liberty Convention" which he and his cosigners specifically noted was not to be a meeting of the Liberty party alone. "We . . . earnestly invite all who desire to cooperate for the deliverance of our beloved, and otherwise glorious country, from its greatest curse and most appalling danger," the circular announced.

The convention, which met in Columbus in June, scrupulously avoided the question of nominations. By October Chase noted with gratification that even a Liberty party meeting in Boston did not touch on the presidential question, preferring to wait.[18]

The more Chase worked to broaden the party, however, the more Birney and his supporters labored to restrict it. Political abolitionism of the sort pursued by the party in 1844 had plainly not worked, yet Birney's reaction was to withdraw to the safer, purer position of moral instructor. He and his friends accordingly resisted the concept of building coalitions. Lewis Tappan recoiled at the thought. "Monstrous!" he exclaimed. "The Liberty Party will join no other party. . . . We adopt no doctrine of expediency, but go for principle." Birney agreed. The defeat of the Liberty lay not in its ideological or tactical rigidity, but in its abortive attempt to be flexible in 1844. To appeal for help from Whigs or Democrats would only corrupt the party more. "Out of our ranks," he observed, "all public men are of the Whig or Democratic party. How can they be abolitionists?" Deepening this conviction was Birney's personal desire to prove Garrison wrong, to show that a political party could indeed be fabricated on immediate abolition and remain pure and effective.[19]

The breach between the two factions thus became ideological and tactical at the same time. If one argued that the goal of the abolitionist, political or otherwise, was an immediate end to slavery, then coalition with a major party was unthinkable. If one argued the reverse, that immediatism was unrealistic, then a coalition based on expediency was logical and violated no ideological canons. Yet a basic similarity between the two groups led them to defend their positions in the same way. Both acted on the supposition that a public informed of the truth would act accordingly. The role of the agitator-teacher was to provide this information and patiently await the inevitable surge of moral outrage against slavery. Since the abolitionist was now committed to some form of political action, it became necessary to use political—as well as moral—texts as a basis of education. Almost simultaneously each faction turned to the Constitution for evidence.

A careful explication of the Constitution would answer one overriding question: did the federal government have the power to abolish slavery, or did it not? In the answer to this question all others would automatically be resolved. If the Constitution was in fact an antislavery document, then the sole mission of the Liberty party would be to present that fact to the electorate which, once informed, would demand appropriate action by the major parties. The call for a coalition would be exposed as an ill-conceived and useless grab for power. If, on the other hand, the Constitution could not be proved antislavery, then the need for a coalition could be justified as a gradual means of obtaining the political influence required to change it. Either way both ideology and tactics would be served.

The spokesman for the anti-coalitionists was William Goodell of New York, a close friend and adviser of Gerrit Smith. Goodell had been active in the antislavery movement for years and eagerly embraced the doctrine of immediatism. He had edited the Boston *Emancipator,* had helped form the Liberty party, and in general was a studious, prolific writer of antislavery tracts and editorials. He had long been convinced that ample powers existed within the Constitution to strip the South completely, and in one stroke, of her slaves. In 1844, partially in reply to Garrison's charge that the Constitution was a proslavery document, he placed his convictions on paper in a tract called *Views of American Constitutional Law, in Its Bearing upon American Slavery.*[20]

Long, tediously researched, and tediously written, *American Constitutional Law* was a grand attempt to persuade the world that slavery existed outside the American political system, that it had no basis in law, and that, in fact, it ran expressly against all constitutional rights and powers. Goodell announced:

To say as some do, that the National Government, in its organic structure, is *neutral* on the question of liberty or slavery, is directly to contradict its express professions. . . . To represent, as do others, that the Constitution is partly in favor of slavery, is to represent that it is a house divided against itself which can not stand. . . . To say that it can secure *general liberty,* and at the same time guaranty *local slavery* . . . is to affirm the greatest of moral absurdities.

With this in mind, Goodell set out to prove that, in all cases, the Constitution favored abolition.[21]

Goodell's arguments were rambling and tortuous, but they centered on four primary themes. One was the basic axiom that the national government was, in all cases, paramount over the states. "Whatever . . . in the action of any of the States," he wrote, "conflicts with the Constitution of the United States, whatever conflicts with the laws of Congress, made in *accordance* with, and 'in *pursuance*' of, the grand objects of that Constitution, is unconstitutional, illegal, null, and void. It can not have the *authority of law.*" This maxim was vital to Goodell's entire interpretation, for it provided, in the federal powers, an important tool with which to dismantle the slave system. Without the supremacy of national law Goodell's schemes could easily be thwarted by the slave states. "If the question of *slavery* is left, exclusively, to the State Governments, then the whole question of *liberty* is left exclusively to the State Governments, and the National Government becomes a mere nose of wax—the fifth wheel to the coach, a nullity, by which no man can be bound." Goodell rejected this as absurd.[22]

If the federal government was indeed superior, then the second step was to show just how it could be used against slavery. Goodell first appealed to the letter of the law. The commerce clause provided a handy weapon. Since Congress had power to regulate commerce among the states, it could easily control the slave trade, and even abolish it. "If the slave States persist in holding the slaves as 'goods and chattels personal,' " he declared, "the *law* of 'goods and chattels personal' attaches itself to them . . . securing to Congress, under this clause of the Constitution the right of exercising the same powers over *slave* property and *slave* commerce, as over any *other* property and commerce." This, he added, presented a dilemma to the slaveholder, who necessarily had to call his slaves property or else relinquish title to them.[23]

As a third defense, Goodell invoked less specific clauses in the Constitution to bolster his case. The preamble, he noted, contained much that argued against slavery. The last phrase, "to *secure* the blessings of LIBERTY to ourselves and our *posterity,*" was in Goodell's view a clear call to eliminate slavery. "It means," he stated, "to overthrow the deadly antagonist of liberty, to wit, SLAVERY." More explicit was Article 4, guaranteeing each state a "republican form of government." Goodell defined republics as being essentially non-aristocratic and committed to preserving equality of all citizens in the political process. Quoting loosely from Jefferson and Madison, Goodell observed:

"The United States" have therefore "guaranteed to every State in this Union" a government *founded—based* upon "the equal rights of EVERY CITIZEN, in his *person,* and *property,* and in their *management.*" Can human language express a more full and unequivocal guaranty than this, of the abolition, by "the United States," of all the slavery in "every State in this Union?"[24]

Goodell must have realized that the provision in Article 4 for the return of fugitive slaves undercut his other arguments, so he turned, finally, to the Fifth Amendment for support. Every human being, he charged, "deprived of liberty *without* indictment, jury trial, and judgment of Court, is . . . *unconstitutionally* deprived of liberty." Thus slavery was illegal, and could be banned. Too, though the original Constitution may have drifted astray by permitting the reclamation of fugitives, the Founders had set matters aright by the Fifth Amendment, which superseded all previous articles and corrected their mistakes. The amendment, he argued, "being an . . . *alteration,* a *repeal* of all that shall be found to conflict with it in the original instrument . . . provides for the abolition or restriction of slavery as effectually" as if abolition had been provided for in the beginning. The fugitive clause, then, had been amended out of existence.[25]

Overlying all this was an appeal to moral law. Goodell frankly admitted that he was no lawyer, that his arguments concerning the Constitution had been "formed more in the light of what I call *first principles* than of *legal technicalities*. . . . I rely less on what is called 'Strict Construction' and even 'the rule of the Supreme Court' than I do on the great ends of civil governments, and the mission of the law." No one, he argued, could doubt that the lofty ideals of the preamble *"include* the abolition of slavery." More importantly, the Constitution itself was valid as law only insofar as it reflected moral law, God's divine plan. Men were incapable of creating law; they could only *"discover* and obey, not *construct,* the laws of the political world." Goodell pleaded for "fealty to *justice,* not to parchments." Goodell's interpretation, then, was an ideal tool for the agitator-teacher. It used reason and logic as evidence, and supported them both with a transcendent appeal to morality.[26]

These arguments were unacceptable to the coalitionists. In no way did the coalitionists wish to plead a case that the Constitution supported slavery, but they were too aware of the ambiguities in the document to argue that it favored outright abolition. To pursue Goodell's line of thought at the polls would open the cause to ridicule by a public who would be convinced only by precise reasoning. In short, the agitator-teacher could not afford to be disgraced by slipshod rationales. Chase in particular disliked Goodell's interpretation. It offended his lawyer's mind, and it gave powers and prestige to the national government that were incompatible with his Democratic attitudes. Nor could he endorse the assumption that underlay Goodell's explication—that slavery should be abolished immediately and in all the states.

With Bailey's encouragement Chase attempted to use the Constitution for more modest goals. He could find nothing in the document which gave the federal government explicit power to emancipate slaves in the South. He concurred with Bailey's conclusion that the Constitution was "neither a pure pro-slavery, nor a pure anti-slavery instrument." It might, however, be useful in keeping slavery out of the territories. Gradualist that he was, Chase's whole course in advocating coalition was to undermine the power of the South piecemeal until her position had become so eroded that she would fall of her own weight. To constrict and confine slavery was his overriding objective. If the public could be made aware that slavery had no constitutional right to expand, then a working coalition based upon that principle could be fashioned. Slavery would begin its slow exit into oblivion.[27]

The question for Chase, then, became not one of showing that the federal government could abolish slavery, but that it had no connection with it whatsoever. The answer lay in turning slavery into a purely local institution. Slavery, he argued, "can have no rightful support or sanction from national authority, but must depend wholly upon State law for existence and continuance." While the Constitution could not abolish slavery, neither could it support it. "There is not a line of the instrument," Chase observed, "which refers to slavery as a national institution, to be upheld by national law." Hence Chase maintained that there could be no slavery in the District of Columbia, on ships at sea, or in the territories. He was willing to leave it alone in the South, but elsewhere he advocated "direct aggression" against it.[28]

There was a problem here of which Chase, a careful lawyer, was acutely aware. If slavery depended entirely upon state law, how was one to explain the fugitive clause of the Constitution and the resulting fugitive slave act of 1793? These seemed to prove that Congress could perpetuate slavery by requiring the return of a fugitive to his master; thus the national government in effect was obliged to contribute to that "existence and continuance" of slavery which Chase said was totally a state matter. The problem was pressing since Chase lived in Cincinnati, where runaways from Kentucky and the South regularly appeared. It was doubly crucial, for if slavery had even a veiled endorsement in the Constitution, a slaveholder might sue for the right to take his property into areas under federal control—the territories.

Chase had his opportunity to protest the fugitive act when an elderly Ohio farmer, John Vanzandt, concealed nine blacks in his wagon and helped one escape two slave catchers. The case ended in the Supreme Court in 1846, with Chase and William Henry Seward arguing for Vanzandt. The facts of the indictment were simple: the slaveowner was suing Vanzandt for the price of his lost slave, plus a penalty fine. Chase, however, used the case to plead that the entire fugitive clause, plus the act of 1793, was repugnant to the Constitution.[29]

He did so along two basic grounds. First, he echoed Goodell, as his friend Seward would do in 1850, by declaring that returning fugitives from service was inconsistent with the higher law, which both the Constitution and the Declaration of Independence recognized. "Whether restrained or not by constitutional provisions," he argued, "these are acts beyond any legitimate legislative authority. There are certain vital principles, in our natural government, which will ascertain and overrule an apparent and flagrant abuse of legislative power." It was hopeless, then, to attempt to enforce a provision for slavery with the same document that embodied the higher law of liberty. To do so would be to go "directly against natural right."[30]

But while Goodell had argued that slaves, as property, were covered by the Constitution and were hence subject to federal oversight, Chase declared that slaves were not property at all. "What is a slave?" he asked. "I know of no definition, shorter or more complete, than this. A Slave is a person held, as property, by legalized force, against natural right." Echoing Goodell, he noted that the Fifth Amendment had removed the "legalized force" used in the recapture of fugitives. Since the fugitive clause described "person[s] held to service," Chase could use that clause, plus the Fifth Amendment, to condemn itself. "It is vain to say that the fugitive is not a person," he wrote, "for the claim to him can be maintained only on the ground that he is a person." Yet the Fifth Amendment had neatly interceded its authority between the master and the slave by guaranteeing all persons "due process."[31]

There were both advantages and disadvantages to this interpretation. On one hand, it returned to the slave his humanity and his protection under the Constitution. But on the other hand, since Chase explicitly denied that the Fifth Amendment extended to the states, it took away one of Goodell's main justifications for advocating direct abolition. Bailey agreed, "We are strictly a State-rights man," he noted, "and will never consent to any act of the General Government, however good its object, if it violate the constitution, and trespass on the rights of the State."[32]

It must be remembered, though, that direct abolition was not Chase's goal. In giving up one battle he was attempting to win another. He wished to sever the Constitution's connection with slavery. While it was true that slavery offended the natural law of the Creator, the whole context of human history proved that such rights were repeatedly abridged by earthly powers, who constantly made laws contrary to natural rights. "Such a law," Chase observed, "may be enforced by power; but the exercise of the power must be confined within the jurisdiction of the state, which established the law." In short, an unjust law could only be enforced by those who made it.[33]

This led Chase out of his conundrum and into his most powerful indictment of the fugitive clause. "The very moment a slave passes beyond the jurisdiction of the state, in which he is held as such," he argued, "he ceases to be a slave: not because any law or regulation of the state which he enters confers freedom upon him, but because he *continues* to be a man and *leaves behind* him the law of force, which made him a slave." In other words, while the Fifth Amendment could not protect a slave in the South, it could and did protect him when he entered an area of freedom. This included any area under federal control—including the territories.[34]

It also included free states. Chase based his case on a limited interpretation of the Constitution. "The constitution establishes a government," he argued, "declares its principles, defines its sphere, prescribes its duties, and confers its powers." Beyond these specific limits it could not go, and any enforcement of rights granted in the Constitution were a matter for the individual state to decide. By this reasoning the South could ignore the Fifth Amendment, but by this same reasoning Ohio could ignore the fugitive clause. "It is, in the strictest sense, a clause of compact, and the natural . . . inference from its terms, seems to be that its execution, like that of other compacts, is to be left to the parties to it." If, therefore, a free state chose to free fugitives or refuse to return them, the federal government could sit blamelessly aside, unconcerned and uninvolved.[35]

With this view of limited government, neither Chase nor Bailey could accept the doctrine of immediate abolition. A congressional act of such nature was constitutionally out of the question. "An act of that kind," Bailey noted, "would require an army to enforce it, and this, of itself, would disorganize our system of Government. But we intend no such thing. Emancipation must take place, if peaceably effected, by the voluntary action of the people of the slave States." Both Bailey and Chase believed that natural law, which could be neither hurried nor held back, would finally resolve the problem. "EMANCIPATE, EMANCIPATE," Bailey appealed to the South, "and trust to those laws of Nature." In the meantime all the federal government could legitimately do was to cut off all its support—direct or indirect—for slavery.[36]

These arguments in defense of Vanzandt were useful to the

coalitionists in two ways. First, by making slavery a local institution, unprotected by federal law, Chase had attacked the root of southern justifications for taking slaves into the territories. With constitutional evidence of this nature in hand, political abolitionists could shift their attention to the territories—an approach that was more acceptable to voters than direct abolition. Second, those who hesitated to join the antislavery cause because they had felt constitutionally compelled to protect slavery could now act more aggressively. This would make the idea of an antislavery coalition more feasible, and vastly improve Chase's chances of creating such a merger. In sum, although Chase failed to save Vanzandt from conviction, he had helped describe an enormously persuasive course for political action.

For Chase it was a fortuitous event. Within a few months of his appearance before the court, the Wilmot Proviso appeared in Congress. This short but broad resolution was ideally suited to the constitutional interpretation Chase had proposed. He immediately recognized that Wilmot had given him one more tool with which to fashion a coalition.

During 1845 and 1846 the debate over broadening the Liberty party intensified. The coalitionists worried especially over the possibility that Birney would lead the party again in 1848. Birney, wrote a correspondent of Chase, "does not possess the political sagacity necessary to carry forward the great enterprise." Others agreed. William Slade, a former Liberty congressman from Vermont, confided to Giddings that the party required "some other man than Birney for a rallying point." A broader coalition and a new candidate were necessary. Liberty men must "lay down a platform for action as *broad as possible,*" noted a friend of Chase. "We have been too *poetical*—we must become more *political* & *practical.*"[37]

When Birney was seriously hurt in a fall from his horse in 1845—an event which made it likely he would not run again—Chase redoubled his efforts to lead the Liberty party into a coalition. He was so aggressive in his pleas that his friends warned that the party might split irrevocably. "Friend Chase," a correspondent advised, "our overweening desire to impress our individual views upon the Liberty movement has been the bane of the party at the East. Let us in Ohio avoid it." But Russell Errett, a Liberty leader in western Pennsylvania, urged Chase to push ahead. Movements were afoot in New York and Massachusetts to quash the drive for a coalition, perhaps by renominating Birney despite his injury. "If the men of the West, the battleground, do not Concert and Combine their opposition," Errett declared, "the Eastern men . . . will ride them down."[38]

The coalitionists received encouragement from events in New Hampshire. There John P. Hale put together a loose band of antislavery Democrats and Liberty men who, working with the Whigs, placed two antislavery spokesmen in the Senate. The coalition was short-lived, but it forced the regular New Hampshire Democratic party to adopt opposition to slave extension. It also provided an example of what could be accomplished when Liberty men cooperated with other parties.[39]

Many observers failed to see these developments in New Hampshire as an omen, chiefly because they underestimated Hale. "John P. Hale is one of your fat, good-natured, fun-loving, joke-telling Yankees," observed Giddings's future son-in-law George W. Julian. "He is a *good* fellow, & perfectly destitute of any thing like affectation or pride. He is a natural born *democrat* in his feelings, & hence his strength among the people. He has a clear head & ready wit . . . but is constitutionally lazy, & never labors." Julian's estimate was accurate, but incomplete. Hale's persistent sloppiness and his barroom manner obscured his absolute hatred of slavery. A lifelong Democrat and a congressman in 1845, he was ready to give up what little power he had achieved rather than support the annexation of Texas, as the state party required. In January, 1845, he publicly refused to join the Democrats' demand for annexation. A month later the party dropped him from the ticket.[40]

Almost immediately Liberty men in New Hampshire flooded Hale with letters of support, many of them urging that he remain in the race as an independent. Hale's friend and fellow Democrat Amos Tuck proclaimed that he was tired of the "dictation of small men" in New Hampshire and was ready to form a new coalition. Hale was amenable, having become convinced that the regular Democrat organization had dumped him unfairly and without giving his arguments a fair hearing. Hale stayed in the race, an "Independent Democrat."[41]

For over a year the election for Hale's congressional seat remained undecided, as Hale drew enough votes away from the Democrats to prevent the necessary majority for any candidate. All that time the Liberty men had been moving steadily over to Hale's support. By 1846, with the help of the Whigs, who were ravenously hungry for control of the statehouse, a coalition had formed. The Whigs agreed to send Hale, not to the House but to the Senate, in return for the coalition's support for Anthony Colby, the Whig gubernatorial candidate. Also, a Liberty man was allowed to fill out a short, unexpired Senate term.[42]

Hale's bargain with the Whigs was founded purely on expediency; his coalition with the Liberty party he hoped would be more permanent. Many of the Democrats who had sided with him, however, were not so eager to remain permanently outside their old party. The regular Democrats recognized this, called to the bolters to return, and, as part of their appeal, included anti-extensionism and the Wilmot Proviso in their platform. It was a persuasive move, for by March, 1847, the New Hampshire Democrats were again in firm control of the state. Hale had his Senate seat, but he had lost his party. The turn of events, he confessed, was "as unexpected as it was mortifying."[43]

The Liberty party, however, had not forgotten Hale. Throughout 1845 and 1846, when the coalition was functioning well, Liberty leaders from all parts of the North began to see Hale as a remedy for the confusion into which the party had fallen. Chase, for example, urged Hale to abandon the Democrats entirely and help form a new party.

Taking the name of Democrats which justly belongs to us, [he wrote] & contending for Liberty for all as the consequence of Democratic principles, we can compel the whole body of the existing Democracy except such parts as are incurably servile to come upon our ground, the absence of the serviles will be more than compensated by the accessions of true friends of Liberty from the Whigs . . . In one word I desire to see the Liberty Party completely merged in a True Democratic Party, organized not in one State only but in every State. . . .

Others, less desirous of a new party than Chase, saw Hale as one who could, at the very least, reinvigorate the Liberty men. Ellis Gray Loring of Boston urged Hale to address a Liberty convention there. "I am satisfied," Loring wrote, "that you can infuse among the rank & file a spirit, that will manifest itself in high toned resolutions. . . ." During the autumn of 1846 Hale's mail was filled with similar letters.[44]

Hale's growing popularity among Liberty men did nothing, however, to alter the strong feelings among many of the leaders that, whoever was the presidential candidate in 1848, the party must remain pure. Some, such as Theodore Foster, a prominent abolitionist and a friend of Birney, looked upon events in New Hampshire with undisguised contempt. The Liberty party, Foster wrote, "is intent on political suicide, either generally, by a national antislavery union, or locally, after the fashion of New Hampshire." Similarly, in 1846 the state Liberty convention in Massachusetts summarily rejected any coalition with Whigs or Democrats, no matter how attractive the immediate gains might be. "We must vote for our own men," they announced, "and keep entirely away from those parties." Birney, recuperating in Michigan, agreed. The growing call for Hale, or any other man, was blended, among eastern Liberty men especially, with an increasing stridency about keeping the Liberty party distinct. Regardless of who was the nominee in 1848, the eastern Liberty men were determined that the party would not give in to a coalition. Purity had to be preserved.[45]

On one crucial point, however, Birney and his friends changed. While they continued to insist that any candidate of the Liberty party be openly committed to abolition, they did agree that the platform should be broadened to include stands on other issues that might attract a wider range of voters. Birney began to take positions in 1844 on such items as the tariff and banks, on which he sounded modestly Whiggish. By 1846 he and Gerrit Smith had decided that the best course was to allow Liberty newspapers and speakers to endorse other planks, but with the clear understanding that abolition remain the primary and most pressing topic. The "one idea" was kept as paramount, but it could be surrounded with other issues. The one thing that could not be compromised, at least in 1846, was the choice of candidate. He, whoever he might be, must favor abolition[46]

So the Liberty party, like the Barnburners in New York and the Conscience Whigs in Massachusetts and Ohio, entered 1847 more divided than ever. Only one thing was certain. With a presidential election not far away, some sort of crisis would soon be met. Some, such as Chase and Sumner, looked forward with eager anticipation, hopeful of a new party. Others, such as Birney, were apprehensive. Still others, such as Martin Van Buren, remained cautious, hoping that their regular parties would bend to the rising tide of anti-extensionism in the North. During 1847 this anti-extensionism crystallized around the Wilmot Proviso.

CHAPTER FOUR

THE WILMOT PROVISO

JAMES K. Polk anticipated a short war with Mexico. Against the superior resources of the United States, the Mexicans could offer only weak leadership, frequent coups, and an army that was sorely undersupplied and underpaid. All that prevented an early, decisive victory for the Americans were the intense heat, bad water, and difficult terrain of northern and central Mexico. Yet these very factors could easily cause the war to drag on into an extended and probably costly campaign. With this in mind Polk prepared a dramatic move in the late summer of 1846. He asked Congress for an appropriation of $2 million to tempt Mexico to the bargaining table. There he hoped that the enemy could be persuaded—with the help of hard cash—into ending the war early and ceding New Mexico and California. On August 8 he sent his bill to Congress, hopeful of speedy approval.

Polk had overlooked one serious drawback to his bill. While in most respects it was a sound political move, promising diplomacy rather than bloodshed, it was the first measure to deal specifically with the territories between Texas and the Pacific. California and New Mexico were both empty, underpopulated lands with no fixed government and few established traditions. There were as yet no slaves there. It was precisely this question, however, that disturbed many northern congressmen. The United States, it appeared, was moving inexorably and swiftly west. Whatever the present condition of California or New Mexico, they would soon be filled with American settlers who would naturally attempt to re-create their old habits and institutions on the frontier. If slavery were introduced there, the Cotton Kingdom would possess a huge new empire.

David Wilmot was one congressman who feared such a result. Wilmot was a freshman in the House who had supported Polk loyally on almost every issue. He was, like Polk, an expansionist who had frowned on abolitionist attempts to prevent annexation in 1844 and 1845. He accepted slavery in Texas as inevitable and natural. But Wilmot also believed that the lands west of Texas should remain free. They had been so under Mexican rule; any effort to introduce slavery where it did not already exist was both morally wrong and politically damaging to the North. Moreover, Wilmot was facing re-election in a district where antislavery sentiment was strong. He did not want to open himself to the charge that he had helped extend a corrupt institution.

With the aid of other Democrats such as Jacob Brinkeroff of Ohio, Wilmot put all these reservations into a single amendment to be attached to the appropriations bill. On the hot August evening that the House received Polk's bill, Wilmot moved:

That as an express and fundamental condition to the acquisition of any territory from the Republic of Mexico by the United States, by virtue of any treaty which may be negotiated with them, and to the use by the Executive of the moneys herein appropriated, neither slavery nor involuntary servitude shall exist in any part of said territory, except for crime whereof the party shall be duly convicted.

After a surprisingly brief debate the appropriations bill passed the House with the Proviso attached and went to the Senate. There both the bill and the Proviso died for lack of a vote. The clock ran out in the middle of debate.[1]

For five months the Proviso lay dormant. Few screams of protest greeted it in the South, where newspapers generally dismissed it as fatuous and inconsequential. In the North hardly a journal marked its appearance. Barnburners, caught up in the battle to reelect Silas Wright, gave it little thought, as did antislavery Whigs in Massachusetts and Ohio, deeply involved in their own campaigns. The Liberty press was almost mute on the subject.[2]

When Congress reconvened for the winter session, however, the Proviso reappeared. Polk again sent down his appropriations bill, swollen this time to $3 million. Wilmot was quiet, but on January 7, 1847, Preston King, the amiable, quixotic Barnburner from upstate New York, offered the Proviso anew. King had consulted no one, not even Wright, and he gave little indication of precisely why he thought the Proviso so necessary. "I thot [sic] it well," he remarked simply, "to present to the House the bill . . . to chaw on—the free principle is what I want & all I want. . . ." But King's effort failed. Polk considered the amendment "foolish" and worked quietly against it, and southerners, now thoroughly alarmed, blocked it at every step.[3]

The Wilmot Proviso, however, was not dead. When antislavery congressmen realized the potential behind it, they began work to tack it on to every bill concerning the territories, while several newspapers in the North adopted it as a war cry against the South. More than any other issue, the Proviso became the focus of the swelling opposition to slavery.

The strength of the Wilmot Proviso was its utter simplicity. In a single, tangled sentence, Wilmot had reduced the various plans to combat the slave power into one move, keeping slavery out of the territories. It was a catalyst, and its importance as such cannot be overstressed. Before the introduction of the Proviso northern antislavery had existed as a collection of largely unstructured attitudes—all hostile in one way or another to the peculiar institution—without any overlying form or structure. Conscience Whigs, Barnburners, and Liberty men acted in isolation. Because of ideological and tactical differences the left hand never quite knew what the right hand was doing, and neither was aware of the actions of the feet. The Proviso offered a program that was rigid enough to support all three groups yet flexible enough to allow each to pursue its own emphasis. It was an indispensable means by which ideological variances could be translated into a unity of action.

Barnburners, for example, saw the Proviso as an effective way of resolving their party crisis. The war had disrupted the unity of the Democratic party by linking slavery to territorial conquest. Now the two could be separated. The war was a fact, the Albany *Atlas* admitted; not to support it was an act of near treason, both to the country and to a Democratic president. But Barnburners could now point out, with perfect ideological consistency, that slavery was not a proper objective of the hostilities. Slavery was a state institution, upheld solely by state law. It could not be introduced where no law supported it. "The Democrats of the Northern respect, and will protect the South in its State sovereignties and the institutions dependent upon them," the *Atlas* promised. In return, the South must agree that slavery be kept strictly local and that no war be fought for its expansion.[4]

The Proviso was also necessary for party unity. If slavery moved into new territories on the heels of Polk's troops, Radicals foresaw a massive defection of northern Democrats to the Whigs. The northern Democracy, Silas Wright noted, had stood by the rights of property of the southern fellow-citizens and insisted upon the full and quiet enjoyment of their constitutional rights in regard to such property. [But, he added,] it is as manifest as the light of day, that no part and no party of the free States will consent that territory be purchased or conquered to extend this institution where it does not now . . . lawfully exist.

If the South attempted to introduce slavery into California or New Mexico, party unity would dissolve, and "the politics of the Union will be geographical."[5]

This was an effective tactical argument as well as an ideological one. Supporting a war for continental expansion would help stabilize the Democratic party in the North and heal the wounds left by the campaign of 1844. Barnburners could once again prove their fidelity to the party that had nurtured them. At the same time they could adopt, with all sincerity, an ideological stance that was increasingly popular in the North, and one that made them distinct from Hunkers, southerners, and their other enemies within the party. Free territory and the Wilmot Proviso thus became a means of helping— not disrupting—the Democrats while simultaneously opening a path by which the Barnburners could return to power. As yet no thought of bolting, of forming a third party, had seriously entered the Barnburner mind. It was far more consistent and potentially more rewarding to work within the traditional organization.

To prove that the Wilmot Proviso was consonant with Democratic ideals, however, it was necessary to link the concept of free territory to republican values. Here the Barnburners sharpened and slightly modified the role of the free workingman in the creation of a republican society. The territories would automatically take on the traditions of those who populated them. Slave territory was, by definition, monolithically agricultural. Free territory, on the other hand, offered the promise of diversification—a diversification that gave fullest expression to the talents of the independent citizen. If the West were free, the *Post* explained, "in a few years the country will teem with an active and energetic population, and its resources will be developed in every possible manner that human ingenuity or enterprise can invent." This encouraged the natural inventiveness of the republican mind.[6]

It also dignified labor itself, and here the Barnburners sounded a theme which was to become central to the antislavery cause over the next decade. "We in the free states are bound to uphold and sustain the respectability of labor," the *Post* announced. To work at one's own pursuits, to succeed or fail as one's talents allowed, were essential to a republican society. Yet the presence of slavery contaminated the republican dream by making labor irksome. "The degradation of labor which results from a system of compulsory servitude, has a contagion that infects with dishonor all who are associated with it," the *Atlas* explained. "But the citizen of the North is taught to look upon labor with pride, and has learned to compel for it respect." The Proviso promised that this contagion would be kept out of the territories.[7]

The argument for free labor carried advantages. In comparing slave labor to free, Barnburners implicitly contrasted a system that was essentially black to one that was white. "The white race is the predominant interest on this continent," the *Post* had declared during the Texas crisis. ". . . It is as degrading white labor, as affecting white freedom, that we of the North detest [slavery]." Turning this idea to political advantage, Barnburners could easily brand anyone who did not resist the extension of slavery as an untrustworthy defender of white rights. "At a single vote," the *Post* remarked, "they would bow down the millions of industrious freemen of the north to work in the same fields and in the same shops with those who have no civil rights, no personal rights, and who are kept in ignorance approaching barbarism. . . ." Thus, to protect free soil was to protect the white race—and, incidentally, to play upon racist fears in the North.[8]

Stripped of its racist overtones, the proviso appealed to men of other, gentler persuasions also. Chase was ebullient. He recognized that Wilmot had phrased the Proviso in almost the precise terms that Thomas Jefferson had used to draw up the Northwest Ordinance in 1787. The ordinance, one of the final acts under the Articles of Confederation, had organized the Ohio and Indiana territories and had provided, as Chase pointed out, that "there should be neither slavery nor involuntary servitude within the territory, otherwise than in the punishment of crimes." By coincidence, Chase used the ordinance to bolster his defense of Vanzandt before the Supreme Court in December, 1846, barely four months after Wilmot had acted.[9]

The ordinance—and the Proviso—aided Chase's argument for non-extension in two ways. First, he noted that the ordinance added further proof that the founders had every intention of abolishing slavery as soon as practicable. The ordinance, being a "deliberate, well considered act," was designed for the "perpetual maintenance of the genuine principles of American liberty, declared to be incompatible with slavery." Second, Chase elaborated on those "genuine principles." They were "the principles of natural right and justice the obligation of which . . . is derived, not from any agreement or consent, but from the essential constitution of man and society."

These were two of Chase's best arguments against slavery, taking in natural rights and the revolutionary heritage in one sweep, and he recognized eagerly that the Proviso was an excellent vehicle for presenting them to the electorate. Large sections of the Liberty press, particularly in the West, agreed, and took up the cry.[10]

Most of all, however, Chase rejoiced that someone had come forward with a definite proposition to make slavery strictly local, supported only by state law with no basis in the United States Constitution. Until Wilmot's move Chase's contention that slavery had no legal connection whatsoever to the Constitution had been simply one of a myriad of opinions held by antislavery devotees. Now, with a resolution before Congress, and significantly one that had come from outside the Liberty ranks, Chase's views assumed greater stature. After arguing for years that the time spent trying to get the Congress to abolish slavery in the South was time wasted, after years spent pleading that the only proper, constitutional means to strike at the peculiar institution was in places of direct federal control such as the territories, Chase suddenly saw his arguments given national prominence by a freshman congressman from Pennsylvania. Heady with optimism, Chase dashed off more letters to antislavery Whigs and Democrats. He was sure that the Proviso, if properly used, would unite the antislavery forces in the North. A similar debate over extending slavery into Missouri in 1819–20 had ended in compromise with the South, but, he observed, "the oven is hotter now than then."[11]

To Conscience Whigs the Proviso was a godsend. Since 1844 they had fought to make antislavery the announced creed of the Whig party in the North. Always they had faced the charge that they were too radical and too closely identified with abolitionists for their goals to be acceptable. With the Proviso, however, Conscience Whigs could ignore these charges and defend their views as part of acceptable northern values. Few of them really believed that abolition was to result from the struggle anyway; the most they had wanted was to strike a blow against slavery, remove all support of the national government from it, and perhaps in the process make a start toward eventual emancipation. Moreover, some, particularly Sumner, were moving towards Chase's position that there was nothing that the federal government could do about slavery directly, and that the only way to attack it was in the territories and the District of Columbia. Hence the Proviso was ideal. It simply proposed to limit the expansion of the institution, and to that end Conscience Whigs counted on a great deal of support in the North.[12]

The Proviso was also a convenient reply to Webster's "no

territory" stand on southwestern expansion. Northern Whigs needed a means by which they could both oppose slavery and keep the support of their southern allies. "No territory," warmly proposed by Webster, Thomas Corwin, and the Boston *Daily Advertiser,* seemed to offer this possibility, but ran counter to the general expansionist temper of the voters. Sumner for one rejected such a course absolutely. "The iron hand which is now upon California will never be removed," he declared. The best alternative was to take the Southwest and apply the Proviso to it. "It is then of vast importance," he concluded, "that we should be prepared for this alternative, & not be cajoled into the simple cry of 'no more territory.' "[13]

Thus, during 1847 the Wilmot Proviso took on increasing importance. Preston King hammered on the Proviso in the House while Silas Wright urged John A. Dix to do likewise in the Senate. Sumner opened a correspondence with King and wrote more frequently to Chase. For all three factions 1847 became a year of movement away from their old parties and toward a new coalition based on the "bold broad principle of nonextension."[14]

With the Proviso as the issue, Chase redoubled his efforts to build a new antislavery coalition. This had always been his primary concern, and he moved ahead now with a sense of urgency and optimism that he had seldom known, writing letters, making speeches, and scratching off editorials for the *Philanthropist* and Bailey's new paper in Washington, the *National Era.*

To complete this task, Chase renewed an old argument and introduced a new one. To his friends among the Whigs and Democrats, he repeated his conviction that neither of the old parties was fit to deal with the slavery question. "If I were persuaded (as I am)," he urged Giddings, "that there is now no reasonable prospect that either the Whig or the Democratic party . . . can . . . be relied on for cordial, inflexible & uncompromising hostility to Slavery & the Slave Power, I would (and of course do) abstain from cooperation with either." He pleaded with Giddings and Sumner and others to do likewise. But Chase realized that party ties were strong, and that to suggest a new party in 1847 was premature.[15]

Therefore Chase proposed simply that an "antislavery league" be formed, open to all, which would monitor the national conventions of the major parties and work to prevent the nominations of slaveholders such as Zachary Taylor or compromisers such as Lewis Cass. It was basically a sound plan. It allowed antislavery Whigs and Democrats to work within their organizations in order to make the Wilmot Proviso part of a national platform. Chase knew that there was a slim chance that one of the parties might choose a Proviso candidate. Silas Wright, for instance, who had openly approved of the Proviso, was in a good position to become the Democratic nominee. If that happened, Chase and the coalitionists would be free to merge behind him, adding their numbers to the already ponderous influence of the northern Democracy. But Chase's plan left him another option. If Wright and all other Proviso supporters were rejected in the conventions, then Chase would be waiting with his league to form a new party. Either way Chase would have his coalition.

The Liberty party itself, however, threatened Chase's scheme. While the Proviso had met warm enthusiasm in Ohio and the West, it found tepid support among conservatives in the East. The Proviso simply did not go far enough, did not attack slavery directly in the South, as Tappan, Birney, and the eastern conservatives wished. It sidestepped the elaborate constitutional arguments developed by Goodell. The Boston *Emancipator* was blunt: "What . . . have we to do with the plans and movements of the Wilmot Proviso men? Plainly, nothing—nothing at all so far as the policy of the Liberty party is concerned. . . . They are not fighting our battle, nor are we in any way responsible for their policy." The proposal to unite the Liberty party behind a Proviso candidate, the *Emancipator* protested, meant "the abandonment of the Liberty Party." Edward Wade of Ohio saw the Proviso as a "greatly enlarged edition of the Missouri Compromise." Lewis Tappan agreed: "Giddings &c want all to unite—Liberty Party men—Conscience Whigs &c—under the Wilmot Proviso flag & elect the best man we can find, Silas Wright, W H Seward, or John P. Hale. How," he complained, "can Liberty men do this?"[16]

During 1847 the struggle between the coalitionists and the conservatives centered on the timing of the Liberty national convention. Coalitionists well knew that if conservatives succeeded in calling a convention before the Antislavery League had time to jell, the proposed coalition was in deep trouble. Chase fully expected to outmaneuver his opponents, for he had managed to postpone a convention for two years already, and he was confident that most of the party membership supported him. His mail was heartening. "I may safely say," wrote an Ohio friend, Adams Jewett, "that every man among us is decidedly in favor of waiting. . . ." Even the normally conservative Chicago *Western Citizen,* edited by Zebina Eastman, favored waiting. "Political affairs are in an unsettled state, in their revolutionary stage," Eastman wrote, "and not knowing what a day or an hour may bring forth we cannot act understandingly in this important business at this early day." The Cincinnati *National Press* (formerly the *Philanthropist*) called loudly for waiting until 1848. Complaints that postponing the convention would destroy the party were myopic, the *Press* charged. "There is such a thing as sinking the great objects of party organization, in the mere desire to preserve the party itself." Chase concurred. "We are Liberty men, I trust, for the sake of Liberty, & not for the sake of Party." Thus pushing aside conservative objections, Chase proceeded with his plans for an Antislavery League.[17]

In all his calculations, however, Chase had overlooked John P. Hale. Chase liked Hale; he had welcomed his cooperation with the Liberty party in New Hampshire, and he sometimes mentioned Hale as a possible candidate to lead a coalition. But Chase assumed that Hale too favored waiting until 1848. Hale himself was undecided, but his friends within the Liberty party were not. In May, 1847, Eastman placed Hale's name in contention for the Liberty nomination. "I came to this conclusion," Eastman informed Hale, "that you were with us in heart and hand, in purpose and action, all but in name." Even the *Emancipator* spoke favorably of Hale, but with the important qualification that he abandon the Democrats before being nominated. "It will be soon enough for him to be nominated by the Liberty party," the paper announced, "*after* he shall cast in his lot among us, by fully identifying his political fortunes with the destinies of that party."[18]

These movements surrounding Hale were significant in two ways. First, they demonstrated that Chase's incessant pleas that the party settle on someone less radical and better known than Birney were having some success. They also indicated that Hale was becoming a tool used by the eastern Liberty men against the coalitionists. As much as conservatives distrusted Hale, they preferred him to a total dissolution of the party.

In June the conservatives moved decidedly to stop Chase and the coalitionists. Acting on the advice of Joshua Leavitt of the *Emancipator,* the national committee of the Liberty party, which comprised one member from each northern state but which had never met, suddenly called for a convention to be held in October. Totally unexpected, the call was signed by a bare majority of the committee members, all conservatives and all easterners. The coalitionists had been outwitted, and the *Emancipator* gloated. "It is to put a stopper on all these machinations of men, who, whatever may be the purity of their intentions, are too credulous or too short-sighted to be safe guides in such an emergency," Leavitt declared, "that we have been so strenuous for the speedy accomplishment of our national nomination."[19]

Thoroughly outmaneuvered, the coalitionists clutched for some means of regaining their power. A few, especially Chase, Bailey, and James W. Taylor of the Cincinnati *Press,* noted that the convention was not bound to nominate, and that it could still decide to postpone action until the spring. Others, particularly Henry B. Stanton of New York, began serious work to see that Hale, and not a conservative, was the nominee. Stanton appealed to Hale to set aside all reluctance about being chosen, "believing," as Stanton explained, "that as events are now shaping a much larger number of votes can be concentrated on you than on any other person."[20]

Hale remained unsure, but slowly his doubts faded. His closest adviser, Amos Tuck, carefully questioned his supporters in New Hampshire and noted in early August that a nomination "will have a very bad effect in this State, and will identify you with a very small party, a faction, in the nation." Hale agreed until a few days later, when Stanton drew both men into a conference and convinced them to reconsider. When Silas Wright died later that month, Tuck abandoned all hesitation and pressed Hale to accept. With Wright gone, Tuck argued, there was no other prominent northerner but Hale likely to appeal to antislavery Democrats. Sensing these movements, Chase publicly and privately urged Hale to decline until the spring. His efforts were futile, for by October Hale consented. "My own inclinations most decidedly are peremptorily to decline the nomination," he informed Tappan, "but my friends have judged differently, & I yield to them."[21]

Hale was by no means unopposed. Gerrit Smith, the wealthy abolitionist from Peterboro, New York, refused to make any deals that, in his opinion, compromised the integrity of the Liberty movement. With support from William Goodell and other radicals, Smith formed a "Liberty League" and held his own convention in June, 1847, a full month before the national committee met.

Goodell, in issuing the call for the radical convention, proposed two things. First, the Liberty party must take a decided stand on all major issues confronting the country, including, of course, slavery, but also the tariff, cheap postage, and banks. Liberty men must do so, Goodell declared, to broaden their appeal and to "escape ultimate absorption in one of the other political parties." Second, a convention was necessary to block Chase and the coalitionists. Goodell and Smith vigorously denounced any plans for a nonpartisan antislavery league. "That the Liberty party could long survive such a policy," Goodell stated flatly, "it were idle to pretend." When the radical convention met at Macedon Locks, New York, it resolved to fight the coalitionists, and Hale, to the end.[22]

Smith's move was not popular among conservatives such as Tappan or moderates such as Stanton. Although they agreed that Liberty men should not yet form any alliance, they did not like Smith's plan to transform the party into an organization for general reform. Eastman voiced the conservatives' objections to Smith's general reform party perfectly. "We do not consider the formation of a political party the surest and shortest way of remedying all the political evils which exist—the universal panacea. Political parties should be founded only upon fundamental principles of government—mere measures of reform can be sooner carried by operating upon the organizations already existing." As abolitionists, Tappan and Stanton respected Smith, but they could not tolerate his peculiar politics nor his schemes. In that respect they were in agreement with Chase.[23]

After the Macedon Locks convention moderates and conservatives—led by Stanton and Tappan—assumed control of the Liberty party in 1847. Stanton occupied a middle ground between coalitionists such as Chase and "one idea" men such as Tappan. He did not favor postponing the Liberty convention, because he was unimpressed by the prospects of General Zachary Taylor. Taylor would fail to get the nomination of either major party, Stanton felt, because he was not a party man. The result would be a tired replay of 1844 with Whigs and Democrats both acting out the traditional issues. Antislavery men would naturally find this unacceptable and would flock to the Liberty party. Tappan, on the other hand, normally did not participate actively in party machinations, but he sincerely felt that Smith's move spelled disaster. In June he had rejected Hale out of hand. Later he changed his mind and concluded that, if the convention indeed must be held, Hale was the best choice around. For Tappan Hale's October letter consenting to a draft was also a means of thwarting Chase. Both Stanton and Tappan were swimming to the same shore: Chase would work to postpone the convention; Smith would threaten to bolt entirely. Hale, standing in the middle, could be brought forward as a compromise.[24]

The plan worked nicely. When the convention met in late October, Chase, as expected, attempted to delay the proceedings until spring. The convention immediately split between East and West, with the latter following Chase. A vote on Chase's proposal was repeatedly postponed, while excitement and talk of dissolving the party flew from both Smith and the coalitionists. At the height of the debate, however, Tappan brought forward Hale's letter. That threw the convention into more turmoil. The haggling continued for another day, as the conservatives worked furiously to make their compromise work. Finally their efforts succeeded. Combining with Smith's faction, the conservatives voted down the movement to wait. Then they shifted alliances and, with the help of the dejected coalitionists, nominated Hale by an overwhelming majority over Smith. Stanton's *Emancipator* was ecstatic. "The Convention could not have made a better selection."[25]

Chase, however, was grim. He had won concessions only in the platform, where he had thwarted Goodell and Smith. In place of Goodell's proposal to commit the party to direct federal abolition of slavery, the platform called simply for "the exclusion of slavery from our national territories, the prohibition of slaveholding in all places under the exclusive jurisdiction of the National Government, and discouragement of it in the States by national example and recommendation." It was bitter compensation to Chase, who still hoped that 1848 would bring a new coalition. Bailey was less optimistic: "I see few symptoms of robust vitality in the Liberty Party," he wrote. "What with its universal reform dreamers, its hairsplitting metaphysicians, its theoretical politicians, its bigots, and its pharisees and impracticables, the building of its tower is in a fair way to be arrested by confusion of tongues and general scatteration."[26]

Stanton, the man who had engineered it all, faced the future with mixed emotions. He had made the best of a bad situation, he felt, for he had greatly feared that Smith would succeed. Besides, Stanton recognized coldly that, if the major parties did break apart in 1848, Hale could be dropped immediately in favor of another man.

While Chase vainly tried to postpone the Liberty nominations, Conscience Whigs in Ohio and Massachusetts were rapidly approaching a crisis in their own party. As Zachary Taylor's exploits on the battlefield gained fame, the old general from Louisiana became increasingly attractive to president makers among both Whigs and Democrats. Remembering William Henry Harrison's smashing victory in 1840, leaders from both parties were aware that an uncommitted military hero such as Taylor possessed enormous potential as a presidential nominee. His political convictions were unknown; he had made no damaging statements to identify him with any particular faction of either party; he carried an aura of heroism and accomplishment resembling that of Andrew Jackson. By early 1847 a Taylor movement was in full swing in both the northern and southern factions of each party.[27]

But Taylor was not acceptable to the Conscience Whigs. He was, most damagingly, a slaveholder—a fact that all but excluded him from consideration by any antislavery group. In addition to that, he was the foremost general in a war that Conscience Whigs universally detested. Taylor's continued silence on all political topics made him triply suspect. Giddings's new Cleveland paper, the *True Democrat,* openly questioned the advisability of nominating Taylor. "Party obligation," the *True Democrat* noted, did not bind Whigs to support any candidate "not known to be opposed" to the extension of slavery. "It is nonsense to talk such stuff to men of principle and common sense," the editor concluded.[28]

But Conscience Whigs badly needed a candidate of their own. Casting about, they first considered Justice John McLean of the Supreme Court, who had made himself perenially available for the Whig nomination and who just as perenially had been passed over. McLean was opposed to slavery, but on the crucial question of the Wilmot Proviso he balked. The Proviso was, to his cautious mind, too radical a step. Conscience Whigs soon abandoned him, and turned to Senator Thomas Corwin of Ohio.[29]

Corwin had catapulted himself to national prominence in early 1847 with a stunning attack on the Mexican War. He hated the violence, considering it an open act of American aggression against an innocent neighbor for questionable purposes. "If I were a Mexican," he roared to Congress, "I would tell you 'Have you not room in your own country to bury your dead men? If you come into mine we will greet you with bloody hands, and welcome you to hospitable graves!' "[30]

Corwin's speech made him an instant favorite among antislavery Whigs. Charles Francis Adams was euphoric. "There has not been in America since the revolution," he rhapsodized, "such a chance for a man to make an everlasting reputation as is now before him." Henry Wilson began mentioning Corwin as a nominee within days after the speech, as did Sumner, who urged that Corwin begin immediate travels through New England to solidify support among antislavery Whigs there. "His presence," Sumner declared, "would awaken an intense enthusiasm." Giddings wrote to Horace Greeley of the New York *Tribune,* urging that Corwin be nominated as quickly as possible, if necessary by a meeting held before the regular Whig nominating convention. "Corwin's early nomination," Giddings predicted, "may save us from defeat by preventing the nomination of a man on whom we cannot unite."[31]

But Corwin's popularity declined quickly among the Conscience Whigs. Greeley shrewdly predicted that Corwin would never consent to run as the candidate of the Wilmot Proviso forces. "In spite of what the public supposes, Corwin is a *timid* man," Greeley informed Giddings. "I don't know any body more afraid of wetting his feet. The moment a cannonade is opened upon him . . . he will duck under water and leave us in the lurch." Greeley's estimation was only partly true. While Corwin had few fears of political battle and controversy— his speech demonstrated that—he had no intentions of running as the candidate of a faction. Corwin was, above all else, a devoted Whig, who feared another fiasco such as that of 1844. To run as a Proviso candidate would gut the party in the South and insure defeat. "Is it right," Corwin pleaded to Sumner, "to present my name to be used with the prospect of such a result?" To underscore his distaste for being the Conscience candidate, Corwin explicitly disavowed the Wilmot Proviso in a speech at Carthage, Ohio, in September, 1847. Antislavery Whigs, who never understood that Corwin loved the Whig party more than he hated slavery, were perplexed. "He has taken up the chain at the wrong end," Adams observed drily.[32]

Thus, with no strong candidate to present to the nation, Conscience Whigs were forced to renew their efforts to win over their state organizations. For Giddings and the Ohio antislavery Whigs, this meant a period of waiting during 1847. Giddings renewed his correspondence with Hale in New Hampshire, hoping to find in Hale's coalition some plan by which Liberty men could be persuaded to combine with Whigs. Giddings still believed that such an alliance was feasible, but with no major state elections occurring in Ohio in 1847, there was little he could do but wait.

Massachusetts Conscience Whigs were more active. Ever since their humiliating defeat at the state convention of 1846, Sumner, Adams, and the rest alternated between open despair at ever reuniting the party and fervent hope that Massachusetts Whiggery might still be saved. With the presidential race fast approaching, however, Conscience Whigs realized that they would have to make their influence felt in their home state quickly or else lose all hope of preventing the nomination of a slaveholder at the national convention of 1848. The state convention scheduled for September, 1847, would clearly be decisive.

While Conscience Whigs worked on their own plans to dominate the convention, so did Daniel Webster and Abbott Lawrence. Webster as always coveted the presidency and hoped that his "no-territory" stance would make him an acceptable compromise candidate at the Whig convention of 1848. In order to be a serious candidate, he of course needed the endorsement of his state party. This conflicted with the aspirations of Lawrence. Lawrence was attracted by Taylor's prospects of nomination. A Taylor campaign offered the best chance for Whig victory, and, not incidentally, the general would need a northerner to run as vice president. Lawrence, with his excellent commercial ties to the South, could reasonably expect to join Taylor on the ticket. For Lawrence to succeed, however, he had to stop Webster.[33]

At the convention the Conscience faction became an unwitting pawn in this feud. When Stephen C. Phillips offered a resolution that no nominations be made, Lawrence set his delegates to work for its passage. Webster naturally rallied against the move and only barely secured its defeat. Outmaneuvered, both Conscience and Lawrence Whigs granted the senator his wish. Webster received his endorsement.[34]

There still remained the question of the platform. Conscience Whigs were willing to accept a Webster nomination so long as he was committed to the Wilmot Proviso. Here they met resistance from both Webster and Lawrence. Webster vainly appealed to them to accept his no-territory position; Lawrence skillfully introduced a general statement opposing slavery, one which made no mention of the Proviso. In this way Lawrence succeeded in keeping the platform vague—and his own prospects for the vice presidency alive. Outnumbered, Conscience Whigs went down to defeat.

Mortified, the Conscience men rode home to Boston in puzzled gloom. Ignorant of Lawrence's intentions, they were unaware that they had been used to foil Webster. They had, they believed, expressed the sincere wishes of the great majority of the Whigs in Massachusetts, and they ascribed their defeat to pure trickery and cloakroom politicking. Thoroughly frustrated and angry, they were convinced that they could no longer function honorably in the Whig party. They now fully expected Taylor to be nominated, and, with that, the Whig party to dissolve. For their own part, they resolved to make their principles heard the best way they could. "The struggle will now probably take a fiercer character," Adams observed.[35]

When Silas Wright left the governor's mansion in January, 1847, New York Barnburners entered a time of crisis and adjustment. They were now without real power as Democrats, either in the state or in the nation. A presidential campaign was approaching, a campaign in which they must reassert their influence in the party or dwindle away. An unpopular war was raging which threatened not only their own power but that of the Democracy itself. As Wright journeyed through the snow to his home on the St. Lawrence, he concluded that all these problems could be resolved by a single move—endorsement of the Wilmot Proviso. "The principle asserted is clearly right, and its assertion now is . . . not merely expedient, but positively necessary," he advised Dix. "The question is now in a shape it never before has and never before could have assumed."[36]

As Wright and other Barnburners pondered the implications of the slavery question, they began to merge the fortunes of the Proviso with those of their party. To their minds, the Proviso was in perfect accord with the republican principles they had long cherished. The loyal defense of those principles was the mission of the Democratic party and the reason for its success. It was logical, therefore, to rest the hopes of the party on the vigor with which Democrats supported the Proviso. At a single blow a vital element of republicanism could be preserved and the Democratic party rescued from defeat. There was no other way. The "singleness and intensity of feeling of the people of the North on this subject," the *Atlas* remarked, made it imperative that the Democracy concede to the public will.[37]

The Proviso also offered a means of reestablishing the Barnburners as the voice of New York Democrats. Hunkers, they reasoned, owed too much to Polk to be able to support a move which he disapproved, yet the tremendous popularity of the resolution in New York would put pressure upon them to take a public stand on it. Thus caught between the demands of Washington and those of the voters, Hunkers would be forced to make a choice. Either way they would lose. Wright's loss in 1846 had removed all Democrats—not just the Barnburners—from power in the state, and Hunkers were just as anxious to win the next election as anyone else. If they rejected the Proviso, they would lose the state. If they endorsed it, they would be no different, in Polk's eyes, from the Radicals, and would lose their grip on his patronage.

Hunkers realized their problem and sought a middle ground, one in which they could support free territory and Polk at the same time. "We would prohibit slavery in the new territory . . .," the *Argus* declared. But, the editor added, "We would not attempt to do it *now.*" If the Proviso were passed, conservatives reasoned, sectional conflict would ensue, and the war would be fought for nothing. "The Wilmot Proviso is simply an abstraction" which would become "inoperative" the moment a new territory became a state. Its passage would do nothing other "than to array the South compactly against the North, and to divide the North with itself." Moreover, under the Proviso southerners would refuse to join in annexing any new territory, and the whole object of the war would be lost. Finally, the *Argus* pointed out, the real intent of the Barnburners in supporting the Proviso was to enhance the fortunes of one "who is regarded as a candidate for the presidential office"—Silas Wright.[38]

Indeed, the possibility of a Wright nomination weighed heavily on the minds of both factions. Wright was such a loyal, popular, and steadfast Democrat that his chances at the nominating convention could not be overlooked. His name carried great prestige throughout the North, and as the heir to Van Buren he commanded a deep following among potential delegates. Conservatives naturally feared him; radicals leaned upon him as their surest defense.

Wright's popularity soared in April when he released a letter endorsing the Proviso. "If the question had been propounded to me at any period of my public life: Shall the arms of the Union be employed to conquer, or the money of the Union be used to purchase, territory now constitutionally free, for the purpose of planting slavery upon it? I should have answered, No!" The Wilmot Proviso, he added, was "the answer to this question." Wright warned Polk that if "the administration wishes to acquire the territory for the extension of slavery," he would consider "the administration wrong and the declaration right." In short, he approved of everything Preston King and the Barnburner press had been saying. But he did not want to become president.[39]

Barnburners conveniently ignored that fact, for they desperately needed him to stop Lewis Cass. Cass had considerable support outside Radical ranks; he was especially popular in the West. In late February, Cass condemned the Proviso as unconstitutional and began a steady trek towards substituting the concept of "popular sovereignty," which he perfected in January, 1848. Popular sovereignty proposed to remove the federal government entirely from legislation concerning slavery by allowing the territories to settle the issue themselves. It was a tidy compromise, and one that could be marketed in both sections. It also worried Barnburners, who more than ever needed Wright to stop it.[40]

In August, however, the Radicals saw their hopes literally die. Wright had spent the summer working incessantly on his farm, toiling for long hours among his crops in muggy heat. He was fifty-two years old, and had not picked up a hoe or plow in years. During August he frequently found himself out of breath, exhausted, with a tightness in his chest. On August 27, as he read his mail at the local post office, pain filled his chest and spread to his neck and left arm. Within hours he was dead.[41]

The effect among Barnburners was catatonic. Months of work spent making Wright and the Proviso irresistible were gone. "All these anticipations," the *Atlas* mourned, "are dashed and turned to ashes." Azariah C. Flagg was bitter. "The consequences to flow from Mr. Wright's withdrawal from the State of action, are not easily foreseen," he complained to Dix. "Woodbury, & March & Cass and Dallas, will all spring forward to take his place in the confidence of the democracy of New-York. The democracy must consider them all as *Regicides.*" Dix contemplated the future: "I see no hope of rallying the Northern democracy," he speculated, "unless it be on Mr. Van Buren."[42]

Wright's death did more than just dishearten the Radicals; it left them leaderless, and factions within the Barnburner group began to appear. On one hand stood Radicals such as Flagg, Dix, and, off in retirement, Martin Van Buren. Like Wright, they favored making no deals with the Conservatives at the upcoming state convention. If Radicals did so, Wright had warned, "we shall sink our ship under us." But they shared Wright's caution and circumspection. They had learned from long experience to swallow temporary humiliation in favor of long-term gains, and, however much they detested the Conservatives, they were not apt to act rashly.[43]

On the other hand stood younger men such as King, William Cassidy of the *Atlas*—and John Van Buren. These men had not been in the party as long as Flagg, and they lacked his patience or his concern for party unity. They were impetuous and intractable, and during May and June they had quarreled bitterly and openly with the *Argus* group. They had adored Wright, however, and as long as he lived they had heeded his advice to confine their activities to newspaper battles. With Wright gone, they became unpredictable, angry, and confused. They remained in that condition until the state convention met in late September.[44]

At stake in the convention was the nomination for state comptroller, an office which Flagg had held for years and which had given the Radicals tight control of state finances. Also at stake was a proposition to make the Wilmot Proviso the official policy of the Democracy of New York. Radicals knew well that if they lost on either point, their influence in New York would slip drastically, and their chances of nominating a Proviso candidate for president in 1848 would be crippled. Flaunting Wright's memory, the Barnburner press dared the Conservatives to challenge Flagg as they had challenged Wright in 1846. "Does any man believe that the game of last fall can be repeated?" the *Atlas* taunted belligerently. Privately, however, Radicals were worried. They had lost much of their force when Wright died, and in the confused month after his death they had neglected to maintain their normally high standards of organization. By the middle of September Flagg and the Proviso were in trouble.[45]

When the convention met at Syracuse on September 29, the Conservatives were in complete control. In several counties they had put up their own slates of delegates in opposition to the Radicals, and at the convention they frustrated Barnburner attempts to prevent them from being seated. In two long days of bitter fighting, the Hunkers reduced the Radicals to an impotent minority by repeatedly passing over Barnburner delegations for Conservative ones. Even John Van Buren was refused as a delegate. That done, they discarded Flagg and nominated their own candidate for comptroller. Then, as a final insult, they turned down Van Buren's renomination for attorney general.[46]

Seething, the Radicals prepared for one last confrontation. On the last day, October 1, David Dudley Field, a young Barnburner from Manhattan, rose to present a resolution for the platform. New York Democrats should "faithfully adhere to all the compromises of the Constitution," Field announced, but they must declare "their uncompromising hostility to the extension of Slavery into territory now free, which may be hereafter acquired by any action of the Government of the United States." Field's resolution went beyond the ground taken by the Wilmot Proviso, and was an obvious slap at Cass. It was a shrewd attempt to embarrass the Conservatives, but it failed entirely when the Hunker chairman ruled it out of order, refused to consider a roll call on it, and declared the convention adjourned. The break had come.[47]

Utterly humiliated, the Radical press turned upon their enemies in a smoking fury. The entire design of the Hunkers, charged the *Atlas,* was "to erase those principles which the Democracy have written on their banners, in order that the votes of New York for the Presidency, be put in the market, and sold to the highest bidder." Conservatives intended nothing less than that New York Democrats "recede from those avowals of 'a free soil for free labor' which have gushed from the hearts of the people." The *Post* included Polk in the scheme. "Unaided, these wolves in sheep clothing could never have betrayed the state. The more formidable enemy lies beyond our reach." The "immense patronage of the general government," the *Post* concluded, bolstered by an unholy war, had helped Conservatives attack "the last stronghold of democracy lying between them and the accomplishment of their political schemes." To thwart this conspiracy, the younger Radicals prepared to purify their party. On October 12 a call went out for a Radical convention to be held at Herkimer near the end of the month. Soon the *Atlas* placed Field's resolution under its masthead as a "cornerstone" for the movement and a challenge to the Hunkers. There it stayed for four years.[48]

From his beloved farm at Lindenwald Martin Van Buren watched the entire spectacle in despair. He shared his dead friend Wright's opinion about the Wilmot Proviso, but he cringed at the course of the *Atlas* and the younger men. Too late he realized that he had committed a grievous mistake. Without quite knowing it he had pursued his retirement only too well. He was still the symbol of the Radical Democracy, but he was no longer its leader. Nor was Flagg. Only Wright had been energetic enough to restrain the younger, less experienced members of the group, and Wright's death left a void that Van Buren was unwilling to fill. Now, helplessly, he watched the disintegration of the party he had worked all his life to organize.

His despair deepened when Flagg informed him that the *Atlas* had consulted no one among the older Radicals in calling for the Herkimer convention. "As I took ground against a convention in any form," Flagg wrote, "I can have very little influence in cooling the ardor of those political hotspurs, from whose indiscretion we have suffered as much as from any other source." When the *Atlas* call appeared, Van Buren was grim. The "call of some of our well meaning friends for a *Mass State* Meeting is so unwise," he lamented, "& so directly playing into the hands of their bitter opponents" that he foresaw only disaster. What good, he asked, could come from the Herkimer meeting? Separate nominations would be useless, for the Conservatives had already risked openly splitting the party at Syracuse, and if the Radicals formally bolted, they would share the blame for defeat. Nor was it advisable to reassert the Proviso. Support for the Proviso was a "course eminently calculated to command the favor & approbation of all right minded democrats at the North," Van Buren declared. "But its assertion as a *party cry,* is an other and a very different thing." That would be merely "an apple of discord" in the party. The only result to follow from the Herkimer meeting, Van Buren concluded, would be to make the Radicals look like traitors to the party and erase what influence they had left. Nor did it ease his mind that his own son was leading the movement.[49]

John Van Buren's course defined the movement to bolt. He had always been the dashing heir to his father's glory, but he had not inherited the ex-President's patience, or his thick skin. He was struggling for power and prestige to which he felt divinely entitled, but the action of the Hunkers at Syracuse left him frustrated and outraged. Furthermore, he had taken his father's defeat in 1844 personally and placed all blame for it upon the heads of the Hunkers and their southern allies. With the close of the Syracuse convention, he became intractable and reckless. "I will never submit to imposition & rascality a moment," he explained. "I want to square the yards with them." If that meant smashing the party, then so it must be.[50]

The convention that met at Herkimer was almost anticlimactic. With John Van Buren leading the way the delegates repudiated the proceedings at Syracuse as a fraud and resolved to support only a committed Wilmot Proviso man for president. Moreover, they determined to hold another meeting in February, 1848, this time to nominate their own representatives to the national nominating convention in June. Significantly, when the *Evening Post* reported the proceedings of the convention, it headlined its columns "FREE SOIL, FREE LABOR, FREE TRADE, AND FREE SPEECH."[51]

CHAPTER FIVE

1848

DURING the early months of 1848 a dispersed and unconnected movement began to unify. Liberty men, Conscience Whigs, and Barnburners all began to look outward, to seek means by which their particular causes could be reinforced by the aid of others. The outlines of a national organization slowly took form. Giddings's paper in Cleveland, the *True Democrat,* expressed the feeling in March: "There are friends of Freedom in the Free States, enough to control the next Presidential election. For this purpose, they must unite. They must lay aside their party bickerings and party prejudices, and come together and labor for the salvation of the Constitution and the cause of Liberty."[1]

"Coming together" was not a simple process. There was, first, the immediate need of fashioning some organizational framework upon which to build an anti-extensionist coalition. Following that were the problems created by the influx of thousands of supporters who were not themselves professional politicians. Over all were the changes a vast, interstate coalition would demand of the ideological foundations of antislavery politics. All these changes had been occurring to some extent since the introduction of the Wilmot Proviso. But during 1848 it is notable that they tended to follow each other in a predictable succession. As the organization of protest became more effective, it attracted new followers. As more people joined the movement, ideology changed.

The most effective organizer was Salmon P. Chase. Almost alone among the supporters of the Proviso, he possessed the necessary organizational skills, combined with the luxury of having no strong party ties, to enable him to pursue a coalition singlemindedly and without looking back. Chase worked both publicly and privately. In countless letters to sympathetic politicians he dismissed the old parties—including his own Liberty party—as hopelessly incapable of meeting the crisis in the territories. He applauded Barnburners and Conscience Whigs alike for their resistance to the slave power. And he begged John P. Hale to set aside his nomination by the Liberty party. Appealing especially to Hale's ambitions, Chase noted that Silas Wright's death had removed the only realistic alternative to Lewis Cass. Certain that the Barnburners would bolt their party after the nomination, Chase raised the possibility that the New Yorkers might turn to Hale. The Liberty nomination, however, "encumbered" Hale's chances by identifying him with a radical faction. Chase urged him to cast it off, and Hale, thoroughly confused, took the matter under consideration.[2]

But letters to individuals were not enough. A new coalition must also give the ordinary voter a means of participation in order to excite his sympathies. Another convention of the Liberty party was out of the question, so Chase returned to the only other means he knew, the mass rally. In March, working closely with Bailey, Chase issued a call for a "people's convention" to be held in Columbus in mid-June. The timing was critical. Chase was counting on the Conscience Whigs and the Barnburners to quit their parties after their respective national conventions. The People's Convention had to be early enough to capitalize on the emotional unrest that would follow, yet late enough to leave time for the revolts to spread. If the People's Convention could seize the right moment, it would lead to the calling of another convention later in the summer. That convention would be the start of a new party.[3]

It was an excellent plan, but one that met problems. Chase could not afford to broadcast his real intentions in calling the convention. It would seem too crass and calculating, particularly among those who still regarded political parties as suspect. Moreover, there were many in the regular parties who still clung to the hope that their organizations would nominate a Proviso candidate. Giddings and Palfrey, for example, refused to sign even the call for the convention. "Any attempt by us here to get up a Convention," they agreed, "would be assailed as a political manuveur." Thus Chase was forced to bide his time, await developments, and hope for the best.[4]

While he did so, Conscience Whigs underwent an unexpected crisis. In December, 1847, Robert C. Winthrop chose to run for Speaker of the House. Conscience Whigs there bluntly refused to support him, recalling his vote for the war appropriations bill a year earlier. Giddings, Columbus Delano of Ohio, and Palfrey each denounced Winthrop as one who had helped perpetuate an unjust and costly war. Their action very nearly cost Winthrop the job.[5]

The unanticipated effect of the affair was to bring Conscience Whigs in Ohio and Massachusetts closer together. The Boston press furiously denounced Palfrey for his vote, branding him with every synonym for traitor. Palfrey's friends naturally rallied to his defense, with Sumner in particular opening a lashing attack on Winthrop through the pages of the *Courier*. Boston Whigs, who well remembered Sumner's earlier attack on their favorite son, returned the fire. The *Atlas* dismissed Sumner for his "personal malignity" and his "vindictive determination" to destroy one of the most promising political careers in the state. Sumner was stunned.[6]

Casting about for help, he turned to Giddings. Giddings had noted Sumner's course with pleasure and had chafed at the rebuttal of the press. Hoping to rescue Sumner's case, he charged that Winthrop had in fact done more than simply vote for the appropriations bill: he had urged northern Whigs in caucus to support the war itself. If true, this would have rendered all Winthrop's later attacks on the war false and hypocritical. Sumner accepted the story without question and placed it in the *Whig*.[7]

Giddings's story, unfortunately, lacked proof, which Cotton Whigs immediately demanded. Giddings wrote desperate letters to members of the Whig caucus, searching frantically for some shred of evidence to support his claim. None came. Lamely Sumner tried again to make his charges stick, then quietly dropped the matter. The whole affair had been disastrous. "My own position in it is painful," he reflected, "while the influence of us all is materially affected by it." Giddings was chagrined. "It seems as though I am to live in hot water during life," he sighed.[8]

A crisis of this sort, however, was precisely what Conscience Whigs needed. They had existed apart from each other, separated by hundreds of miles, ever since the annexation of Texas. Now they began to communicate more frequently—first offering condolences and moral support, then calling for positive action. Each group, moreover, practiced a type of moral politics that made such controversies endurable, even invigorating. Giddings, for example, was at first depressed. Then he took heart. His stand against Winthrop had won him new friends who applauded his course and shared his defeat. He felt a spirit of solidarity that transcended state lines. "I am satisfied that my vote against Winthrop . . . has increased my moral power both in the house and throughout the country," he wrote to his son. "I am of the opinion that I was never as strong in the District as I am to day."[9]

But Conscience Whigs were unable to use their new-found solidarity effectively. As their letters multiplied, they of course began to talk seriously about the upcoming national convention. All agreed that Zachary Taylor must be stopped, and to do so they sorely needed a candidate of their own. This, their most pressing need, was also their most difficult task. All the possibilities—Corwin, McLean, Webster, even Henry Clay—had serious liabilities. They were either too cautious, too uncommitted, or too conservative. None was eager to be the candidate of a radical faction. The lack of a candidate seriously hampered the Conscience Whigs' efforts at organization. The Winthrop episode had shown that, when given a specific issue, they could work well together. Without some focal point of activity, however, Conscience Whigs were gripped by inertia. Still Whigs, they had not made a conscious decision to erect an alternate party—an attitude which was in marked contrast to that of Chase.

Giddings was dimly aware of this fact, for in the interim between the Winthrop episode and the Philadelphia convention he began to realize that Chase possessed a tactical advantage which gave him great flexibility in organizing antislavery protest. Chase was not a party man; he had no ties that must be painfully severed before he could act. Thus the People's Convention, an amorphous mass rally with no discrete political affiliation, could be an effective means of tapping dissent without giving the appearance of being a factional revolt. If the convention did nothing else, it at least gave the dissidents a common project on which to work—a semblance of motion. It also gave Chase the air of a man who was in control. This disturbed Giddings, but he refused to participate in organizing the meeting; he was still a Whig.[10]

So were the Conscience Whigs in Massachusetts. They had been badly burned by the Winthrop controversy, yet they had not been excommunicated from the party. They remained delegates to the Philadelphia convention, but they were delegates without a candidate. Neither in nor out of their party, Conscience Whigs were seized by a kind of paralysis that enervated their attempts at action. In this state it became obvious that the critical move toward a revolt would come from someone else. Far removed from Ohio, they could not sense the growing power of Chase as Giddings could. The Barnburners, on the other hand, were near and obvious, and on them the Conscience

Whigs relied. Without the Radical Democrats, Adams concluded, "we can do nothing out of the Whig party." Thus, as the national conventions neared, it was the Conscience Whigs who were the least effective in organizing their protest.[11]

Barnburners were active, yet they too were caught between loyalty to their party and a growing impulse to secede. The Herkimer convention of October, 1847, seemed to be an act of outright secession on the part of Barnburners. Yet these same men were anxious to preserve their identity as Democrats and to participate in the national nominating convention. Their ties of party were too strong, their stake in the nomination too great, for a hasty withdrawal from the Democracy.

Accordingly, in the early weeks of 1848 the Radicals attempted to prove their party loyalty once more. The Herkimer convention had called for another such meeting in the same city in February to select delegates to the national convention. Discarding this move, Radicals used their small majority in the regular state party caucus to schedule yet another meeting, to be held in Utica, for the same purpose. Their reason was, again, to make certain that the delegates who appeared in Baltimore in May would have the unquestioned approval of the New York party. Conservatives, not to be outdone, used their own slim majority in the state central committee to call for an alternate convention in Albany. The two conventions met, selected their respective delegates, and prepared for a confrontation at Baltimore. Now two sets of delegates, each claiming to be the true representatives of the New York Democracy, would present their credentials to the national party.[12]

To undermine the Hunker delegation, the Radical convention at Utica attempted to portray themselves as loyal Democrats—idealists who had not compromised essential party principles. The Wilmot Proviso was more than a prescription for the future of the territories; it was an infallible test of who was a true Democrat and who was not. "By a fortunate accident, or a special providence," the convention declared, "the assumption by slaveholders of a new and indefensible position on the subject of slavery, has enabled democrats to stand forth in their natural and true attitude, as the champions of human freedom." The rival Hunker convention was simply a demonstration that those who rejected the Proviso were not Democrats. Hunkers had "formally and in a body, abandoned the democratic party and set up for themselves." This left the Barnburners as the only unsullied defenders of the republican faith.[13]

To combine principles and partisanship effectively, Barnburners also needed a candidate. Cass was obviously unacceptable, and unfortunately no other northern contender had emerged to replace Silas Wright. Without an acceptable alternative, however, Barnburners would go to Baltimore minus a crucial bargaining tool. In the vacuum created by Wright's death, they turned to a familiar name, Martin Van Buren. Tentatively, almost humbly, John Van Buren broached the question to his father. Would the elder Van Buren allow his name to be presented "as the choice of the democracy of this state?"[14]

Van Buren replied with a careful evaluation of the political situation and a program for action. He applauded the "constitutionality and justice" of the Proviso and predicted that when its principles were fully comprehended in the North the resulting outcry would "turn the tables" on the Hunkers. But, however right the Proviso might be, slavery was a political bombshell. "The unavoidable tendency of the slave question," he wrote, was "to break the party as a national one." This no good Democrat could accept. Barnburners must remember that their "overriding concern" was for the "integrity of the Party," and act accordingly with caution and tact.[15]

Hence Van Buren counseled patience. Whoever the convention nominated, Barnburners must cheerfully submit. Cass was anathema, but Van Buren preferred him to a breakup of the party. Moreover, he was looking ahead to 1852. Taylor would probably win in November. If he did, Barnburners could calmly remind other Democrats that they had urged the party to nominate a Proviso candidate and had been disastrously ignored. If, on the other hand, Cass won, Radicals could say that they had buried their own desires, had worked diligently for the party, and would command a share of the patronage. Either way the faction would be strengthened. But if the Barnburners bolted and Cass lost, they would open themselves to the charge that they were "indifferent to the general success of the party" and that they wanted only "to revenge past injustice." This would undermine their influence in 1852. Only two possibilities merited a break. One was the admission, in any form, of the Hunker delegation; the other was the renomination of James K. Polk.

These were thoughts from a shrewd and practiced politician. Van Buren's incredible patience, his calmness in the face of crisis, and his ability to look ahead had seldom failed him. He was confident that the convention would accept the Radical delegation, in which case the scenario he had drawn would paint itself over time. He did not foresee the convention's problem in seating the New York delegates, so his natural course was one of caution. For that reason he declined to be mentioned as a candidate. It would only disrupt the party and be interpreted as "revenge." "Upon this I feel a degree of delicacy about my position . . . ," he concluded, "that I cannot consent to have it frittered away."

The Baltimore and Philadelphia conventions, however, dashed the hopes of Barnburners and Conscience Whigs. At Baltimore Democrats pondered the rival demands of the Hunkers and the Barnburners, then concluded to admit both delegations, giving each an equal share of the state's vote. This pleased neither faction, and both sat sullenly in their chairs refusing to take part in the proceedings. Ignoring them, the convention proceeded with the task of nominations and, on the fourth ballot, chose Cass.[16]

Although Cass had won easily, his support was not well distributed among the delegates. He had won only about one-seventh of the northern delegates, the rest came from the West and South. Even in the South he was unpopular. Popular sovereignty implied that slavery could be barred from as well as admitted to the territories, and when it came time to insert this doctrine into the platform the entire Florida delegation, with two Alabamians, walked out. More significantly, however, the Barnburners had already left. Immediately upon hearing the roll call that nominated Cass, they delivered a short farewell and left for New York.

The Philadelphia convention fared only slightly better. Taylor's men had come full of confidence and promises, and Conscience Whigs had come in despair. Like Cass, Taylor required four ballots to win the nomination. Unlike Cass, he did not insist upon a platform. He did not want one, for his strategy was to remain discreetly silent on all disturbing issues and count on the squabbles of the Democrats and the loyalty of the Whigs to give him victory. The delegates concurred. They made their nomination, and refused to consider the drafting of a platform.[17]

Conscience Whigs were furious. Their only hope was that the convention would bind Taylor to a document that frankly and explicitly endorsed the Proviso. When that did not happen, their loyalty to the Whig party evaporated. As they filed out of the hall, Charles Allen of Massachusetts pronounced an early epitaph to the party. The price of party unity, he declared, was "the perpetual surrender . . . of the high offices and powers of the government to the South. To these terms, I think, Sir, the free states will no longer submit. I declare to this convention my belief that the Whig party is here and this day dissolved."[18]

In fact, neither convention could have acted much differently.

Professor Richard McCormick has suggested that the second party system of Whigs and Democrats was "artificial" in that it was the only political arrangement ever to combine roughly equal followings in both North and South. Each party was under an unbreakable obligation to mute sectional tensions, and could do so only by avoiding moral issues such as slavery. They worked reasonably well so long as they took stands on economic problems, for central banks and high tariffs had their supporters and detractors in all sections. Slavery tended to split these parties along sectional lines. Whoever took a strong stand against slavery would likely win votes in the North, but lose them in the South, and vice versa. This problem was especially delicate in the race for president—the only really national office for which they competed. Thus Cass's platform of popular sovereignty was no more than an attempt to bridge the two sections by removing the slavery question from the hands of the federal government. Taylor's silence was even more effective, for it ignored the issue entirely. The dreams of both Barnburners and Conscience Whigs, then, were doomed from the start by the very nature of the parties to which they belonged.[19]

With the nominations of Taylor and Cass, a new party at last began to form. Three separate conventions, all held in June, provided the catalyst. The People's Convention met in Columbus on June 21; irate Barnburners convened at Utica on June 22; Conscience Whigs assembled at Worcester on June 28. Each gathering told much about the tactical abilities and ideological motivations of the men who led them.

Chase had watched the proceedings at Baltimore and Philadelphia with undisguised glee. Without firm party ties himself, he knew far in advance of the major parties' instinctive need for compromise, and the probable consequences. A third party, he assumed, was inevitable. It would be a party that focused on the single issue of slavery, but— being composed of so many different elements—it, too would have to seek some ideological compromise. Barnburners had been raised as Democrats, Conscience Whigs as Whigs, Liberty men as abolitionists. Whatever the current status of these factions, their sentiments must be appeased.

With a keen appreciation for old party loyalties, Chase and his advisers agreed that the People's Convention must make no nominations. Barnburners in particular must be handled with discretion. "They are so situated that they must lead off as 'democrats,' & in the 'regular' way, or perish," Henry B. Stanton explained. A similar situation prevailed among Conscience Whigs, although this latter group was not so accustomed to exercising political power as the ex-Democrats. On the night of Taylor's nomination Chase's friend Stanley Matthews had sat with Wilson, Allen, and others to plot strategy. All concurred that a coalition needed time to form and set August as a likely date. Meanwhile Matthews advised Chase simply to declare principles at Columbus and wait for future events. Chase agreed. On his advice the convention declared itself "inflexibly determined" to resist the expansion of slavery and called for a national meeting at Buffalo in August. Nothing was said about a nominee.[20]

The following day Barnburners met at Utica. Despite their apparent unity, Radicals were deeply divided over the question of separating from the Democratic party. The *Atlas* had summoned the gathering on a note of frank revenge: "The men who in the Baltimore Convention boasted that 'they could get along without New York' will learn that it is New York that can get along *without them*." Some of the older Barnburners disagreed. "I am for preserving our organization on the State tickets," Flagg observed, "maintaining our creed in resolutions, and the character of the men to be returned to Congress, and let the rank and file give Cass such a blow at the ballot boxes as will make dough faces shy of this state hereafter."[21]

Martin Van Buren—who did not go to Utica—occupied a middle ground. His political sense had failed him at Baltimore, for he never expected the convention to seat both sets of delegates. Now confronted by a crisis, he began to admit the desirability of a break. He wrote to Blair:

New York has too recently humiliated herself before the Democrats of other States, or rather has been too grossly humiliated by them to adopt any measures which seem to contemplate cooperation on their part. She cannot afford to have her invitations to the path of honor & duty a second time scorned. She should therefore maintain her position with firmness & dignity, though . . . it be solitary & alone.

Yet, while Van Buren appeared to approve a new party, he was in fact urging Barnburners to sit out the election and vote for no one for president. Regarding Cass and Taylor, he informed Butler: "If no other candidates than those before the country are presented, I shall not vote for President."[22]

The Utica convention had every intention of presenting other candidates. What Van Buren had interpreted as abstinence they saw as acquiescence to run. When Butler presented the letter to the delegates, they immediately dragged the ex-President out of retirement and nominated him in a frenzy of tears, cheers and—as one reporter noted—"hysterical screeches of laughter." In fact, the observer added drily, "the delegates were perfectly wild with excitement."[23]

Reluctantly Van Buren allowed his nomination to stand. He obviously did not want it; he was a party man—more so than almost any other man of his time. He believed in the spoils system, had made it the cornerstone of party regularity. As such, he could not complain when bad fortune sometimes followed good. So the question remains. Why did this, the supreme Democrat of the age, allow his name to be used against his own party? It is a question that he never specifically answered, but the solution probably lies within the context of the very partisanship he seemingly brushed aside.

If one recalls his earlier letter to his son, in which he urged Radicals to accept the decision of the convention so long as the Hunkers were not admitted, a pattern to Van Buren's thoughts emerges. His instincts told him that the Wilmot Proviso was right, but that it signaled the onset of a wrenching debate in the national party. The South must be given time to realize that the principles of free territory and free labor were indispensable to the northern Democracy. Treated calmly, southerners would ultimately adjust. He had hoped that a Democratic defeat in 1848 would drive this point home to southerners, and that their own devotion to the party would convince them that compromise was better than a continuing series of Whig presidents. He had wanted to work with southerners inside the party to arrange this compromise, but the events at Baltimore had convinced him that only a severe blow—an actual disruption of the party—would now bring concessions. Barnburners, in effect, must take a calculated risk in a game of raw power. The party could not win with a divided New York Democracy. It must be taught that lesson with a bold, almost desperate act of secession. By breaking the party in New York, he hoped to save it nationally, though the task would take four years.[24]

Van Buren's more immediate reason for splitting the state party grew from the situation in New York itself. Van Buren had long known that no person, no faction, could achieve national power without first securing its own local political base. The New York Democracy was currently weak, divided, and impotent. It would become even more so after the election, when Polk was no longer available to support it through patronage. The national party would then demand a drastic restructuring of the organization in New York, which would of course entail some serious compromising with the Barnburners. When that restructuring took place, Van Buren and his lieutenants meant to be there, dictating terms. Thus reestablished as an essential element of the New York party, Barnburners could go into the canvass of 1852 with a long list of demands that, if the party were to win, must be met. He had, in sum, chosen another route back to power when the first one had been closed at Baltimore. This question of leverage, of power used to its fullest, was partly the reason Van Buren was so willing to negotiate at the national convention on every point save one—the seating of delegates. Platforms could be made fuzzy enough to satisfy everyone. Candidates were open to compromise. Power was not.

By comparison, Conscience Whigs were fully the equals of the Barnburners in their disappointment with the nominations, yet they lacked the same political leverage. Neither Massachusetts, Ohio, nor the states of the Old Northwest—all areas where Whigs and Liberty men were the most likely to join a new party—were as critical to the presidential election as New York, which alone possessed more electoral votes than these states combined. Hence the loss of New York alone would be more damaging to a candidate's chances than any of the others. Moreover, Conscience Whigs were not nearly as organized as Barnburners. They lacked the discipline and minute attention to detail long practiced by the New Yorkers—and imitated by Chase.

Still, the Worcester convention provided Conscience Whigs an opportunity to express their protest. In many ways the Worcester meeting resembled the People's Convention. Milling about the town common, the delegates spent most of their time listening to elaborate ideological orations from Sumner, Adams, and others. They were not there, however, to make nominations, and the convention scrupulously avoided endorsing any potential third party candidate. Van Buren was congratulated; Daniel Webster was applauded for withholding his support from Taylor. Beyond that the only positive act of the convention was the appointment of a central committee to coordinate the moves of Conscience Whigs with other dissidents. Having done so, they resolved to await developments at Buffalo.[25]

On August 9, 1848, the long-awaited moment arrived. Oliver Dyer, free lance reporter, political observer, and developer of a "new method" of rapid writing, was there observing the scene as the delegates crowded into Buffalo. "Long before the hour for the organization of the Convention," Dyer reported, "an immense concourse had assembled under the tent in the Park to listen to a few preliminary remarks and speeches, and encouragements and exhortations to unity, and expressions of determination 'to put the thing through,' 'no giving up,' 'no compromising,' 'free soil and nothing else.' " Speakers mounted the podium almost at will, haranguing the crowd, detailing the sins of the old parties, and extolling the merits of the Wilmot Proviso. Their listeners cheered and applauded, all the while milling about and fanning themselves in the heat. In the middle of one speech the platform on which Dyer and other reporters sat collapsed, "capsizing ink, paper, table, reporters and all, spoiling our gold pen, rasping the epidermis from our shins, and committing sundry other outrages of a similar nature." The Buffalo Convention was underway.[26]

It was quickly apparent that two conventions—not one—had gathered in Buffalo. Between ten and twenty thousand had appeared, some as delegates but most as volunteers or spectators. Not all were thoroughly committed to the Wilmot Proviso. A few were disgruntled partisans of the losers at Philadelphia and Baltimore, diehard advocates of Clay, Webster, and the rest. Others advocated cheap postage, land reform, or prohibition. By far the greatest number, however, subscribed to one of the three major factions that made up the new party, and their presence in Buffalo was an obvious boost to the morale of the leadership. Here was material for a mass movement. On the other hand, the sheer number of the delegates and the endless variations in their political persuasions created a delicate problem in drafting a platform that would appease them all.[27]

Accordingly, a second convention took shape, in the form of a committee of "conferees." Six were taken from each state, three from each congressional district, the total being divided equally among Whigs, Democrats, and Liberty men. (They met, significantly, in a Universalist church.) These conferees formed the core of the new party's leadership. With few exceptions, they recognized that tact and compromise were essential if the party were to tap the sentiments and labor of those outside. Almost predictably they selected as chairman the one man who had contacts among them all, Salmon P. Chase.[28]

The first business of the conferees was the platform. A strong statement of principle was clearly mandatory, given the nature of the party. The conferees, however, undertook their task with two especially pressing problems in hand. One was the very newness of the coalition. Six or even three months before Free Soil had existed largely as a diverse collection of state factions with no central core. These factions knew each other primarily by reputation, with a certain amount of distrust included. Unlike the regular parties, they had not sat in common before; many were meeting each other for the first time. Hence it was difficult to gauge how each would act, and even more difficult to determine what each considered crucial to the platform. Some would doubtless insist upon including one point or excluding another. To satisfy all would not be easy.

The second problem concerned the thousands who made up the mass convention. Prior to the convention most of the movement toward a coalition had been taken at the initiative of a small group, the factional leaders within the various states. These leaders had acted within a limited political field. New York Barnburners, for example, were a diverse and combative lot, but one could assume a certain continuity of intent and purpose among them. Conscience Whigs behaved in similar ways. Liberty men, on the other hand, were deeply divided. To translate these local concerns into a national organization that was immensely larger and more complex required tact and flexibility. If the platform were to be useful, it must provide a common thread of sentiment to knit these factions together; it must also be infinitely elastic. With this in mind the conferees began their task.

The final document was notable for what it said and what it did not say. Chase had clearly dominated the committee's secret deliberations, for much of the platform drew upon arguments he had developed in the Vanzandt case. The first five resolutions attempted to remove the federal government from all connection with slavery, and appealed to law and history for proof. Slavery was a creation solely of the states. Therefore the platform proposed "no interference by Congress with Slavery within the limits of any State." But, the Northwest Ordinance, the Fifth Amendment, and the Declaration of Independence demonstrated the founders' intent *"not to extend, nationalize, or encourage,* but to limit, localize, and discourage, Slavery." Nothing in the Constitution had changed this policy. The aggressions of the slave power, however, had succeeded in overturning the original course set down by the founders. In the most important resolution the delegates declared that the federal government must separate itself from the perpetuation of slavery. "WHEREVER THAT GOVERNMENT POSSESSES CONSTITUTIONAL POWER TO LEGISLATE ON THAT SUBJECT, AND IS THUS RESPONSIBLE FOR ITS EXISTENCE."[29]

The next five resolutions dealt with the territories. In attempting to extend slavery to the West, southerners had forced a bitter question upon the North. The delegates' "calm but final" answer was simple: "No more Slave States and no more Slave Territory. Let the soil of our extensive domains be kept free, for the hardy pioneers of our own land, and the oppressed and banished of other lands seeking homes of comfort and fields of enterprise in the New World." An act of Congress was necessary to establish this policy, which must be extended not only to the Southwest but Oregon as well.

The remaining resolutions moved beyond the slavery issue and dealt with other concerns. The platform called for cheap postage and governmental retrenchment, river and harbor improvements—which were an object of *"national concern"*—free grants of public lands to settlers, and an early repayment of the national debt through a tariff for revenue. There was no endorsement of a central bank or subtreasury system, no mention of the late war with Mexico, and curiously, no expressed mention of the Wilmot Proviso, although its spirit was included in the resolutions on the territories.

Several points must be made about this platform and the way in which it served Free Soilers during the campaign. First, it was most acceptable to Barnburners, who used it as a starting point for their defense of free labor and republican values. In terms little different from arguments they had earlier used against the money monopoly or the power of vested corporate wealth, they portrayed slaveholders as "aristocrats" who were attempting to use their political base in the Congress to "control the affairs of government in such a manner as to defeat every measure that opposes their particular interest." This was a favorite theme, hammered out in countless variations whenever an ex-Democrat addressed an audience. By portraying a raging war between independent citizens and conspiratorial aristocrats, Barnburners tied their defense of free territory directly to their republican heritage. Even Jefferson's name was used as a weapon in this struggle. "The distinguishing feature of Mr. Jefferson's mind and policy, above all other, was that of hostility to slavery," noted the *Post* in a shameless bending of the truth. The Democrats at Baltimore had nominated a man who "openly repudiated the doctrine and principles of Mr. Jefferson, in regard to the extension of slavery." It was time, they concluded, to return the country to its original values.[30]

Conscience Whigs, on the other hand, found the platform less useful. It said nothing about the moral duties of either the individual or the society to resist corruption and promote progress. The word "moral," in fact, did not even appear. The document took no notice of the government's responsibility to inculcate high values among its citizens or to provide for their moral growth. The whole tone of the resolutions—from the disavowal of any intent to meddle with slavery in the state to the call for repayment of the national debt—was distinctly Democratic. There was scarcely a plank in it that could be identified as an elaboration of Whig values. Undoubtedly, this was the work of Chase.

What the platform did offer to former Whigs was an affirmation of federal responsibility for the extension, or non-extension, of slavery. The conferees had specifically noted that the duty of the federal government was to remove itself from any and all connections with the institution, wherever it had the constitutional power to do so. Moreover, an act of Congress was necessary to protect the territories from the encroachments of the slave power. Conscience Whigs seized on this point to give the document a Whig caste. It implied that government, through Congress, could take positive action concerning the moral welfare of its citizens. To restrict and confine slavery indicated a national policy of moral fulfillment. In effect, it offered the means for redefining Whig ideals of progress and moral reform through the confinement of slavery and the extension of freedom. "Henceforward," Sumner proclaimed to a rally, "PROTECTION TO MAN, shall be the new AMERICAN SYSTEM."[31]

Former Liberty men found the platform least appealing. Only one plank, that which called for a separation of the government from all ties to slavery, was closely reminiscent of the Liberty platform of 1844. While this was important—was, in fact, the resolution that summarized all the rest—it was essentially a negative position. Because of the necessity of appealing to a diverse coalition, the conferees had not inserted any language into their final draft that advocated any positive action against slavery. One could imply, for example, that to end the government's protection of slavery meant abolition in the District of Columbia, but that action was not explicitly stated. Barnburners were almost certain to oppose such an idea. Like Conscience Whigs, moreover, Liberty men were disturbed at the failure to deal with the moral struggle between slavery and freedom. To them the platform was a rather dry account of the political conflict which avoided the inherent sinfulness of slavery. It was, in sum, short of the mark and uninspiring.

Thus, when Liberty men discussed the platform and the new party, they urged patience and forbearance. Joshua Leavitt, who had made a dramatic conversion in supporting Free Soil, attempted to convince Liberty men that the ultimate benefits of the coalition far outweighed its temporary shortcomings. "What have we lost?" he asked. "Not one of our principles—not one of our aims—not one of our men." Abolitionists were now dealing with people who did not share their zeal or conviction, but who were at least heading toward the proper goal. "Let us do our duty to these new relations which the providence of God and the misconduct of men have brought us into," Leavitt concluded. "In this throng of freemen . . . those who do the best service will have the most effect in forming its character."[32]

The absence of any call for abolition or direct federal action against slavery raised the second point about the Free Soil platform: its deafening silence concerning race. This omission must be seen as a further result of the need to give Free Soil a national base and as evidence of the influence of Barnburners in forming the party. Only two years before, the New Yorkers had succeeded in maintaining strict property qualifications over black suffrage in their state. They had, moreover, chosen to emphasize the theme of keeping the territories open to free, white labor as part of their defense of republicanism. Arraying the republican concept of an independent citizenry against the quasi-feudal nature of slavery—which was built upon dependency and force—the *Post* stressed the "brutish level" of black workers in the South. The latter toiled at their jobs amid squalid surroundings reminiscent of a prison "watched by an armed man night and day." "By the inevitable necessity of such a state of things," the *Post* concluded, "the position of white masons, carpenters, barbers, etc., is also reduced in their neighborhood, to the level of these degraded beings. It is as in the case of a score of infectious sick, side by side with a score of healthy persons; the healthy do not purify the sick, but the sick contaminate the healthy." David Wilmot was even more specific. "The negro race already occupy enough of this fair continent" he told a rally. "Let us keep what remains for ourselves, . . . for the free white laborer." Amid sentiments such as these the platform's silence on race was a matter of necessity; silence avoided an embarrassing topic.[33]

That Conscience Whigs and Liberty men acquiesced in the omission, however, suggests that they too remained ambivalent about black rights. Certain Liberty men—especially those who refused to join Free Soil and turned to Gerrit Smith's Liberty League—remained anxious that the black not be forgotten or set aside. Yet others, notably Leavitt, steadily backed away from a clear defense of black rights. They had been doing so for at least four years. The Liberty platform of 1844, which contained forty-four resolutions, had made only two cryptic references to black rights, one urging the "restoration of equality of rights" in all the states and the other inviting blacks to participate in the party. By 1848 even this obscure language had disappeared in the rush toward a new coalition. During the campaign former Liberty men tended to emphasize the social and political corruption induced by slavery rather than the need for a national policy of black equality. Yet, after the pressure of the campaign had passed, several Liberty men, including Chase in Ohio, attempted to deal with the problem locally by removing voting restrictions in the northern states. This implied a recognition of reality: racial inequalities could best be solved through piecemeal, local action, but not through a national political party.[34]

Conscience Whigs were perhaps the most vague on the issue. Most endorsed the Barnburners' concept of free labor but without its blatant racism. And in the years following the election Whig Free Soilers in Ohio, Wisconsin, and Massachusetts were far more likely than Democrats to join abolitionists and former Liberty men in attempting to repeal local black codes. A few, such as Charles Sumner, publicly defended the rights of blacks to enjoy the same privileges of education, voting, and transportation as whites. Yet the striking fact is that, with certain exceptions, Whigs seldom took the lead in these efforts. Where black codes were repealed and constitutions revised, the most vigorous activists were most likely Liberty men. During the campaign Conscience Whigs gingerly avoided the subject. It was hard enough to convince voters of the absolute necessity to forsake their regular parties to keep distant territories free; harder still to convince them that blacks shared a place in northern society. Hence the most distinguishing characteristic of the Conscience Whig position on race was its absence.[35]

The third point to be made concerning the platform involves the planks which did not pertain to slavery. Again the conclusion is that the influence of Barnburners was paramount. Cheap postage, governmental retrenchment, a tariff for revenue, and homesteading were all malleable enough to be used in various ways, but the overall tone they presented was Democratic. Governmental retrenchment, for example, was a logical extension of the Jeffersonian doctrine of limited government. A tariff for revenue did not imply protection for domestic manufacturers. Homesteading was an adjunct to free labor in the territories. It suggested that an independent citizenry, tied to the soil which they worked, needed room for expansion in order to promote "the interest of all the States of this Union." Repayment of the national debt echoed the republican concept that indebtedness was merely another form of dependency, to be resisted like all the rest. While most Whigs would have recoiled at the thought of an insolvent government, this wholesale reduction in the ability of the state to borrow contradicted their own ideal of vigorous social institutions. Only the demand for river and harbor improvements seemed to reflect the American System, yet even this was advocated primarily by western Democrats. Mired in bad roads and hampered by snags, they were far more anxious for federal aid than their counterparts in the East.

A final point to be made about the platform concerns its relationship to the nomination. Knowledgeable observers such as Chase, whatever their personal inclinations toward a candidate, had long realized that the Barnburners would be central to the strength of the new party. After the Utica convention it was clear that some prominent Barnburner, probably Van Buren, would be presented to the convention as a nominee, and that without such a man the New Yorkers would be disinclined to wage a vigorous campaign. Thus the Democratic leanings of the platform were there by design. They provided a standard which any Radical Democrat could raise, yet they were vague enough to appease Whigs and Liberty men. A careful attention to Democratic sympathies and a careful omission of disturbing topics such as black rights were the surest prescription for keeping the Barnburners loyal to their new party. Moreover, Liberty men such as Henry B. Stanton sensed that certain concessions to the New Yorkers regarding the platform might allow Barnburners to accede to Van Buren's wishes and withdraw his name.

These considerations were evident when the nominating process began. Chase surprised Conscience Whigs by withdrawing McLean's name completely for the justice only a week before had adamantly refused to be drafted into the race. Then Stanton explained that, since the platform was acceptable to Liberty men, Hale had decided to set aside his Liberty nomination and offer himself to the new party. Finally, in a surprise move, Benjamin F. Butler announced that Barnburners no longer insisted upon having Van Buren as their candidate. "It may happen, in the course of the deliberations of the Convention," the ex-President had written on August 2, "that you become satisfied that the great end of your proceedings can . . . be best promoted by an abandonment of the Utica nomination." Now, with the platform in hand, the new party was committed to principles that were compatible with the Democrats'. Barnburners, Butler concluded, were willing to grant Van Buren's "uniform desire never again to be a candidate for the Presidency." With that, balloting began.[36]

And Van Buren won. In the committee the vote split cleanly along party lines. Liberty men, except Chase, sided with Hale, while Democrats supported Van Buren. Conscience Whigs, with no candidate of their own, held the balance. Swallowing Van Buren was hard, but Whigs grimly acknowledged that there were more northern

Democrats than Liberty men and more support for Van Buren than for Hale. Moreover, Hale himself was an ex-Democrat, so there was absolutely no chance that a candidate for Whig leanings would lead the party. Reluctantly Stephen C. Phillips turned the Massachusetts delegation to Van Buren, and the rest followed. At that point Joshua Leavitt laid the Liberty party to rest and moved that the nomination be made unanimous. To balance the ticket and give it added prestige, the committee chose Adams as the running mate.[37]

On the night of August 10 the committee presented its choices to the convention. When Van Buren's name was announced, "Hats, and banners, and handkerchiefs were waved, and cheer followed cheer," and the nomination was instantly approved. Then the committee brought forward Adams. "The cheering at this point was terrific," Dyer observed. After a few concluding speeches, the tired and happy delegates adjourned and left for their homes. They took with them a slogan: "Free Soil, Free Labor, Free Speech, Free Men." They called themselves Free Soilers.[38]

The Buffalo convention had clearly demonstrated the relative strengths of each of the three factions that made up Free Soil. Radical Democrats were strongest because they possessed the largest pool of voters, concentrated in a critical state. They were also the most organized, the most professional, and the most difficult to appease. Conscience Whigs represented a potentially enormous body of support, but one that was diffused throughout the North and only loosely tied by organization. Liberty men commanded the fewest votes, were split and divided by Gerrit Smith's defection at Macedon Locks, and were the least acquainted with systematic party politics. For all these reasons and more the platform and the candidate were most useful to the New Yorkers.

But while the platform was flexible enough to be used by all three factions, Van Buren's name on the ticket was an obvious embarrassment to Whigs and Liberty men. "The first question naturally arising in the mind of an antislavery man," the Chicago *Western Citizen* observed, "is this,—Can he be trusted, after his long course of servility to the slave power . . . ?" Answering its own question, the paper appealed to the cause, not the candidate. "For ourselves, . . . we look not to the man, but to the circumstances in which he is now placed. We will not soil our conscience, nor lower the dignity of our manhood, by offering any apology for Mr. Van Buren's former political errors. It is not necessary. Let by-gones be by-gones." This seemed to be the only defensible ground—to emphasize principles and ignore Van Buren's past. "We will stand by our principles, though the heavens fall," wrote the Ashtabula *Sentinel*. "The mere instrument to be used to establish those principles is of but little consequence, in comparison with their inestimable value. Whatever may be said against Mr. Van Buren (and there is much), it cannot be charged that he ever violated a pledge or abandoned his friends." On that ambiguous note Free Soilers turned to their strategy.[39]

Ideals had to be presented effectively, and so Free Soilers set out to organize their forces. Here the Barnburners were the most experienced. For three decades they had paid minute attention to the details of operating a political party, and although the rift with the Conservatives had seriously weakened their power, they remained superb party craftsmen. At the local level they worked by school districts, drawing up lists of voters, crossing off confirmed partisans on either side, and concentrating on the undecided. By spreading the work among many volunteers, they were able to reach thousands of ordinary citizens who might have been ignored or overlooked otherwise. At the state level they relied on newspapers and frequent small rallies to spread their message and publicize their candidates. But they were always careful to see that most of the work was done among small groups. They seldom used the mass meeting, nor did they import famous speakers from other states.[40]

The situation was different among the Conscience Whigs and the Liberty men who joined Free Soil. Most were rank novices at the political game; compared to the Barnburners, few had ever held political office. This inexperience was evident in the way they presented their message. In Massachusetts, for example, lines of communication among the Free Soilers in the towns were poor. Most of the state meetings were called by Free Soilers in Boston. Although Worcester, in the center of the state, was the favorite rallying point, the condition of the roads and the expense involved in getting there meant that the gatherings were few and attracted only the hardiest and most committed voters. At the meetings one was likely to hear a speaker brought in from outside the state. Giddings went to Massachusetts on one such tour; John Van Buren was invited for another. As popular as these meetings were, they did not reach deeply into the electorate, and they did not place the Free Soilers there in close contact with as many voters as did the system of the Barnburners.

As the organization of the party differed from state to state, so did the strategy. In New York, for example, Free Soilers looked for their greatest strength in heavily Barnburner districts where devotion to Van Buren ran high. Though opposition to Taylor was rife within the New York Whig party, Free Soilers correctly assumed that Van Buren's presence on the ticket would drive most antislavery Whigs back into their old organization. Too, no major New York Whig leader—not Greeley, not Seward—endorsed the new party, and it was unlikely that their followers would join the Free Soilers. On the other hand, the Free Soilers did count on winning most of the Liberty vote. Accordingly, when the state Free Soil convention met, a Barnburner, Dix, was chosen to run for governor alongside a former Liberty man, Seth M. Gates, for lieutenant governor.[41]

In Massachusetts the party enjoyed a broader base. Although the non-extension movement there had generally been led by Conscience Whigs, Van Buren's nomination was popular among Marcus Morton's band of Radical Democrats. Morton of course felt little love toward the Conscience Whigs, but he had been so long shut off from influence in the national party by his Democratic rival David Henshaw that he rushed to Van Buren's support shortly after the Utica nomination. Free Soilers expected at least one-third, and possibly half, of Massachusetts Democrats to follow suit. At the state convention Free Soilers attempted to balance these elements by pairing Stephen C. Phillips with a Free Soil Democrat. With this arrangement they prepared for a fusion of the two factions in November.[42]

In Ohio the Free Soil campaign took a different course. Despite Chase's hope that the Democrats would eventually unite with the Free Soilers, astute political observers knew that the best source of Free Soil votes lay among disaffected Whigs on the Reserve. Since slave extension was massively unpopular among Reserve Whigs, Free Soilers, Chase included, suggested that the two parties merge in the state contest; if that plan worked well, Taylor's prospects in Ohio might be demolished in November. Before any merger could take place, however, it was necessary that Seabury Ford, the Whig nominee for governor, renounce Taylor explicitly. But Ford doggedly resisted all attempts to make him either endorse or reject Taylor. "I came to the conclusion," he advised Chase, "that an avowal on my part against General Taylor was certain defeat, and an avowal in his favor nearly as certain." Though Ford resisted Chase's pleas that he publicly endorse Van Buren, it was an open secret that he regretted Taylor's nomination. In any case, antislavery men considered Ford preferable to the Democrat, John Weller, who supported Cass. Confronted with a choice, then, Free Soilers decided not to run a man against Ford. It was a wise move, for it traded Whig votes on the Western Reserve for Van Buren in exchange for Liberty votes for Ford. In October, Ford was elected by less than 350 ballots.[43]

In other states the Free Soil campaign assumed a variety of forms. In New Hampshire Hale buried his disappointment at losing the nomination. With Tuck he struggled to rebuild his old coalition of antislavery Democrats and Whigs, and Liberty men. In Connecticut Senator John M. Niles abandoned the Democratic party and set out to preach the Free Soil gospel to the countryside. Pennsylvania Free Soilers cooperated in electing the Whig candidate for governor in October. Alarmed, regular Democrats redoubled their efforts to convince Wilmot's Free Soilers to vote for Cass. As the election approached, Pennsylvania remained doubtful. In all these states Free Soilers counted more on winning votes in the country and in the small and medium-sized towns than in the cities, where the regular party organizations were strongest. Giddings orated to the factory workers of Lowell, Massachusetts, while Niles went for the "shoemakers & mechanics in the villages."[44]

In the national campaign Free Soilers hoped to win votes by shaking party loyalties through a careful appeal to the slavery issue. For Whigs and Democrats these objectives were reversed. The surest path to victory was to maintain voter regularity by ignoring or blurring the slave question. In this Taylor and the Whigs were more successful. Taylor preserved his silence on the territories as his campaign workers attempted to keep Whig voters in the fold. In the South they pointed to their candidate's ownership of slaves and noted that Cass's popular sovereignty would possibly limit—not extend—slavery. In the North they repeated Taylor's promise to follow the will of Congress concerning the territories. Cass, on the other hand, was weakened by his own words. In his own way Cass had acted with a certain amount of courage in presenting his compromise on slavery; he had not totally avoided the issue as Taylor had done. Yet any stand on slavery was open to attack. One that could be read two ways was—as Whigs demonstrated—doubly vulnerable. State elections in early October simply verified what was becoming obvious: Cass was in deep trouble everywhere except in the West.

On election day the expectations of the Free Soilers, the best hopes of the Whigs, and the worst fears of the Democrats were all realized. Taylor won solidly in every section but the West and edged Cass by over 100,000 votes out of almost 3 million cast. In every section Taylor's popular vote exceeded that of Clay in 1844, a tribute both to the disorganization of the Democrats and to the perseverance of the Whigs. Cass, on the other hand, fell short of Polk's total in 1844; only in the Northwest and South did Cass do as well. Clearly, Van Buren's defection had hurt him. In New York alone Cass lost over 100,000 votes to the ex-President. Van Buren also crippled Cass in Pennsylvania. Although Taylor would have beaten Cass there even if the latter had won all of Van Buren's 11,000 votes, the Free Soil vote turned what might have been a close contest into a rout. In the electoral votes Cass's victory in Ohio almost offset his loss of Pennsylvania, but his failure to win New York was disastrous. Van Buren's strong vote in New York handed Taylor the state's 36 electoral votes, and when the electoral college met, Cass lost by precisely 36 votes. Clearly, if the Barnburners had given the same staunch support to Cass that they had given Polk, Taylor would have lost.

For Free Soilers the results were reason neither for joy nor for gloom. They had not picked up any electoral votes, but in their first campaign they had secured one-tenth of the popular ballot, a respectable number for a party that had formally organized barely three months before election day. As expected, they did well in New England. They beat Cass in both Vermont and Massachusetts, taking about a third of the ballots in each state. In New York they gained their largest tally; Van Buren polled 120,000 votes, better than Cass, but only about half of the Whig vote. In Ohio they did disappointingly poorly. While Van Buren ran on the Western Reserve, the rest of the state remained firmly locked to the old parties. In Cincinnati, Chase's home, Free Soil failed miserably.

Still, the returns showed many signs of promise. Van Buren had run well in several states of the North; in only five had he failed to get at least 10 percent of the vote. Moreover, he had drawn from both Whigs and Democrats. While the Free Soil vote in New York was overwhelmingly from the Barnburners and that in Ohio primarily from the Whigs, the party was more balanced in other states. In Massachusetts, for example, the Free Soilers had done very well among Morton's Democrats who contributed almost half the Free Soil vote there. In New Hampshire, where ex-Democrat Hale was in charge, the Free Soilers rallied fully one-third of their support from the Conscience Whigs. Nor was Free Soil limited to any one class or occupation. As Niles of Connecticut had predicted, the returns suggested that the movement appealed to farmers, craftsmen, and professional men alike.

There were also good signs for Free Soil in the Old Northwest.

Although the party ran poorly in Ohio and Indiana, it captured many Whig and Democratic votes in northern Illinois and southern Wisconsin. Moreover, its strength in Michigan, while not overwhelming, was well distributed across the state. The total number of votes cast for Free Soil in these states was not large, but the possible impact on state politics was great.[45]

But the returns also raised questions concerning the roots of the Free Soil vote. In aggregate terms, the new party appeared to draw substantial support from both Whigs and Democrats. When the local returns were compared to the nature of the Free Soil leadership in each state, however, a pattern emerged. Where Democrats contributed to the Free Soil vote, they generally did so under the aegis of men who had loyally followed Van Buren in previous elections. Morton in Massachusetts, Brinkerhoff and Tappan in Ohio, Niles in Connecticut, Francis P. Blair, Jr., in Missouri all were fast friends of the ex-President. This suggested, although it did not prove, that Van Buren's name on the ticket and the Democratic slant of the platform were crucial in attracting Democrats to the new party. It was doubtful, of course, that any loyal Democrat would have forsaken his party had he not been favorable to the principles of the Wilmot Proviso. But in an age of intense party rivalry and high voter loyalty, something beyond principle was necessary to ignite dissent. For antislavery Whigs the presence of a slaveholder on the national ticket was the spark. For antislavery Democrats it was the presence of an acceptable, even exciting, alternative to Cass in the Free Soil nominee. This meant, in practical terms, that Free Soilers were dependent upon the continued dissatisfaction of Barnburners to keep their movement alive over the next four years.

In effect, Free Soil was not a perfect fusion of antislavery dissidents, but a federation. Liberty men, Conscience Whigs, and Radical Democrats each constituted a distinct element, with different leaders and different reasons for joining the coalition. They had worked well together during the national campaign, where the interests of one complemented those of the others. After the election, however, the party would face an entirely new political situation. State and local concerns would confront Free Soilers, and these would place new demands upon unity and cooperation. It remained to be seen how well the three factions would be able to set aside their traditional hostilities and work together. This problem was complicated by the fact that Free Soilers had not run well in the state races. In most states their base of power was fragile and—more importantly—divided among the factions.

For the moment, however, Free Soilers were content. Preston King was especially jubilant. "The late election," he rejoiced, "is only the Bunker Hill of the moral & political revolution which can terminate only in success to the side of freedom."[46]

CHAPTER SIX

COALITIONS AND DIVISIONS

FREE Soilers tended to see the campaign of 1848 as all-important to their movement. In many respects, of course, they were right. Without the revolts at Philadelphia and Baltimore, there would have been no Buffalo Convention; without the Buffalo Convention there would have been no Free Soil party. An important segment of northern opinion would have had no outlet for expression and protest. All these things the campaign provided, and—with the benefit of hindsight—it is clear that American politics were never again quite the same.

But to have judged the whole future of the Free Soil party on the basis of one national campaign, as many of its members did, was a mistake. The roots of this mistake were not hard to find. Free Soilers waged their campaign primarily as a political statement of national values. These values were of diverse origin and could only be brought together under a vague, almost non-programmatic platform. But the essential function of the party during the campaign was to explain that platform to a national audience in hopes that an entire country could be persuaded that it could no longer comfortably contain two distinct versions of the democratic ideal. The choice of Van Buren was a tactical necessity in presenting this message as loudly as possible: he was a man of national repute who could win substantial numbers of votes. That a campaign fought with these objectives could attract a tenth of the electorate and materially affect the outcome of the election gave credence to Sumner's prediction that Free Soil was "destined to triumph."[1]

What all too many Free Soilers forgot in the turbulence of the campaign was the dual nature of their movement. Free Soil was grounded in values that were national in scope. Its ability to argue those values was most effective in a national contest. But the party itself existed primarily as a collection of state coalitions, not all of which acted from the same motivations and none of which could draw on the excitement of a presidential campaign in the years between 1848 and 1852. With so few Free Soilers going to Congress, the success or failure of the party would be hammered out in the states. With a strong political base in the states, Free Soil stood an excellent chance of carrying its momentum into 1852. Without such a base all its efforts then would be hampered.

The persuasiveness of ideology would be of little help here. By 1848 those who had joined Free Soil had undergone four long years of explaining—to themselves as well as others—the values that sparked their protest. After 1848 there would be no new major interpretations to be added to their position; most of their goals, in fact, would outlast the party and reappear as part of Republicanism in the 1850s. In the interim, however, Free Soilers would face the same irritating dilemma that had plagued them before 1848: how to prove that a national issue was inextricably entwined with state and local concerns.

Ideology could, on the other hand, become a brake to the future success of Free Soil. The party was, after all, a group of factions, each of which interpreted the goals of the movement differently. Each of these factions had a political past that linked it either to one of the major parties or to abolitionism. Burying these differences had been hard enough during the campaign, as the choice of Van Buren had shown. To ignore them in the states was even harder. Yet the differences had to be tamed if the party were to survive. Creating temporary coalitions with either of the major parties—coalitions based on expediency in a quest for power—offered Free Soilers their best hope of gaining political offices. And offices, particularly highly visible ones such as senatorships, were ideal pulpits for the Free Soil cause.

To obtain these offices required discipline and sacrifice. Party organization had to be tight, almost regimented, if Free Soilers were to use their small numbers to advantage. More importantly, Free Soilers had to be willing to subordinate all other questions and all former party preferences to the goal of winning office. Caught up in the intense rivalries of the second American party system, Free Soilers had little room for sloppiness or hesitancy in pursuing their quest for office. Tragically for the party, they failed.

Two states, Ohio and New York, best show the seeds of this failure during 1849. In Ohio divided loyalties and personal rivalries tore the party apart even as it was making substantial gains in both state and national arenas. In New York, where organization and discipline was predictably advanced, the lure of old fidelities to the Democratic party proved irresistible. Free Soilers there quickly abandoned their cause.

A few days after the election of 1848, Joshua Giddings turned from national affairs and considered the position of the Free Soilers in his home state of Ohio. The party had not done as well there as he had hoped, but it had captured the Reserve and had sent a sprinkling of men to the state legislature. There the Free Soil members were likely to enjoy a measure of power that outweighed their numbers, for Ohio was neatly split, as it had been for years, between the Democrats and the Whigs. Giddings was optimistic that the handful of Free Soil legislators could determine the balance of power. "I think the free soil men should let the old parties understand that we do not intend to make war, but peace between them," he noted. "Not to give one power over the other but to hold the scales of justice with an even hand."[2]

Politics in Ohio was a maze, however. With Free Soil help a Whig governor, Seabury Ford, had been elected in October, but in November the state had turned to Cass for president. State policy shifted just as capriciously. Whigs instituted state banks one year, and Democrats dissolved them the next. Giddings realized apprehensively that his party contained men from both the old parties, and there was no way to tell if they could set aside their old differences and work together in a common cause.

Two problems in particular threatened the unity of the new party. One had originated months before in Cincinnati. Hamilton County, which contained that city, had traditionally sent Democrats to Columbus. A sizable portion of the district was Whig, however, and the five legislators from the county were Democratic only because they were elected at large. In February, 1848, a Whig legislature had ruthlessly gerrymandered the county, splitting it into two districts, one of which was certain to select Whigs. The Democrats had agonized furiously, declaring the whole affair fraudulent and unconstitutional—which it was. In the October elections Democrats had proceeded to elect five representatives at large as they had always done, while the Whigs, acting under the new rules, had chosen two of their own. Now the two Whig seats were being disputed, and a prolonged and bitter fight at Columbus loomed.[3]

The other question concerned a possible U.S. Senate seat. Senator William Allen, a Democrat, friend of Benjamin Tappan and enemy of

James K. Polk, was finishing his term. He wanted to be reelected, but he had bitter enemies in his own party, not the least of whom was Samuel Medary of the powerful *Ohio Statesman*. Whigs naturally wanted the Senate post for one of their own men; so did Free Soilers.

But no party was certain to win the seat because of the situation in Hamilton County. Whigs and Democrats each had won 30 seats in the house, excluding the 2 disputed seats. Free Soilers had sent 10 men to the house, 5 of whom had been elected with Democratic help, 3 with Whig, and 2 who were independent. In order to control the house, which helped select the senator, the Democrats needed the aid of 5 of the Free Soilers, plus both of the seats at issue in Hamilton County, for a total of 37 out of 72 votes. The Whigs, in turn, required both seats from Hamilton County plus the 3 Whig Free Soilers and both independents. The situation was equally tense in the state senate, where Free Soilers also held the balance of power.

Perceptive Free Soilers, including Chase and Giddings, instantly noted that the situation in Columbus gave them power beyond their numbers. Whigs and Democrats each desperately wanted possession of the two votes from Hamilton County. Without control of the house neither party would be able to direct state policy. Free Soilers were thus in a position to bargain. In turn for throwing their support to one of the major parties on the Hamilton County case, they could legitimately claim that party's votes for a Free Soil senator. The first long step would be taken toward building a genuinely national base of power for the insurgents. But, as Giddings and Chase both knew, the prize could be won only through hard work and difficult negotiation, all of which required the utmost unity within the new party.

Two problems threatened these Free Soil hopes. One was the division among the Free Soil members of the legislature. Former Whigs tended to support the redistricting of Hamilton County; former Democrats pronounced it unconstitutional. As time for the winter session drew near, there was little indication that either group was willing to compromise even to preserve party unity.[4]

There was also the growing rivalry between Chase and Giddings. Both had been active in the antislavery movement for years, and both coveted the Senate seat. Chase had led the movement of the Free Soilers in Ohio ever since the People's Convention at Columbus in June. He had seized the initiative in organizing the new party in bargaining at Buffalo, in setting up rallies and speakers, and in extending his ties with the Conscience Whigs in Massachusetts and with the Barnburners in New York. On the other hand, Giddings, though he had been slow in breaking with the Whig party, was in complete command of the antislavery forces on the Reserve. Neither man completely trusted the other. Their personal styles clashed: Giddings was personable but slow; Chase was pompous but relentless. Both were ambitious to the core.

Giddings feared Chase, however, and moved to block his plans. To a Whig Free Soiler he urged that, since "Mr. Chase and other gentlemen will be at Columbus at the commencement of the session, with the intention to have a perfect and thorough organization throughout the states . . . , the Reserve should be fully represented . . . there." Giddings also made it plain that he welcomed the opportunity to become a senator. "My name is sometimes inserted among the Candidates for the Senate," he observed. "I will not disguise the fact that I should feel highly gratified with the appointment on many accounts but I also desire no sacrifice of the paramount interests of humanity on my behalf." But, he added, "should my election be deemed beneficial to the progress of the revolution now going on I should be pleased to receive it."[5]

Chase, however, was hard at work perfecting his own plans. In September he had begun weighing the possibilities for a coalition with either the Whigs or the Democrats. Although his sympathies on economic policies lay naturally with the Democrats, he was realistic enough to know that most of the Free Soil strength in Ohio came from Whigs on the Western Reserve and that, if he was to gain anything from a coalition, he must have their support. With that thought in mind he declined a proposed Free Soil nomination for governor and threw his weight behind Ford, the Whig. It was a move that his close adviser in Cleveland, James A. Briggs, approved. Endorsing Ford, Briggs wrote, "will in my opinion be of benefit to you on the Reserve *for future use.*"[6]

Nevertheless, Chase kept alert for overtures from the other side. As he expected, the Democrats, with no federal patronage behind them, seemed receptive to the idea of working with the Free Soilers. In November Wilson Shannon, a Democratic ex-governor, offered an outright deal—Shannon to go to the Senate with Chase to be made a judge of the state supreme court. It was the signal that Chase had been waiting for, for now he knew that the Democrats were in trouble and would need Free Soil help. He ignored Shannon's offer. If the Democrats would give up a seat on the court so easily, they might be forced to relinquish the senatorship with a little hard bargaining.[7]

Now began three months of intrigue. When the state representatives began drifting into the capital in early December, the issue uppermost in everyone's mind was the Hamilton County case. The two Hamilton Whigs, George Runyan and O.M. Spencer, were there, their seats challenged by Democrats George Pugh and A.N. Pierce. Moving quickly, the Democrats disregarded the fact that all previous sessions had convened at ten o'clock on the morning of December 4, assembled during the night, and began the work of organizing the state House to their liking.[8]

When the Whigs realized what the Democrats had done, they marched into the hall and demanded that Spencer and Runyan be seated. The Democrats refused and admitted Pugh and Pierce; the Whigs, in turn, stalked out. The next day the Whigs reappeared, took their seats across the aisle from their opponents, and proceeded to organize separately. At the end of each day the Whigs left while the Democrats stayed behind, taking care that Whigs would conduct no business without them. In session, night and day, exhausted Democrats kept constantly on guard. Their chairman remained on duty, two prize bulldogs and a spittoon at his feet, challenging the Whigs to act without him. But the Whig refusal to answer the roll left the Democrats without a quorum. The situation was deadlocked. "Our Legislative Hall has become a perfect bear-garden," the *Sentinel* sighed. "Transactions have occurred there that would disgrace an Irish wake."[9]

For the Free Soilers it was a golden opportunity to seize the initiative and make a deal with one of the parties; yet they held back. The *True Democrat* bluntly pronounced the Democrats wrong. "The only difficulty we see in the quiet organization of the House," the editor declared, "is the admission of the two Cass men from Cincinnati. They are not entitled to seats." Most of the Whig Free Soilers from the Reserve agreed, and their three representatives at Columbus took seats on the Whig side of the House.[10]

Chase, however, remained quiet. Observing the events at Columbus from his home in Cincinnati, he noted that five Free Soil legislators had sided with the Democrats. Furthermore, the two independent Free Soilers, Norton S. Townshend and John Morse, were attempting to act as peacemakers, offering resolutions that would have organized the house first and then have gone on to the Hamilton County question. If the Democratic Free Soilers stood their ground and if Townshend and Morse drifted into the same camp, then a coalition with the Democrats was almost a certainty. In mid-December Chase received word that, if four or five Democrats could be persuaded to support him for senator, Townshend and Morse would both vote to seat Pugh and Pierce. Reading that, Chase hurriedly packed his bags and caught the train for Columbus.[11]

At Columbus the situation remained confused. After trying repeatedly to get the house organized, Townshend and Riddle finally convinced both the Whigs and the Democrats to reject both sets of contenders, organize, then take up the Hamilton County case anew. With massive reluctance and great suspicion on all sides, the representatives agreed. On December 23, nineteen days after it had first been scheduled to meet, the legislature of Ohio finally convened.[12]

Chase now moved to forge a working relationship with the Democrats. Only one day after Townshend had successfully resolved the crisis over organizing, the Free Soilers assembled in their state convention at Columbus, with Chase in complete control. Working far into the night in his hotel room, he drafted a platform that repeated all the traditional Free Soil ideas about slavery in the territories and the Wilmot Proviso, plus several unabashedly Democratic planks on economic policy. On the day of the convention Chase's friends forced it through, specifically adding that the Free Soilers were not bound to act with other parties solely on the basis of opposition to slavery. The platform was a clear signal to the Democrats, who eagerly turned their attention to Chase's plans.[13]

With help from Townshend and Morse Chase now began to be more specific about the price that the Democrats would have to pay for Free Soil cooperation. To gain a point he had advocated for years, Chase first demanded that the Democrats join in repealing the Black Laws, which had ostracized Ohio Negroes for decades. In return for that Townshend and Morse announced that they were ready to vote to admit Pugh and Pierce and to help elect a Democratic speaker for the house. The Democrats tentatively agreed but still expected to send one of their own men to the senate.[14]

What they had not fully grasped was that, even with Pugh and Pierce, they would still not hold a majority of the legislature without Free Soil help. When the balloting for senator began, Chase would be standing by, ready to remind the Democrats that they owed their power to the Free Soilers and ready to call in the debt. As January began, Chase prepared to put his strategy into effect.

Whig Free Soilers watched these developments with mounting alarm. Even as Chase emerged as the strongest Free Soil candidate for senator, the *True Democrat* dismissed his chances out of hand. "Mr.

Chase is a young man—and high honors yet await him," the editor noted. Then he added curtly, " 'Work and Wait,' is a good motto." Riddle was more concerned. "Chase is a noble man," he advised Giddings, "but as ambitious as Julius Caesar. And he has certainly favored the Democrats to an almost dangerous extent. That he did this from convictions that they were in right I am anxious to think. That Townshend & Morse did so I am most certain." But Riddle remained edgy.[15]

While Riddle and the *True Democrat* complained of Chase's ambition, they failed to see similar forces at work among Whig Free Soilers. Several of their party, especially Nathaniel Chaffee and Reuben Hitchcock, were consulting and cooperating almost daily with the Whigs, looking to the same sort of arrangement that Chase was negotiating with the Democrats. Chaffee in particular was determined to keep Hamilton County divided and to wrest concessions from the Whigs on that point. The major difference between these maneuverings and Chase's was the fact that neither Chaffee nor Hitchcock was pledged to one single candidate for senator. This meant that Giddings was not being uniformly supported by the members of his own faction. Hitchcock desperately wanted to be senator himself, although his chances were slim. Thus Giddings's only steadfast support came from Riddle and from the newspapers on the Reserve.[16]

Giddings himself was perplexed. He refused to concede that Chase was in a better position to obtain the Senate seat than he. He had the votes of the Whig Free Soilers, he thought, plus some support from within the regular Whig organization. Moreover, he had been the voice of Ohio antislavery for almost ten years. Logically the Senate seat seemed to be his. But Giddings had misread the events at Columbus. From some unknown source, probably Townshend, he heard that Chaffee was trying to arrange a deal to give the Free Soilers state offices while the senatorship went to a Whig. The information was false, for not even Chaffee was willing to go that far, yet Giddings believed that it explained and even justified the course of Townshend and Morse. "I do not know that it is true," he remarked concerning Chaffee's alleged scheme. "Yet I really think there is much truth in it, and Morse & Townshend seeing it could see no way to break it up" except to cooperate with the Democrats. "I make no calculation on Senator," he added, "but I am as far from giving it up as ever."[17]

But while Giddings waited impatiently for news from Columbus, Chase was busy cementing a coalition with the Democrats. In early January, with the debate over whether to seat Pugh and Pierce still raging, he finally reached an agreement. Townshend and Morse were to vote to admit the two Democrats to the house and to cooperate in filling the speaker's chair and certain judgeships; in return, the Black Laws were to be revoked, Free Soilers were to be given some state offices, and, most important, Chase was to become senator. On January 9, after days and weeks of haggling, Townshend and Morse began the deal by helping choose a Democratic speaker.[18]

Instantly Whig Free Soilers on the Reserve were alarmed. "Messrs. Townshend and Morse," the *True Democrat* warned, "the party to which you belong, your constituents and your own characters, too, require that you should give good reasons for this conduct, which, if good, is not appreciated."[19]

Townshend answered with a direct slap at the Whig Free Soilers. He had voted for the Democrat, he explained, in order to "prevent the free soil party from being swallowed up by whiggery." He charged that too many Free Soilers were little more than Whigs in disguise, trying to overrun the party. Against this he and Morse had rebelled, "not willing to be sponged up and identified with whiggery under any guise." His action echoed the private sentiments of Chase, who confided to Hamlin: "I approved of the intention of Messrs. M. & Townshend, because I thought it the only way to save the Free Democracy from identification with Whigism . . ."[20]

As if in further reply to the *True Democrat,* on the night of January 26 Townshend and Morse voted to admit the two Democrats from Hamilton County. The Whig Free Soilers were outraged. "We think Townshend and Morse have voted wrong, and in the admission of Pugh and Pierce, the Law has been violated," the *True Democrat* stormed. There was, however, little the paper could do but complain, for Chase was now firmly in control of the situation and making plans for the next step.[21]

In Washington Giddings was more sanguine. He was beginning to see that Chase's maneuverings had in fact placed the Free Soilers in an excellent position to dictate to one of the other parties. Chase had used the Hamilton County mess to force the Democrats into a more conciliatory mood; the same circumstances might yet convince the Whigs to act with the Free Soil men. With the Democrats winning the speakership and then the Hamilton case, the Whigs might agree to send Giddings to the Senate in order to stave off further Democratic gains within the state. "As to Senator," he predicted to his son, "if the Whigs come in and support me Townshend and Morse will vote for me and I can be elected. If not they will vote for Chase and he will be elected by aid of Democratic votes. . . . All my letters from a certain quarter," he added, referring to Riddle, "are in deep mourning because Pugh & Pierce were admitted as it will defeat my election. This is mere fudge."[22]

Chase, however, knew that the outcome could go only one way. The Whigs hated Giddings for his defection in 1848. "I do not believe you can be beaten for the Senate," Stanley Matthews noted to Chase, "except by the Whigs voting in a body for Giddings—a contingency not very likely to happen and the very possibility of which is the very thing to reconcile the Democrats most completely to their support of you."[23]

In February, 1849, the Democrats took the first step in completing their part of the deal. With Chase's constant prodding they finally joined with Free Soilers to repeal most of the Black Laws. Although blacks still could not vote, the repeal erased the ban on black schools and the requirement that free blacks post a bond before settling in the state. Even the *True Democrat* set aside its suspicions temporarily. "We think our colored people have great cause of rejoicing, and they have rejoiced," the paper proclaimed. "The repeal of the Black Laws is a great step in the work of Progress and Justice."[24]

The Whigs, alerted by this development, moved to smother the mounting threat of a coalition of Democrats and Free Soilers by nominating John McLean for senator. It was an act of desperation, prompted by the hope that McLean's popularity among the Free Soilers would turn them away from both Chase and Giddings and into an alliance with the Whigs. Chase, however, was not worried. McLean had lost stature among the Free Soilers at Buffalo in 1848, and it was not likely that they would accept him as a compromise. McLean, for his part, wanted no part of such proceedings; when he learned of the Whig action, he quickly declined. Their hopes shattered, the Whigs awaited the inevitable.[25]

After much stalling and final dickering the Democrats at last accepted fate. On February 22, after a series of midnight conferences with Free Soilers, Ohio Democrats abandoned their own man and voted to make Chase senator. The *Ohio Statesman,* organ of the Democrats, welcomed the result with guarded optimism. Chase, Medary noted, was "right on most of the questions, but a little streaked when the subject of slavery is touched—but a staunch friend of the Union." A few days later Medary was more explicit: "It was Mr. Chase or a whig."[26]

Giddings accepted his defeat graciously. He had feared all along that the Whigs would shrink from voting for him; he was also convinced that Chaffee and other Whig Free Soilers had been guilty of bad management and insincerity. Too, it was difficult for Giddings to believe that Chase had acted dishonorably in negotiating a deal with the Democrats. Long experience in practical politics had convinced Giddings that such bargaining was unavoidable, and he did not berate Chase for playing the game so well. When the morning paper brought news of Chase's election, therefore, Giddings was relieved that the struggle was finally over. "I was so far from being mortified at this result that I can say truly it gave me pleasure," he confided to his diary. "I felt it would probably promote the cause more than my own elevation to that office."[27]

Other Whig Free Soilers were not so generous. Riddle was plainly disgusted at Chase's course. Chase's deals with the Democrats were a "zigzag course meandering here and there," designed to seize the balance of power for the benefit of Chase alone, with no reference to the rest of the party. "In so doing," Riddle concluded, "none of us have been permitted to have the least influence whatever in any business nor have we in any respect shared the personal confidence" of Chase and his friends.[28]

Beyond that was the galling question of reconciling the election of a man with Democratic economic sympathies as the representative of a party composed overwhelmingly of ex-Whigs. Despite their attachment to the new party, neither the *True Democrat* nor most other Free Soilers from the Western Reserve could completely set aside their affection for the Whig party. "As we view Locofocoism," the editor had declared earlier, "it is as destructive to the welfare and interests of the people of our State as the locusts were to 'every green thing' in Egypt. It must be destroyed." It was not surprising, therefore, that Whig Free Soilers watched Chase's dealings with concern; he was offering the Free Soil party for sale, they felt, to an implacable foe.[29]

Puzzled and hurt by Chase's successful dealings with the Democrats, Whig Free Soilers conveniently forgot that they had been perfectly willing themselves to bargain and to politick with the Whigs, and in the weeks after the election they retreated into attacks on the party system itself. Ignoring the fact that no Free Soiler, not even Giddings, would have gone to the Senate without some sort of bargain, the *True Democrat* cried out against compromises and coalitions. "This is not a kind of political morality that we expected to see . . . ," the editor shrieked. "Out with such ethics! away with such hypocrisy! It smells of corruption." A few weeks later the paper was more direct. "We can have no coalitions! It would smother free and earnest expression of thought and action. It would sell the principles of freemen for the offices of party, and make a mockery of all our efforts in behalf of freedom." It was lofty rhetoric, but bad politics. Birney and Tappan had used the same anti-party sentiment four years earlier to keep the Liberty party small, and had succeeded only too well.[30]

Stunned by these blows against his character and his honesty, Chase tried to make peace. Hastening to make amends, he scratched off a letter to Riddle. "I had told you," he explained, "when I was first in Columbus, that if the Freesoil cause could be served thereby I would withdraw my name wholly from the canvass for Senator. You, then, expressed yourself decidedly against any such step." Then Chase noted that Free Soilers could not "claim all offices" but must give "a liberal support" to the demands of any party which would cooperate in return for placing Free Soil candidates into key positions. He had settled on the Democrats for two reasons. First, the "principles" of the Free Soilers and the Democrats were compatible, and second, the Whigs, who had control of the White House, would not be inclined to bargain with the new party so long as they enjoyed that power. On the other hand, the Democrats, shamed by Cass's defeat, would be ready to "progress in the direction of Freesoil." To Chase the outcome was predictable, almost inevitable, and he scolded Riddle and the Whig Free Soilers for leaving "too much to others" and then complaining of the result.[31]

Chase explained his position more elaborately to Giddings. In Chase's opinion, the Free Soilers had had two alternatives open to them. Either they could nominate a full slate of candidates for state offices and probably win nothing, or else they could concentrate on one or two important offices, giving the others to whichever party was willing to cooperate. The latter course had been good strategy, Chase felt, and he was hurt that he, along with Townshend and Morse, had taken so much abuse for what had happened.[32]

The damage to Chase's reputation was perhaps the sorest blow inflicted at Columbus. As he left for Washington in early March to begin his duties, he left behind a storm of doubts, accusations, and suspicions that did not bode well for his future career. One nagging word hung over his future like a dark cloud: ambition.

Certainly Chase was ambitious. Few men ever gain high office without ambition. But it was unfair for Whig Free Soilers to think of him simply as a plotting Macbeth, ready to stab his friends for political spoil. For almost a decade Chase had honestly believed that the future successes of political antislavery lay in converting the Democratic party. To him the Democratic ideology of restricted power and special privileges to none blended well with the attack on human bondage and the entrenched southern "aristocracy." Moreover, he had stated his ideas many times, openly and candidly, to whoever would listen.

While Chase's intentions were sincere and his bargain with the Democrats was sensible, all his protests of innocence showed a certain naiveté. Granted that Giddings probably had never had a real chance at becoming senator with the help of the Whigs, it was still foolish of Chase to proceed with his plans without making more attempts to win the approval of Whig Free Soilers such as Riddle. In his secret bargaining Chase had inevitably raised suspicions that he was binding up Free Soil for sale to the Democrats. The magnitude of his mistake did not dawn on him until after the affair was finished and the damage done.

But the real problem at Columbus lay in a simple lack of party discipline. Every Free Soiler wanted to see the Black Laws repealed; all demanded that one of their men go to the Senate. The trouble was that Whig Free Soilers wanted to remain Whigs on all other matters, while Democratic Free Soilers wanted to remain Democrats. This was fatal to party harmony. "The truth is," John C. Vaughan wrote to Chase, "we have not forgotten our old party feelings—and until we do, until we realize where we are, and what we have to accomplish, we shall not have the influence that we might or should exert." The ramifications of this were apparent from the start at Columbus. Any sensible observer would have seen that bargaining with one party meant not bargaining with the other. It was incumbent, then, upon the Free Soilers to probe both parties for signs of weakness, choose one, and divide the spoils. This was not done. Chase automatically turned to the Democrats; Riddle and Giddings chose the Whigs.[33]

That they did so was undoubtedly due to their old preferences on state fiscal policy. It was curious that a party that had been founded around a broad national principle of opposition to slavery would split itself upon the rock of local politics. Men gathered around Free Soil because it was a lofty issue that appealed to their aspirations and their fears. To allow their party to split over who would control the banks was, to say the least, ironic.

Amid all this bitterness Ohio Free Soilers somehow forgot their success. Despite Chase's overbearing ambition and his heavy tactics, he saw clearly that the Free Soil party needed two things: offices and policies. He himself had succeeded in engineering both. Ohio now had a Free Soil senator, one of only two in Washington, who would enter Congress at a crucial point in the struggle over slavery. When the California and New Mexico issues came up for debate in 1850, Chase would be there arguing for the antislavery position in a way that John P. Hale could not. Moreover, Ohio's Black Laws had been repealed. Chase wisely made that the first item in his bargain with the Democrats, for it gave a platform and a respectability to the movement that no amount of officeholders could offer. Chase and Giddings both knew that the party must show results, whoever led it.

The repeal of the Black Laws also strengthened the positive side of Free Soil ideology. Abolitionists had objected that Free Soil was merely a white man's party, catering to racism and fear of blacks. The repeal had shown that not all Free Soilers were so narrow. Ohio was the only state in which former Liberty men contributed heavily to the Free Soil strength, and Chase's efforts in repealing the code had demonstrated a breadth and a liberality to the movement that was not found in, say, New York. It was a triumph of which Free Soilers could be justifiably proud.[34]

Still, the Free Soilers needed unity, and during the spring of 1849 most members of the party made that their task. Samuel Lewis, who had become disenchanted with Chase, his former ally, pleaded conciliation in the pages of the *True Democrat*. "If I could speak to every free soil man in Ohio," Lewis urged, "whether he call himself Liberty man, free soil, free Democrat, or any other name, my speech would be unite and keep united . . . ." Similarly, the Ashtabula *Sentinel* refused to print any condemnation of Chase, Morse, or Townshend. "We intend our paper shall be devoted to the support of truth and humanity," the paper argued, "and we cannot permit it to be made the instrument of attack upon any man whom we believe to be honestly laboring in the same cause."[35]

Giddings was especially anxious to heal the wounds. He was not so rigid or proud as Chase and was more willing to take the necessary steps to bring the party back together. In early May he convened a "reunion" of Free Soilers in Cleveland. Before the assembly met, he went so far as to consult Townshend on a draft of the resolutions, one of which condemned all coalitions. Townshend objected that such a phrase would be an implicit censure of Chase, and Giddings immediately withdrew it. Nonetheless, the meeting was not happy. Townshend's presence was rankling; Chase did not attend. "I cannot say that anything came of this great convention," Townshend wrote, "except that we came, we saw, but didn't fight." In July, however, Giddings arranged a more general convention of Free Soilers from throughout the North. This time Chase came, along with John Van Buren. Under the veneer of unity, however, the old rifts remained.[36]

Chase had apparently learned little from his mistakes at Columbus. The settlement of the Hamilton County division had been merely postponed, not constitutionally resolved, the previous winter, and Chase was determined to use the same issue to forge a new relationship with the Democrats at the next legislature. Despite the fact that this maneuver had disrupted his party before, he began working to make the Hamilton case an issue in the fall campaign. He reasoned that, if Free Soilers openly opposed the division in their party convention, the Democrats would be obliged to cooperate.[37]

Giddings would have none of this. Regardless of his private feelings on Hamilton County, Giddings had enough sense to realize that the issue had become toxic to Free Soilers. Condemning the division publicly would only alienate many antislavery Whigs who might still be won over to Free Soil. "Our people were nearly all Whigs and of course retain many Whig prejudices and opinions," he wrote to Chase. "They had been accustomed to think that whatever was *Whig* in its character was right," and naturally would support dividing Hamilton County. Giddings also had enough sense to see that Democrats remained weak because of their lack of federal patronage, and would probably be willing to join with Free Soilers under any circumstances.

It appears to me that standing as we must in opposition to the administration, necessity will compel the democrats and free soilers to act together on all matters touching the administration. Therefore if we take an entirely independent position we shall hold in our ranks a greater number of the Whig party than we can if we exhibit any partiality for the democrats.[38]

To his credit, Giddings was not thwarting Chase's ambitions alone. Several Whig Free Soilers, notably Chaffee, were also trying to make the Hamilton case a test question, only taking the Whig side. What Giddings denied to Chase he also refused to Chaffee. Thus, no matter how many letters Chase poured across Giddings's desk imploring him to oppose the division, and no matter how often Chaffee tried to force Giddings to do the reverse, the congressman remained firm. He was the only one to come away from the fracas at Columbus with an untarnished reputation, and he used that power to keep Hamilton County out of the Free Soil resolutions in 1849.[39]

Still Chase persisted. When he finally realized, during the summer of 1849, that Giddings was immovable, he stubbornly went ahead with his own plans. Traveling up and down the state, he made private assurances to the Democrats that the Free Soilers would favor repealing the Hamilton division in the fall. He also attempted to persuade them to set aside their own men and vote for Townshend and Morse. The Democrats nodded approvingly, and Chase entered the fall elections a partner, he thought, in a gentlemen's agreement.

There was a dire lack of gentlemen in the Ohio Democratic party, however. The Democrats, with eyes and ears open to the circumstances around them, were quick to fathom the divisions among Free Soilers. During the summer they tempted Free Soilers with promises of aid until the party was too firmly committed, and too deeply divided, to remain independent. Then, beginning in August, the Democrats systematically abandoned their deal. In county after county they refused to support Free Soil candidates, including, of all people, Norton Townshend. When the elections finally came, the Free Soil vote plummeted.[40]

Struggling to understand what had happened, Chase noted that the Democrats had perhaps overplayed their hand. They still needed Free Soil help to resolve the Hamilton County question, which had reappeared this time in the state senate. Again Chase appealed to Giddings to convince Whig Free Soilers to cooperate. Again Giddings declined. He was determined that the Ohio Free Soil party must remain independent of all coalitions, particularly with the Democrats. Without Giddings's support, therefore, another battle followed at Columbus. The Democrats succeeded, with Chase's help, but as 1850 began Ohio Free Soilers were farther from unity than they had ever been.

Shortly after the election of 1848 William Cullen Bryant of the New York *Evening Post* listed for his readers the three major results, as he saw them, of the campaign:

It has compelled both parties to do homage to the principle of freedom in the territories, and to acknowledge it as an established maxim of political conduct.

It has emancipated the democratic party from the control of the slave power.

It has so disturbed the composition of the democratic party of the north, that it will compel it to reorganize with the principle of free soil in its creed as a settled doctrine.[41]

The last point was crucial.

The Barnburners' hostility to the extension of slavery was genuine. It may have sprung from sources different from that of the Conscience Whigs or the Liberty men, and it may have been tinged with more self-serving fear and hatred of blacks than was just. But nonetheless Barnburners detested slavery and the effect it had upon national policy and the development of the country.

The important point, of course, was that the Barnburners could not separate the fate of the nation from the Democratic party. Their partisanship was complete. When they walked out of the Baltimore convention in 1848, they did so to save the Democracy—and, by extension, the country—from a disastrous surrender to the slave power. The results of the election only served to bolster their convictions. Taylor had never opened his mouth on slavery, had declared his willingness to let Congress decide the matter, and had won. Cass had offered a specific concession to the South in the form of popular sovereignty, and had lost. And so the Barnburners turned their eyes back to the Democracy with the self-congratulatory gaze of men who had been proved right. They also began to abandon Free Soil.

They had never been comfortable as Free Soilers anyway. The very presence of Charles Francis Adams on the same ticket with Martin Van Buren was, to them, an unnatural liaison of polar opposites. Their alliance with committed abolitionists such as Joshua Leavitt was distasteful and strange. Dix had entered the movement only at the elder Van Buren's insistence; so had Flagg and many others. Cassidy of the *Atlas* still carried David Dudley Field's "cornerstone" resolution on the masthead, but he could not bring himself to speak of the bolters as "Free Soilers." Instead, he referred to "our organization," "our party," or, more explicitly, "the free democracy." Of all the prominent Barnburners only Preston King avoided these ambiguities.

There was, then, a basic difference between the Free Soilers of New York and those of Ohio and other states. In Ohio party leaders fully intended to become, in time, the dominant party. Their problem was to maintain an artful balance between temporary coalitions and permanent independence, until the moral force of their ideology crushed one or both of the major parties. Their dissensions grew out of which party to cooperate with, not out of basic goals. In New York, on the other hand, the Barnburners never considered capturing one of the major parties. They were a major party. They had polled over half the Democratic vote in the state and considered the Hunkers the apostates, not themselves. Besides, they had never intended to form a permanent new party; they wanted merely to purify the old one. Naturally, then, they never thought of merging with antislavery Whigs—a step that probably would have made Free Soil irresistible in the state, if the Whigs had consented. Their course was to rebuild the Democracy.

Bryant's warning about slavery remained, however. To enjoy any hope of future success, the Democrats had to take a harder line against slavery. "We expect to make the democratic party of this state the great anti-slavery party of this state, and through it to make the democratic party of the United States, the great anti-slavery party of the United States," John Van Buren proclaimed. "Those who do not contemplate this result will do well to get out of the way . . . ." "We hope to see no further forbearance" on slavery, the *Post* added. "Hitherto it may have been an error; hereafter it will be both a folly and a crime."[42]

The Barnburners were in an excellent position to carry out their plans. Their defection in 1848 had done two things. No Democrat sat in the White House, and hence federal patronage was not available to the Hunkers. The battle would now be fought on more balanced grounds than in 1845. The returns had also scared the Hunkers. Many Hunker leaders, including Marcy and Horatio Seymour, had seen the danger of the slavery issue in the election returns. Never comfortable under Calhoun's tirades anyway, Marcy and others were coming to accept a mild form of Free Soil in the party so long as their own political futures would not be sacrificed to the demands of the Barnburners. Other Hunkers, however, were not so charitable. Croswell of the *Argus* and Senator Daniel S. Dickinson in particular had been deeply hurt by the Barnburner attacks of the past six years. They wanted nothing to do with the Van Burens under any circumstances. Croswell and Dickinson therefore staunchly resisted all moves for reconstructing the party.[43]

In 1849 the push and pull among these factions began. On January 2 three Hunker assemblymen in Albany entered the Barnburners' caucus, proposed a reconciliation, and offered to bargain for either speaker or clerk of the state assembly. The Barnburners pointedly refused to negotiate, but they did offer the highly provocative hint that there was only one Democratic party in New York, and all the Hunkers needed to do was join it.[44]

In February the Barnburner caucus nominated Dix for senator; the Hunkers, still leery of their former foes, balked, and nominated their own man. Both factions lost to the Whigs. That drove home a bitter lesson to the Democrats, Radical and Conservative. As long as the party remained split, Whigs would remain the undisputed masters of New York politics, drawing on their own control of the state legislature and upon federal help sent up from Washington.[45]

In April the Barnburners made another move toward union. Their legislative caucus address called for a convention of all Democrats—

not, however, Free Soilers—at Utica in September. Although the call denounced slavery extension in terms as strong as ever, it was plainly an invitation to the Hunkers to meet together and to patch up the party. A week later the Hunker caucus replied, somewhat less affably, but declaring themselves ready to meet if possible. On May 1 the *Atlas* laid out its demands. Union, Cassidy noted, was imperative to resist the "corruption" of the Whigs. But, he added, it was "vain" and "insulting" to expect the Barnburners to ally themselves with any faction that did not repudiate its ties with slave extension.[46]

At that point the *Argus* stepped in. While the Hunker caucus was controlled by men who wanted reunification, the Democratic central committee was in the grip of Croswell and Dickinson. Setting aside the caucus address, the committee declared that there could be no union on the Barnburners' terms. The Barnburners should have "left the designation of the time and place of holding a convention to their state committee," the *Argus* charged. The Hunker committee then called a convention to meet one week before the Radicals', to preclude any hopes of a joint gathering.[47]

The separate actions of the Hunker caucus and committee were both good and bad signs to the Barnburners. While the committee action made it clear that the road to reunion would be a tortuous one, the fact that the caucus was more receptive suggested that many, perhaps most, of the Conservatives could be coaxed back into a working coalition. The Radicals accepted the committee action with restraint and poise, launching none of their traditional tirades against Hunker treachery. Instead, the *Atlas* begged conciliation and unity. "To accomplish this we will ask no degrading concessions from the other side; we will submit to none ourselves. . . . We desire a union which shall elevate and add honor to all who participate." As proof of its good intentions, the *Atlas* pointed to a meeting in Suffolk County, on Long Island, which had reunited the Democrats there with the mild concession that both sides agreed only on the "evil" of slavery, nothing more. Even the rival *Argus* softened its tone. "The democrats will meet any fair proposition at least half way."[48]

The *Atlas* letter opened the door. In late June John V. L. Pruyn, chairman of the Hunker central committee, offered to hold a joint "consultation" at Rome, in central New York, on August 15. Radicals accepted the invitation with a warning. No union could be made "by obscuring the questions before the party." In short, the Wilmot Proviso must become the official policy of the reunited Democracy. Anything less "would result in getting mere 'goat's wool' and a meagre minority."[49]

An unsigned letter to the *Argus* warned that the meeting at Rome was destined to fail. The two conventions would probably make the situation "worse than before, and spend their time like hostile vessels maneuvering for·the windward, or in fruitless wrangles or discreditable bargains, made in form, to be violated in substance." The writer was at least partly right. The Barnburners sincerely wanted reunion, but they refused to sacrifice their opposition to the extension of slavery to bring it about. Enough Hunkers also desired a reconcilation to override the objections of the *Argus,* but were unwilling to surrender entirely to the Radicals' demands. The Barnburners, in turn, recognized this fact and were ready to compromise on the nominations, if not the platform. With these currents swirling about them, both sides converged on Rome in August.[50]

It was not a happy meeting. Meeting in a Baptist church, the Barnburners quickly drew up a key resolution that declared simply that "the Federal Government possesses the legislative power over slavery in the territories and ought to exercise it so as to prevent the existence of slavery there." It was an open repudiation of Lewis Cass and popular sovereignty. To this the Hunkers replied that they were perfectly willing to "waive all questions as to the regularity of the two organizations, and to pass over without remark the controversies of the last two years." But they could not make slavery a party test. "The democracy of New York is a part of the national democratic party," the Conservatives noted, "which party can only hope to triumph by preserving its ranks unbroken throughout the entire Union. And this cannot be expected or even hoped for, if opinions upon the subject of slavery are allowed to be made matters of party faith." Thus they proposed sidestepping the issue and leaving "everyone to the enjoyment of his own opinions on that subject." The Radicals naturally refused. To have acceded to the Hunker position would have been to disavow their course of the past two years. After much wrangling and sparring, the Hunker convention finally issued a general denunciation of slavery, but repeated that it would not be bound to support the Wilmot Proviso. With that, they left Rome.[51]

But the Barnburners would not be put off. The action of the Hunker leaders had not been welcomed by their followers, and at least one prominent Conservative, Marcy, was ready to repudiate Croswell altogether. In the four weeks following the Rome fiasco, Marcy hinted that he was willing to ignore the Hunker central committee and work again for a reunion. The Barnburners were alert for this and asked only that the regular Hunker convention, scheduled for September 5, ignore the action at Rome and make some move for reconciliation.[52]

At the Hunker convention at Syracuse Marcy and Seymour

constructed a careful plan to bring the two factions back together. First, they declared their opposition to the extension of slavery but said nothing concerning the power of Congress to interfere with it— thus ignoring the Wilmot Proviso. They did, however, admit privately that they and most of the convention delegates agreed that the Proviso was not only constitutional but desirable. Next, in a brilliant move designed both to appease the Radicals and to destroy Croswell and Dickinson, they called for abolishing the state central committee and relying instead on the legislative caucus. Finally, they drew up a list of candidates for office with the stated intention of withdrawing some of the names if the Barnburners cooperated in the election.[53]

The Barnburners consented. At their own convention at Utica one week later, John Van Buren pressed the delegates to accept the Hunker proposition. They did, and shortly afterwards, at a third meeting at Syracuse on September 14, the reunion was begun. Nominees were divided between the groups, and a working arrangement on the slavery question was pieced together. The Barnburners insisted that the convention acknowledge the power of Congress over slavery expansion, but consented to tolerate the "free exercise of individual opinions upon the question." To all outward appearances the New York Democracy was back on the road to cooperation, with the Barnburners apparently in full command. "The fell spirit of disunion which has distracted the democratic party of this state for the past two years," the *Post* rejoiced, "has been exorcised."[54]

Not quite. While the *Argus* had accepted the Barnburners' action, neither Dickinson nor most of the New York City branch of the party liked the results of the Syracuse meeting. On election day, with the Whigs rolling toward another victory, the local committee in the city published a card in the New York *Herald* that vigorously denounced the coalition. The Barnburners, the *Herald* charged, had given away nothing at Syracuse; they still maintained the "test" of "Abolition doctrines" and were determined to close the doors to any Democrat who did not openly approve the Proviso. The *Herald* note infuriated the Radicals to the point that they were prepared once again to bolt the party. King for one was irate, and only the pleadings of Martin Van Buren himself prevented him from walking out of the coalition entirely. In the election the Democrats lost, beaten by their own divisions and by the unity of the Whigs. Yet after the election tempers cooled, and the Radicals and the Hunkers began work again. Van Buren, surveying it all, was hopeful. "The political pot certainly boils strangely," he commented to Blair. "Good must come out of it."[55]

Free Soilers in other states were less optimistic. "We are all much disquieted by the occurrences in New York," Sumner noted to Chase. "I do not judge our friends hastily; but I confess to a feeling that our cause has been sacrificed to a vain desire for the harmony of that ancient omnibus the Democratic party." Chase was also worried about the movement toward reunion. "I hope for good from it. . . ," he mused. "But I hope not without apprehension. The vital point is will the Free Soil Democrats make Free Soil principles an essential condition of their support of a Presidential Candidate in 1852? If they will, all will be well. If not . . . we shall have the work of 1848 to do over again." Most Free Soilers, however, followed Sumner. "Our policy & our duty . . . ," he commented, "are silence & non-intervention at present in N.Y. politics, if we cannot directly co-operate."[56]

So the Free Soil movement ended 1849 on an ambiguous note. In Ohio the party was divided and lacked direction. In New York it was rapidly losing its separate identity in the Barnburners' rush back to the Democracy. In Massachusetts and other states Free Soilers were quiet while they waited for local developments to present them with an opportunity for vigorous action. What none of these groups realized was that events in Washington would soon present them with other problems, other obstacles, which would seriously affect the course of Free Soil in the states. They had underestimated Zachary Taylor—and had forgotten completely Henry Clay.

CHAPTER SEVEN

COMPROMISE AND DISSENT

ZACHARY Taylor took office on March 4, 1849, with one paramount problem confronting him—what course to follow in regard to California and New Mexico. Throughout the summer, with Congress not in session, he remained officially silent on the subject, but in June he dispatched T. Butler King, a friend and advisor, to California to instruct the settlers there to draw up a constitution and prepare to apply for statehood. A similar plan was considered for New Mexico. Taylor apparently did not mind that both territories would likely outlaw slavery. If his simple scheme worked, he reasoned, it would dispense with the vexing questions of slavery extension, the Wilmot Proviso, and southern threats of secession in a single move.[1]

But Taylor's action raised more problems than it solved. Democrats and Whigs alike recognized that he had skirted most of the major issues that were crying for solution. The President's course merely postponed the problem of extending slavery into the territories, a question that was certain to arise over the organization of the huge Deseret, or Utah, territory. Nor did Taylor move to answer southern demands for a stronger fugitive slave bill or for a settlement of the Texas boundary; he likewise ignored northern requests to restrict or abolish slavery and the slave trade in the District of Columbia. Consequently congressional resistance to Taylor and his proposals was quick and massive and came from all parties.

Alternate plans soon appeared. Freshman Senator Stephen A. Douglas of Illinois proposed that Deseret be accepted as a state, with an option to become a territory if the inhabitants there so desired.

Douglas's offer was unrealistic—the area involved was too vast and sparsely populated—but had the virtue of leaving the slavery issue to the Deseret residents, not to Congress. On the other hand, Senator Henry S. Foote of Mississippi offered to organize California, New Mexico, and Deseret as territories with no mention of slavery. Again, Congress would not have to pass on slave extension. As a concession to the South Foote proposed that Texas be divided into two slave states, an act that would increase the number of southern congressmen. Other motions to strengthen or weaken the fugitive slave law also arose. None of these plans, however, not even Taylor's, had any real hope of passage.[2]

In late January Henry Clay moved to resolve the impasse. Realizing that a compromise was inevitable, Clay offered concessions to both North and South. To the North he promised California without slavery, New Mexico as a territory with no mention of slavery and independent of Texas, and an end to the slave trade in the District of Columbia. To the South he offered to have the federal government pay the state debt of Texas, to allow slavery itself to remain in the capital, to leave the interstate slave trade alone, and finally to strengthen the fugitive slave law. On the whole, the South would get major concessions on slavery, while the North would get added representation in Congress.[3]

Clay's proposals were completely satisfactory to almost no one. Southerners were predictably outraged at any concession to the North. Taylor of course would have nothing to do with the plan. He had his own measure, and he feared that Clay was simply trying to overwhelm him as he had tried to do Tyler. Northern Whigs and Democrats alike were concerned that Clay had offered too much to the South and had received too little in return. "I do not think much of Mr. Clay's Compromise as a whole," noted one Whig observer. "It can please nobody. If adopted [it] would bind nobody."[4]

The Clay compromise—with its concessions to the South—was a challenge to Free Soilers in Congress. They were a small and diverse band. Free Soilers never numbered more than twelve in the House; normally they could count on nine or perhaps ten stalwarts—the "immortal nine," as Julian called them. They represented all parties and all parts of the North. Giddings was their leader in fact and in name, although Preston King had more influence among former Democrats. Those who had once been Whigs included Giddings, Charles Allen of Massachusetts, Joseph Root of Ohio, John W. Howe of Pennsylvania, and William Sprague of Michigan. Free Soil

Democrats were King, Amos Tuck of New Hampshire, Walter Booth of Connecticut, and Wilmot. Liberty men had sent Julian of Indiana and Charles Durkee of Wisconsin. Others who often voted with the Free Soilers were Horace Mann of Massachusetts and William F. Hunter of Ohio. In the Senate were Chase and Hale.[5]

From the outset the Free Soilers intended to remain independent and hold the balance of power. The party makeup of the House encouraged their course, for representatives were neatly split between 108 Democrats and 103 Whigs. The problem, as Free Soilers quickly learned, was that neither major party acted as a unit on the slavery issue. Northern Whigs bitterly opposed southern Democrats on slavery extension, but northern Democrats and some southern Whigs favored compromise. Thus Free Soilers were immediately caught up in a maze of alliances and coalitions that seemed to change daily.

The first test of Free Soil strength and unity came early, concerning the election of a Speaker. Democrats wanted Howell Cobb of Georgia, a southern moderate, while Whigs preferred Robert Winthrop. Winthrop was plainly closer to Free Soil sympathies than Cobb, but he had one insurmountable disability: he and Giddings were not on speaking terms. Each had been hurt, in his own way, by Giddings's charge in late 1847 that Winthrop had advocated the Mexican War and had lied to his constituents. It was not likely that Winthrop, whatever support Free Soilers might give him, would forgive Giddings and help place Free Soilers on important committees. It was also unlikely that Giddings, with his damaged pride and reputation, would forgive Winthrop. Though Winthrop might pick up votes from Sprague and Mann, he could not break Giddings's grip on the other Free Soilers in the House.[6]

This became apparent when the balloting for Speaker began. Cobb led on the first vote, with 103 ballots to Winthrop's 96. Wilmot, the Free Soil candidate, had 8. No man had a majority. For over two weeks the contest dragged on, with Cobb steadily sinking and Winthrop never reaching more than 102. Each man offered to drop out and give the race to the other, but this tactic also failed. Free Soilers remained firm.[7]

On December 12 the Free Soil vote suddenly broke. William Brown, a Democrat from Indiana who had temporarily replaced Cobb, unexpectedly came within two votes of being elected. Six Free Soilers, including Giddings and Wilmot, had voted for him. Perceptive Whigs sensed a deal, and George Ashmun of Massachusetts asked loudly if a bargain had "taken place between the member from Indiana and some member of the Free Soil party, in which he had pledged himself to constitute the committees in a manner satisfactory to them?'' ''Common rumor,'' he added, had given him this information.[8]

Common rumor had not lied. Although Brown initially denied the charge, his correspondence with Wilmot was produced, in which he had agreed to place Free Soilers on the committees for the territories, the District of Columbia, and the judiciary. Wilmot made no apology for the deal. Seeing the deadlock, he and other Free Soilers had decided that they had no chance to elect their own man, that Winthrop would probably never treat them well, and that Brown, being a northerner, was better than Cobb. They determined to settle for the committee posts for the single reason that Free Soilers ''and the constituents whom they represented might be heard in this hall.''[9]

The deal would have succeeded if all the Free Soilers had voted for Brown. Their unity broke, however, for three reasons. First, Wilmot and Giddings had arranged the bargain hastily, without consulting each of their followers. This sloppiness of organization ran headlong into the second of Brown's difficulties: Julian completely distrusted him. To Julian, and perhaps others, Brown was no more than a ''pro-slavery Democrat, through and through.'' Julian had no doubt that Brown would have kept his promise to Wilmot, ''but the whole power of his office would have been studiously subservient to the behests of the slave oligarchy.'' Brown in fact later voted for each of Clay's compromise measures. Finally, Brown was a Democrat, and however much Whig Free Soilers such as Root or Sprague detested Winthrop, they still could not tolerate a Democrat in the Speaker's chair.[10]

The drama finally ended on December 21, eighteen days after the House had convened. Democrats proposed that the Speaker be elected by a simple plurality, rather than the absolute majority that had been customary. Free Soilers vigorously opposed this, for they knew that, under the plurality rule, their balance of power would evaporate. The motion passed nonetheless, and within a few ballots Cobb was chosen. To the end most Free Soilers clung to Wilmot, although Tuck vacillated between his own candidate and Winthrop. Refusing to break ranks, the third party had allowed a southern Democrat to become Speaker. For this they were rewarded with a customary blast from northern Whigs, who charged them with being hypocrites. Brushing that aside, Free Soilers sat down to the long struggle between Henry Clay and Zachary Taylor.[11]

Clay, as a good politician, knew that if his compromise was to have a chance it needed the support of the senior senator from Massachusetts, Daniel Webster. Webster, like Clay, possessed immense prestige, but, like Clay, he had been shut out of the formation of the Taylor administration. He also shared Clay's fears for the safety of the Whig party and for the very unity of the nation. It was logical, then, for Clay to seek Webster's support, and seek it he did on a chilling winter night shortly before he introduced the compromise measures. In a long conference with the New Englander, Clay urged him to reject Taylor's plan and fall in line behind the compromise. Webster, tight-lipped, promised to think it over.[12]

Six weeks later, on March 7, Webster stunned New England and the nation with a long speech on the floor of the Senate, fully endorsing the Clay compromise. Ignoring the problem of slavery in the territories, as Taylor proposed to do, would solve nothing, Webster declared, nor would adopting the Wilmot Proviso. Northerners must prepare to make certain concessions, even galling ones, to preserve the Union. But Webster was mostly interested in mollifying the southerners and heading off all talk of secession. He promised, with Clay, that the fugitive slave bill would protect their interests and would be strictly enforced. He assured them that they had nothing to fear from the North and nothing to gain by threatening to secede. All in all, it was an astonishing turnabout for a man who had once claimed the Wilmot Proviso as his own "thunder" and who had briefly considered becoming a Free Soiler.[13]

Free Soilers in every state pounced upon Webster's words. Webster was an "archangel ruined," Sumner charged, one of "the dark list of apostates." The speech was yet another example of the tyranny of the slave power, and Free Soilers hoped that it would shock the northern public awake. "Mr. Webster surrenders to the South," the Albany *Atlas* remarked, and the *Evening Post* added: "At this critical moment, Mr. Webster deliberately leaves our camp . . . to capitulate to the enemy. Of course he is received with clapping hands and shouts of exultation" by the southerners.[14]

Webster was indeed hurt in the North. Even the Boston *Atlas,* which had long been friendly to the senator, was disturbed. "Either we have been, all our life, mistaken in regard to his views, have read him through an inverted medium, or else his late speech is a wide departure from his former course." The paper particularly grieved over his abandonment of the Wilmot Proviso and the principles of the Northwest Ordinance. Robert Winthrop sadly concluded that the speech "would have killed any New England man but Daniel Webster."[15]

But the tremors against Webster soon subsided. Gradually perceptive men realized that the kernel of Webster's speech was not a defense of slavery but of the Union. And it was clear that the Union would be in real danger if some solution to the slavery question were not found. Free Soilers had already refused to concede an inch to the South; southerners would soon meet in Nashville to consider secession. Webster had played a gambit. Once the fury over the speech had subsided, all talk would return to the major question: would Taylor's plan, or Clay's, be accepted?

The answer was by no means clear. Clay's compromise had been assembled into one cumbersome "omnibus" bill and introduced into Congress, where it was immediately mired to the axles. Most members favored at least one of the measures; few liked them all. During June and July Congress slogged through a series of amendments and counter-amendments as senators and representatives sought to modify the bill to suit their individual tastes. The deadlock naturally pleased Taylor, who was all the while working hard for his own plan.

The Free Soilers in Congress were caught in an uncomfortable bind. They had their own plan for the territories, of course. From the beginning of the session they attempted to tack the Wilmot Proviso on every territorial bill, only to see the motion repeatedly voted down. By mid-February it was clear to them that the Proviso had no chance whatsoever and that, sooner or later, either Clay or Taylor would triumph. Six months before they had fought Taylor mercilessly; now they began to reconsider. Taylor was at least willing to have California as a free state, and Julian was impressed by his "unexpectedly manly course . . . in withstanding the imperious and insolent demands of the extreme men of his own section." Joseph Root declared himself "willing, ready, and desirous" to have California organized under Taylor's plan. The problem, however, was New Mexico and Utah. Taylor had done nothing about these territories, and Free Soilers worried greatly that they would be open to slaveholders without the Proviso. Still, compared to Clay's proposals, Taylor's bore up well.[16]

It was the Clay compromise that Free Soilers feared most. Whatever faults Taylor's plan had, the President had left open the questions of slavery in New Mexico and Utah and the District of Columbia. Clay had offered specific concessions on each of these points—none of which pleased Free Soilers—and had gone the extra, fatal step of trying to strengthen the fugitive slave law. For all this antislavery men were to receive no more than California and an end to the slave trade in the capital. To Free Soilers it was not a good bargain. Root insisted that a free government be set up in New Mexico, while Giddings fumed at the blindness of the Clay Whigs. "A generation of Whigs has now risen up," he roared, "who seem not to have known General

Taylor, or his policy, who now turn their backs upon his plan and vote for civil governments in Utah and New Mexico without any exclusion of slavery.'' This, Giddings correctly noted, was no more than Cass's popular sovereignty with a Whig stamp. No less galling was the fugitive slave bill, which Free Soilers regarded as a monster, the ultimate perversion of the Bill of Rights. The only hope of stopping Clay's omnibus of horrors lay in publicly calling for the Wilmot Proviso and privately working in support of Taylor.[17]

But death foiled their plans. Taylor foolishly exhausted himself during Independence Day celebrations in July, contracted cholera, and five days later died. Millard Fillmore was now President, and Millard Fillmore liked the omnibus. Quickly sweeping Seward and the rest of Taylor's advisors aside, Fillmore made Webster secretary of state and his personal confidant. Webster, in turn, proceeded to make support of the compromise the price of official patronage. The Boston *Atlas,* for instance, soon found itself without a government printing contract. The omnibus appeared to be out of the mud and rolling toward success.[18]

It was not an easy journey. In late July a series of parliamentary blunders brought the package to a premature vote, and the compromise failed. Disgusted by his apparent defeat, Clay left for a vacation. In his absence Stephen Douglas took up the measures singly, rather than presenting them in one lump. Brilliantly assembling a different set of supporters for each bill, he deftly guided the proposals through the Senate in August; by early September the House had followed suit, and the Clay compromise was law.[19]

The Free Soilers were despondent. "The consummation of the iniquities of this most disgraceful Session of Congress is now reached," Adams wrote Julian, "I know not how much the people will bear. . . . They have been so often debauched by profligate politicians that I know not whether a case of breach of promise will lie against their seducers." Of one thing Adams was certain: the Free Soil party had "a duty to perform" in arousing opposition to the compromise. "I pray," he concluded, "that they may not leave it undone."[20]

The introduction and eventual passage of the compromise marked a turning point for Free Soil. Before 1850 Free Soilers were confident. They had proved their power to disrupt the party system in 1848, and even their faltering efforts in the states in 1849 had shown that they had the potential to force the major parties to bargain with them. More important, they had an almost reckless faith in the righteousness of their cause. Antislavery and anti-extensionism seemed irresistible; it was only a matter of time before the northern public would join hands with them to crush the slave power.

The compromise was a severe setback. True, the North had gained a free California and an end to the slave trade in the capital, but they had not secured a definite end to the extension of slavery into the territories. Moreover, they were now, each of them, expected to be deputies in enforcing a draconic fugitive slave law. What was most disturbing was the possibility that the northern public, tired of six years of war over slavery, would acquiesce. In each state, then, Free Soilers had to adapt and adjust to the compromise. If popular opinion could be rallied against it, Free Soil would be stronger than ever. If not, the movement would die.

The compromise worked special problems in New York. The Barnburners there were intent upon rebuilding the Democracy, not on perpetuating Free Soil. They were determined also that their new Democracy would not be built upon a diluted version of Lewis Cass's popular sovereignty. Clay's move, therefore, presented them with a hard choice. They could either hold fast to the Wilmot Proviso and risk alienating large numbers of the regular Democrats, or they could accept the compromise, a move that might turn away the more steadfast antislavery elements in their ranks. Martin Van Buren had no doubts as to his course. The reconstruction of his party in New York and the salvation of the national party from southern control had forced him to take a calculated risk in 1848. If the game were to be played to his satisfaction, Van Buren could not afford to lose critical support in New York by clinging stubbornly to the Wilmot Proviso. "If you see Mr. Clay . . . ," he concluded to Blair, "you may say from me that he added a crowning grace to his public life, by his liberal propositions on the Slavery subject, & the able & dignified support of them, which will be more honorable & durable than his election to the Presidency could possibly have been."[21]

The younger Radicals were less charitable. Webster and Clay, the *Atlas* noted, "have entered into a disgraceful competition for the favor of the slavepower." The *Post* even endorsed Seward's "higher law" doctrine of the Constitution, and warned that the compromise would be resisted to the end. "If you take this compromise," Bryant advised his readers, "you take it with full warning that it will not be allowed to last. You buy the jar with notice that there is a flaw in it, and you cannot complain if it breaks in your hands." But, the *Atlas* added pointedly, "let it not be forgotten that this is a Whig Committee, Clay at one end, Webster at the other." The implication was clear. Two prominent Whigs had assumed the burden of defending the South. When Taylor died, the *Atlas* hastened to note that, bad as the old general had been, he had at least stood against Clay and the regular Whigs. "But things are not changed. The Whig opposition has become the Administration itself." A few days later the *Atlas* made its point plain. Taylor's death had increased the need for unity in the New York Democracy in order to resist the Whigs and, by extension, the South.[22]

The separate courses of Martin Van Buren and the *Atlas* represented the two extremes within the Radical group; between them, and as important as either, stood John Van Buren. In February he noted Clay's proposals with some interest and reluctantly concluded that their passage was probably inevitable. Sensing that, he accepted most of the compromise and insisted only on two major points—the early admission of California and the need to keep New Mexico as free territory. He also opposed the fugitive slave law, but much less so than other Free Soilers. Van Buren's opinions were acceptable to most other Democrats, Radical and Conservative, and placed him squarely against Croswell and Dickinson, who supported the compromise unstintingly.[23]

John Van Buren's thinking on the compromise closely paralleled that of an old enemy, Marcy. Marcy had, of course, stood by Cass in 1848 and had thought the doctrine of popular sovereignty much better than the Wilmot Proviso. But Marcy too was disturbed at the arrogance of the southerners in refusing to allow California to enter as a free state. If the southerners continued to block California, he predicted, they would "fail in the attempt and, I fear provoke further agitating measures from the North." Marcy was anxious that the compromise pass, but he, like Van Buren, worried for the safety of northern institutions, and of the Democracy, if the South should gain too many concessions.[24]

Without quite realizing it both the younger Van Buren and Marcy began to reach similar conclusions during the summer, 1850, as to the best course for the New York Democracy. The actions of Webster and Clay had taken much of the heat of slavery off the Democrats, but it was clear that the Proviso was still unacceptable as a basis for rebuilding the party. The best course for both Hunkers and Barnburners then was to denounce slavery in general and demand the admission of California—but no more. Pushing either the Wilmot Proviso or popular sovereignty would only produce trouble and would, in any case, place the New York Democracy in a poor relationship with the national party. During the summer, as the debates over the compromise wore on, the Barnburners, including the *Atlas,* gradually accepted John Van Buren's and Marcy's views.[25]

It would simply not do, however, for the Barnburners to compromise openly and without a fight. They needed another issue—something that would take the focus away from their own pronouncements on slavery long enough for a reunion to form. That issue was Senator Daniel S. Dickinson. Dickinson had long been hated by the Barnburners, but during 1850 he began to fall from grace among the Hunkers also. Both Marcy and Horatio Seymour disliked him because of his ambition and because he did not follow orders well, if at all. Dickinson pointedly ignored the opposition to slavery within his party and supported the compromise from the beginning. He refused to heed legislative instructions to vote against the extension of slavery, even though those instructions had passed the state assembly overwhelmingly. Marcy saw him as a threat to his own position as head of the conservative Democracy and as an unnecessary obstacle to reunion.[26]

During the summer of 1850 lines began to form. In New York City, where Dickinson was popular, his friends gave him an elaborate dinner in which he specifically denounced Free Soil and the Wilmot Proviso. The *Argus* reported this with a warning: "We need not say that his re-election to a station he fills with equal ability and patriotism, is a cardinal point with the Democratic Party of the state, which will not be yielded upon any contingency whatever." But the *Post* replied that most Democrats wanted another senator "who will properly represent the cause of free labor."[27]

This open warfare upon Dickinson made the job of reunion easier for the Barnburners. In March, 1850, the Barnburners and Hunkers both had agreed to meet in a joint convention at Syracuse in September. In the intervening six months Barnburners and Hunkers alike had time to adjust their beliefs to the events in Washington and take sides for or against Dickinson. By the time the convention met, the factions in the New York Democracy had realigned—and proliferated. Most were either "Hards," followers of Dickinson and the compromise, or "Softs," former Barnburners and Hunkers who had softened their animosity toward each other. The former were more unified, for their beliefs were the same and their leader was clear. The latter were more numerous but at the same time were incapable of agreeing upon anything but their suspicion of Dickinson.[28]

At Syracuse the delegates groped their way toward reunion. It was easy enough to knife Dickinson. The votes against him were there, and the senator received not even a word of thanks. Similarly, the Barnburners were willing to share the nominees for state offices. They refused to support Marcy, for old feuds died hard, and Marcy did not want an elective office anyway. But they did join in nominating

Seymour for governor, for the simple reason that Seymour had wisely kept his mouth shut concerning the compromise. "In regard to the subject of slavery extension, we have understood Mr. S. to hold doctrines in common with the mass of the democracy of the State," the *Atlas* explained, "though his withdrawal from public affairs for a few years has not presented him the occasion of action upon them." Silence could indeed be golden.[29]

Getting around the slavery issue itself was more difficult. Neither Marcy nor any other Hunker could be coaxed into an endorsement of the Wilmot Proviso; neither John Van Buren nor any other Barnburner wanted to approve the compromise. Where the compromise was concerned, however, the Marcy Softs and the Dickinson Hards were a unit. On the last day the convention was asked to approve a statement that applauded the "recent settlement by Congress of the questions which have unhappily divided the people of these States." Van Buren vigorously protested, and offered to resolve that the convention only hoped that the issue was settled. He was quickly shouted down, and the resolution passed.[30]

This was the crucial point for Free Soil in New York. Three years earlier the Barnburners would have stalked out. Now they remained, shuffling and mumbling. The *Post* was perhaps the most outspoken against the resolutions. "So far as they relate to the slavery question," Bryant declared, "they are the merest and most pitiable drivelling in the world, and it would be manifestly unjust to make the convention generally responsible to them." But the *Atlas* explained that slavery was so unlikely to be introduced into the Southwest that Barnburners could consistently support the resolutions, although the paper regretted them. To deflect attention from the resolutions, the paper seemed to catch fire with indignation over the fugitive slave act and began printing long tirades against it, as if to prove that no ground had been surrendered. But John Van Buren, in a rare moment of absolute frankness, had given the game away at the convention two days before the resolutions were introduced. He said:

I go heartily for the union of the democratic party. It is a mistake to suppose that I belonged to any other. History has been mistaken and misstated by those who say we had a free soil party. Our addresses were always directed to the Democratic Republicans of the State of New York. . . . I know no other party except that, and never belonged to any other.[31]

In short, the Barnburners had been forced to make a choice. They could either accept the decision of the convention and return to the party, or they could cling fast to the Wilmot Proviso. They chose the former, because that was what they desperately wanted and because they honestly felt that they had broken the influence of the slave power in the New York Democracy. Both John Van Buren and the *Atlas* warned that agitation would continue against the compromise, particularly against the fugitive slave law, and the *Post* cautioned other Free Soilers that, "considering the distracted condition of our party," the result at the convention was the best that could be hoped for. Besides, every Barnburner was still free to oppose slavery in whatever way his conscience dictated.[32]

There was not a little self-deception in all this. The Barnburners had given up much at Syracuse, despite the fact that they had brought most of the Democracy around to at least a nominal opposition to slavery. But by 1850 they were tired. They had fought the Hunkers unsparingly for six long years, always proclaiming that they, not their rivals, were the true Democratic party. Caught up in their own bitterness over Wright's defeat and their frustration and grief at his death, and deeply wounded by the nomination of Cass and the challenge of the Hunker delegates at Baltimore, they had led each other into an unnatural coalition with men whom they had never liked. Having shown their power to disrupt the party and having found a way to preserve most of their opposition to slavery by attacking the Clay compromise, if only as individuals, they looked to the campaign of 1852, in which they expected once again to be a powerful and influential segment of the Democracy. During 1851 they continued to demand free territory and free labor as the price of their cooperation, but for all their talk the revolt of the Barnburners was over. During the summer, 1851, Cassidy finally removed Field's "cornerstone" resolution of 1847 from the masthead of the Albany *Atlas.*

While the Free Soil movements in New York and Ohio met their crises early, that in Massachusetts moved more slowly. The Whigs, though battered in 1848, still held firm control of the legislature, and the next election for senator would not come until 1851. Thus, during 1849, Free Soilers continued their ideological war against slavery and meditated on their prospects. Most were optimistic. "I think the Free Soil party of Massachusetts is the best political party of its size the country has ever seen," Sumner boasted, "containing a larger amount of talent, principle, and sincere, unselfish devotion to the public good than has ever before been brought together in any similar number of persons acting politically; it will yet leaven the whole lump."[33]

But the party had its troubles. When Palfrey ran for reelection to his congressional seat from Middlesex County, north and west of Boston, in the fall of 1848, he had failed to secure a majority, which was necessary for election in Massachusetts. In six tries during 1849 he was unable to win back the seat. Consequently, when Congress convened in December, 1849, there was no representative from Middlesex present.[34]

The deadlock in Middlesex paralleled other problems that plagued the Free Soilers. Throughout 1849, at every Free Soil meeting held in Massachusetts, a growing number of former Democrats began urging a coalition with the regular Democracy and a dividing of the spoils of office between the two. It was not an agreeable plan to former Whigs like Adams, Palfrey, and Phillips. Adams had no love for either of the old parties, but the very idea of coalition with the Democrats disturbed him, as it had in 1848 when he had reluctantly consented to run with Van Buren. "We must now go back once more to our independent and insulated position," he advised Giddings, "and we must reconstruct our system with reference to the present emergency." A coalition with the Democrats, commented Richard Henry Dana, Jr., "would take the virtue out of our party."[35]

Other Massachusetts Free Soilers disagreed. In early February, 1849, Henry Wilson took command of the Boston *Republican,* the party organ, and a few weeks later began to hint that cooperation with the Democrats was desirable. Chase's election in Ohio was proof. Encouraging Wilson in these efforts were Francis W. Bird and Edward L. Keyes, two of the party workhorses in 1848.[36]

Between the two groups stood Sumner. He had long been a Whig and had protested with all the rest that his antislavery activities were merely good examples of Whig doctrine. Yet Sumner had always been more willing than most of his friends to work with Democrats. He had graciously, if not enthusiastically, supported Van Buren in 1848, and he was quiet when the Barnburners began to drift back to the Democracy in 1849. Sumner was a surprisingly gifted politician for one who had never held an elective office, and he realized that compromises often had to be made in order to advance principles. During 1849 he slowly began to favor working with the Democrats. By October he was openly enthusiastic about a union.[37]

The coalition, however, made a faltering start. In September Sumner and Wilson steered the Free Soil convention into making kindly statements about Democratic principles; the Democrats, in turn, sounded remarkably antislavery in their convention a few weeks later. Sumner quickly concluded that a coalition had formed. "With us fusion is complete," he rejoiced to Chase. The state elections quickly erased such optimism. Still working well, the Whig machine smothered all other parties once again. For Sumner and Wilson it was a mild setback. For Adams it was a ray of hope that the Free Soilers would no longer flirt with Democrats. Both eventualities fell into doubt, however, with the introduction of the Clay compromise.[38]

Anyone reading the compromise, or listening to Webster's defense of it, could easily have predicted trouble for the Whig party of Massachusetts. Letters poured across Winthrop's desk, some favorable, some aghast. All concluded that the provisions of the bill, particularly the fugitive slave act, would cause severe problems. Everett thought that any attempt to enforce the law in Massachusetts would be "certainly inoperative" and "wholly distasteful." He refused even to sign a petition backing the great senator's speech. Winthrop was more charitable. He knew the effect the bill would have, but nonetheless thought the speech was "grand." "Many of its most obnoxious things were undeniable truths, which we must all acknowledge and sustain."[39]

Public opinion seemed to flow into two camps, with no vocal middle ground. Supporting the speech were many of the aristocrats and businessmen of State Street, who were eager to see the slavery issue settled quickly. The controversy with the South had thrown a shroud of unease and pessimism over their dealings that was stifling. Their unnatural allies were large numbers of workmen, many of them Irish, who feared that runaway slaves would compete in an already shrinking job market. Against these ranged a broad spectrum of antislavery Whigs and Democrats, Free Soilers, humanitarian reformers and abolitionists, and of course free blacks. When the compromise passed and Webster resigned from the Senate, Free Soilers saw their chance. They had their issue; they also had a Senate seat almost within their grasp.[40]

Free Soilers differed, however, on the best way to reach their goals. Adams still clung to the idea that an independent Free Soil organization was the only proper method by which to preserve the high ideals and the moral influence of the party. That belief brought him into direct conflict with Wilson and, more importantly, Sumner. To Sumner the passage of the compromise and Webster's renewed influence meant only one thing: the Free Soilers had to pursue their coalition with the Democrats more vigorously than ever before.

But Sumner was not willing to jump into a coalition recklessly. A successful fusion depended upon keeping the loyalty of prominent Conscience Whigs like Adams and Palfrey while at the same time taking care not to offend Democrats with extreme antislavery declarations. Sumner decided that the best course lay in cooperation, not outright coalition. On September 9, 1850, one day before the state

Free Soil caucus was to meet, he advised Wilson that he had "no objection" to fusion on a town-by-town basis, but that it was a "step of questionable propriety for our State committee . . . to enter into an arrangement or understanding with the Democrats as to the disposition of offices." Privately, however, Sumner let it be known that a general coalition was the only means by which any substantial results could be achieved.[41]

In the fall elections this informal combination at last won. Even the *Daily Advertiser* admitted that the compromise had been too much for the Whigs. No party gained a majority, but the Democrats and Free Soilers held a slight edge in the state legislature and, under the antiquated rules of the state, that body was called on to choose a governor and lieutenant governor. Also, since Webster's Senate term, filled temporarily by Winthrop, was due to expire, the legislature prepared to select a replacement.[42]

Now began the division of the spoils. The Free Soilers cared less about filling the state offices than they did about sending a representative to Washington, so they quickly agreed to support George S. Boutwell, an antislavery Democrat, for governor. Boutwell was elected, and, in return, the Free Soilers expected the Democrats to cooperate in electing a Free Soil senator.[43]

Sumner was the logical candidate. No other prominent Free Soiler had as much prestige or influence among both Democrats and former Whigs; no other Free Soiler, except possibly Wilson, had been so successful in persuading his party that a coalition was necessary. Both Adams and Palfrey, the only other Free Soil men with influence as great as Sumner's, had placed themselves out of the running. They had rejected all talk of making any deals, and besides they were odious to the Democrats. By the end of 1850 Sumner had emerged as the undisputed candidate of Massachusetts Free Soilers.

He had mixed feelings about the post. Horace Mann, an antislavery Whig whom Sumner had tried to draw into the party for months, noted bluntly in August that Sumner would soon have to "jump into the muddy waters of politics," and Sumner quietly agreed. Sumner knew very well that he alone was the Free Soiler most likely to win. But he remained properly reluctant, unwilling to come out openly in the race. "I would not move across the room to take that post," he replied to Mann. His interest in the coalition was purely to obtain the balance of power in the state for Free Soil. Probably he wished to avoid the charge that he was merely in the antislavery movement for the spoils of office, a point that Boston Whiggery had been at pains to argue for years.[44]

Before he could claim victory, however, Sumner faced grave problems. The Whigs obviously opposed him. Although they were not fully united behind Winthrop, they still vastly preferred him to a man who had challenged and irritated them so greatly for five years. To many Democrats Sumner was equally galling. Marcus Morton disliked the "greediness" with which the Whig Free Soilers demanded the post for Sumner; Morton complained that an antislavery Democrat would be just as deserving. And Caleb Cushing of Newburyport, whose power in the party was immense, balked at the idea of sending an outspoken abolitionist to the Senate for six full years. Such a move might be harmful to the Democratic presidential nominee in 1852. Cushing was perfectly willing to allow the Free Soilers to join in making Boutwell governor, but he hesitated when the question of the senate seat came up. On this question, Everett observed, "the high contracting parties will split."[45]

Sumner and the coalitionists also faced a revolt in their own party. Adams was convinced that the plan to divide offices had "spread disease into the very hearts" of the Free Soilers, and he was highly skeptical that any man, even one with Sumner's lofty moral principles, could long stay uncorrupted by such bargaining. Palfrey circulated a blistering attack on the proposed coalition to the Free Soil members of the legislature. A few weeks later he was rewarded by being removed as editor of the new party organ, the Boston *Commonwealth*. It was an event that further alienated the old Conscience Whigs. When it was rumored that Francis W. Bird, a coalitionist and friend of Wilson, would take over the paper, Samuel Gridley Howe complained that Bird was too willing "to go deeper into this Slough of a Coalition." By the end of January, 1851, the Free Soilers were bitterly divided.[46]

Sumner did his best to reconcile the warring factions, while at the same time carefully tending his own political future. To hesitant Democrats he denied that he was either a radical or a revolutionary, as the Whig press charged, and promised to pursue his ideals through proper constitutional means. He wisely avoided, however, the mistake that Chase had made in Ohio. He was careful to seek the advice of his old friends, especially Adams and Palfrey, and he never once let it appear that he would allow the bargaining for office to compromise his high Free Soil standards. It was not an easy task, nor was he completely successful in allaying fears that he was selling his soul for a mere office. Still, Sumner hung on, watching the proceedings with a keen interest while outwardly retaining an olympian aloofness.

For almost four months, between early January and late April, 1851 a byzantine political intrigue unfolded in Boston. Balloting for senator dragged on with all three groups—the coalition, the Whigs, and Cushing's independent Democrats—remaining adamant. By April it seemed likely that Massachusetts would have no new senator until after the fall elections the following November. Underneath the apparent impasse, however, the fight moved slowly to a decision.

The hardest worker was undoubtedly Wilson. Sumner, because he was the candidate, wisely remained in the background. But Wilson was under no such restraints. He had a natural love of politics anyway, and he spent every spare moment darting in and out of the capitol building, collaring representatives, and demanding that the Democrats keep the bargain. He was not yet as astute a politician as Chase; he had given the Democrats too many offices too eagerly. Still, he persevered. His efforts earned him two rewards: he was fast becoming the most powerful Free Soiler, after Sumner, in the state. He was also gaining a reputation for cunning and ruthlessness. "He is lax in principles," Adams remarked—unfairly, perhaps. Nevertheless, by April Wilson's work began to bear fruit.[47]

No single factor broke the deadlock. Probably it was a combination of sheer exhaustion and impatience to get the business of the state underway, matched by nervousness among the Democrats that they would lose their chance to control the state if the election remained undecided. Also, it is likely that Webster's March 7 speech and his cold vindictiveness toward Lawrence and Winthrop persuaded some Whigs to offer Sumner as a public rebuke for his support of the Clay compromise. Whatever the reasons, during April the tide slowly turned in Sumner's favor, and on April 24, 1851, he gained the prize.[48]

Reactions were, of course, mixed. Though Democrats were hardly eager to send a former foe to such an important post, they had been out of power for so long in Massachusetts that they were content with finally having control of the state. They had an opportunity to initiate needed reforms in the state constitution, particularly in the way in which representatives to the legislature were chosen. Whigs, on the other hand, were predictably furious. They had been shut out of power, and they were incensed at the blow dealt to the fortunes of Robert Winthrop. Sumner's election, the *Advertiser* howled, was the "grossest outrage upon the feeling of the majority of the people of the State, by a combination between two minorities, which we have known to be perpetrated in any of the States of the Union." Disregarding all these attacks, Sumner prepared to leave for the capital.[49]

His party was sadly divided. Although the Free Soil triumph had been productive and successful, it had opened gaps within the ranks that proved impossible to close. Sumner was largely absolved from any bitterness; not so, Wilson, Keyes, and Bird. The quiet but intense campaign of Wilson on behalf of the coalition had sickened Adams, who gloomily resolved to concern himself with politics no longer. Palfrey too remained adamantly against the bargain. As his battle for reelection plodded into its second year, he declined to campaign actively for the Democratic votes that could bring him success. In November, 1851, on the fourteenth try, he went down to defeat.[50]

Slowly during 1851 the Massachusetts Free Soil party began to disintegrate. Palfrey's failure was only one sign of its impending collapse. During that year the editorship of the *Commonwealth* drifted from Bird to a former abolitionist and Liberty man, Elizur Wright, and briefly back to Palfrey. With no firm hand to guide it, the paper failed to provide good, forceful leadership to the party. When Congress assembled in December, 1851, Sumner was strangely silent, biding his time while waiting for a proper occasion to speak out for Free Soil. Sumner had good reasons to keep quiet—he wanted to kill his image as a radical—but his inaction puzzled and disturbed his friends who expected far more from him. The Free Soil party, without quite realizing it, was succumbing to a policy of drift.

Nor did the coalition with the Democrats hold up. Marcus Morton, who had joined the party in 1848 as Van Buren's friend, worked hard against Sumner's election, and after the balloting was over he promptly returned to the Democrats. He resented the *"bare-faced"* intrigue that had put Sumner in office, he later explained to John Van Buren. Moreover, he simply did not trust the former Conscience Whigs, who, he felt, had formed the coalition "merely because they could not obtain from their own party in which they had been ultraists, what in their own esteem they merited," and who had "by the most open and corrupt traffic" grasped for office. Morton was fooling nobody; he had done more than his share of intriguing during his political career. Moreover, he, like Cushing and leaders of the national party, was looking to 1852 and did not want to alienate totally the South. But his reasons satisfied him, and he acted accordingly. With both Morton and Cushing declining to help, there was little chance that a lasting coalition could be secured.[51]

By the end of 1851 prospects for the coalition had not improved. Wilson worked as hard as ever, but with little success. Although he mended his relations with Palfrey and convinced him to run for governor, the Free Soil vote slipped so low in the fall elections that the coalition barely succeeded in regaining control of the state. The

Democrats, still pugnacious and still greedy, demanded that the Free Soilers help in reelecting Boutwell. Tired and beaten, Wilson and his party agreed, but this time they had nothing to gain in return.

With that, the Free Soilers split into two seemingly irreconcilable camps. Wilson and Sumner looked to the future, hoping that 1852 would bring new life to the movement. Adams, on the other hand, bade farewell to the movement. "I have precluded myself," he explained, "from every such position that is predicated upon the junction of men holding opposite opinions in public matters touching Slavery."[52]

CHAPTER EIGHT

"THE WORK IS TO BE DONE OVER"

THE compromise intensified the Free Soil debate over coalitions. A grim realization that Clay and Douglas had offered the country an acceptable bargain combined with a growing awareness that the party was not doing well in the states. No Free Soiler had anticipated this situation. In 1848 the movement had been naively optimistic, certain that the force of values would overcome the weakness in numbers. That had simply not happened. Most northerners were too loyal to their traditional parties, too suspicious of antislavery agitators, to set aside political habits they had held for years. Free Soilers had responded by advocating either strict independence of the old organizations or outright coalitions. As they moved to a final resolution of their dilemma, Free Soilers underwent what was, in effect, a crisis of values.

The course of the Chicago *Western Citizen* was a case in point. Before 1848 Zebina Eastman of that paper had been a Liberty man. In 1848 and 1849, encouraged by Van Buren's showing, Eastman spoke warmly of coalescing with one of the major parties, particularly the Democrats. "It has long been fully apparent," he wrote, "that . . . one or the other of the great political parties of the country would step in in advance and assume the platform and do the work of the lesser reform party, to save itself from overthrow. Such a termination is natural and logical. Nor is it to be regretted." Liberty men, Eastman cautioned, "need not labor under the feeling that the overthrow of American Slavery is any less the fruit of their labors should it be accomplished through the intervention of the old Democratic party."

By 1851 Eastman had changed his mind. Viewing the situation in Ohio and Massachusetts, the editor observed that Free Soilers seemed incapable of agreeing upon any subject other than non-extension of slavery. They promptly fell apart when confronted with state policies that might contradict ingrained Whig or Democratic feelings. Eastman's solution was to avoid these issues entirely through rigid independence. *"Keep clear of all entangling alliances.* The trouble has been that the policy of the slave power has been to keep issues before the anti-slavery people to divide them, or to sponge up their political power."[1]

Chase, Wilson, and Sumner took an opposite view. Granted that Free Soilers came from both major parties, plus the remnants of the Liberty ranks, the best course was to coalesce with any willing partner, give the economic and state field to them, and concentrate upon filling the Congress with Free Soilers. Eventually the presence of a powerful Free Soil contingent in Washington would force the cooperating parties to demand non-extension, and the major battle—the only one that really mattered to a dedicated Free Soiler—would be won. In some respects this position was more idealistic than Eastman's, for it presumed that mortal men could sacrifice inclinations they had developed over decades to the service of one overriding question. It also presumed that the party would be disciplined and united to an almost military degree.

The bittersweet successes of Sumner and Chase and the warfare that surrounded them drove the two sides far apart. In the cold afterlight of what had happened at Columbus, Chase decided that a temporary coalition would not do; Free Soilers must actually merge with Democrats. "I am thoroughly satisfied that a party which confines itself to the Freesoil measure cannot be permanent," he concluded. "It must take ground on all questions so far as they are of practical importance as actually existing political issues. Taking such ground they must be either Democratic or Whig in sympathy. Perfect independence . . . is out of the question." Later he added: "Under these circumstances my opinion is that it is best to organize as the Democracy—the Independent Democracy." Henry B. Stanton agreed. "The Liberty party accomplished great good—but its basis was too narrow for a national party," he reflected. "It did its work & died. The Buffalo party served its temporary purpose & is rapidly becoming extinct. In my sober judgment the day for 'third parties' on the Slavery question is gone."[2]

Nothing could have been farther from the minds of the anti-coalitionists. In the spring of 1851 Eastman voiced what many Free Soilers were beginning to perceive as an irresistible fact:

We once had a Liberty Party of the United States, . . . a National Party—a party of the whole—organized to work on until slavery was abolished throughout the land. . . . It was not conceived for the purpose of meeting any incidental contingency like the right of petition, or the exclusion of slavery from free territory. Such was the confessed position of the Liberty Party of 1840 and '44. To this old path it is evidently the duty of anti-slavery men to return.[3]

This clash of values was nowhere more apparent than in Ohio. As usual, Chase and Giddings were the antagonists. During 1850 Chase found himself in a delicate position. He was at once an increasingly powerful man in Ohio—with a Senate seat and a loyal following of Free Soilers and antislavery Democrats—and a pariah. Acutely aware of this, he resolved not to be shaken from his course. He still believed that the only viable course open to Free Soilers was coalition, or even fusion, with the Democrats.

But Chase did not control the Democratic party of Ohio. Democrats there were eminently practical men: they were ready to use Chase and bargain with him when necessary. They were also proud. They did not enjoy making concessions to a radical. One whose pride had been especially hurt was William Allen, the man who had lost his place in the Senate to Chase. Allen waited patiently during the winter of 1849-50, when the Hamilton County case again plagued the statehouse. Then, when Democrats resolved that issue with Chase's help, he stepped in. Chase expected the bargain to bring the Democrats into another alliance with Free Soil, with the major party adopting an anti-extension platform and the Free Soilers uniting on a candidate for governor. But at the Democratic convention in early January Allen and his lieutenants proceeded to erase any and all mention of the Wilmot Proviso from the party platform. Other Democrats, leery as ever of Chase, agreed. Chase was stung. "I consider it a complete triumph of the Hunker stripe of Democrats," his friend Townshend moaned, "& one that I suppose will compel us to make a Free Soil nomination."[4]

A further blow to Chase's hopes came late in the spring. Like many state constitutions, that in Ohio was outdated and sorely needed revision. In May, 1850, delegates from throughout the state met at Columbus to draw up a new charter. Since Free Soilers and Democrats constituted a majority, Chase and Townshend hoped that the repeal of part of the Black Laws would be extended and written into an untouchable statute. But the Democrats had gone, in their opinion, far enough. While they did not reinstitute the Black Laws, they pointedly refused to allow blacks to vote. Chase's coalition was crumbling.[5]

For Giddings 1850 was a time of reevaluation and change. His battles over the compromise in the House had further convinced him that any concession to the South was both ethically and tactically wrong. He had no faith in the Democrats, and Webster's course convinced him of the bankruptcy of the Whigs. So, while Chase scurried about trying to perfect his cherished coalition, Giddings moved the other way. As his visions of a quick and easy Free Soil triumph faded, he became more and more convinced that the only future for the third party lay in absolute independence. He knew the battle would take years, but, if Giddings lacked Chase's learning and limitless energy, he did have one thing the senator lacked: a bulldog's capacity for patient hanging-on. The *True Democrat* echoed his feelings. "Better be in a minority . . . better stand alone, and be right, than win an office."[6]

Sensing Giddings's increasing radicalism, Chase determined to bring the congressman once and for all into his plans. He had learned not to ignore Giddings in 1849, so in the spring of 1851 he attempted to make Giddings senator. With monotonous regularity the Ohio legislature was once more finely balanced, with the Free Soilers holding the critical votes. To an incredulous Giddings Chase suggested that enough Democrats could be compelled to vote for the congressman if Free Soilers would again cooperate. "They would consider this rather a hard dose," however.[7]

Giddings was not impressed. He allowed his name to be put forward for the Senate when balloting began, but he saw clearly that neither Democrats nor Whigs trusted him enough to grant him the seat. Nor did Giddings trust Chase, who he feared would desert him the moment it became apparent he could not win. "My danger of failure lies near home, among our friends," he confided to his son. "This undoubtedly weakens me."[8]

Giddings had read all the signs correctly. The Ohio legislature plowed through weeks of balloting in early 1851 with no result. As Giddings had predicted, Chase quickly abandoned him, partly because Giddings had given him no encouragement and partly because Chase wanted "some Freesoiler of Democratic sympathies" anyway. But try as he might, Chase could not convince the Democrats to settle on some other man, and Giddings's friends could not make the Whigs give in. "The Whigs sneer at the idea of taking Giddings," Hamlin observed.[9]

It was a dark horse, Benjamin Franklin Wade, who won. Wade was an antislavery Whig, one of the most irascible and pugnacious men in the state. He was the brother of Edward Wade, the abolitionist, who was so infuriated that his brother remained a Whig that he sued him over a family matter in a fit of pure spite. He was also the former law partner of Giddings, with whom he had not spoken since the election of 1848. Wade's election was a Whig compromise. With the voting bogged, Whigs offered their most outspoken opponent of the compromise to tempt Free Soilers. Six agreed, enough to send Wade to the Senate, where he stayed for twenty years.[10]

But Wade was no Free Soiler, and his victory was no triumph for the third party. Chase did not like him; Giddings only tolerated him. The Ashtabula *Sentinel* attempted to portray Wade as a secret Free Soiler who had disowned the Whigs upon hearing Webster's March 7 speech. "We think Judge Wade now stands on correct principles," the editor ventured. Wade rewarded them all a few months later by calling Free Soilers "broken down politicians; political hacks." Free Soilers, in turn, disowned him.[11]

Whatever Wade said or did, nothing changed the fact that the Free Soil party in Ohio had reached a crossroads. There was no longer the prospect of a senatorship before the party, and the new state constitution had dashed hopes of a thorough repeal of the Black Laws. With no immediate pressing business before them, both Chase and Giddings were free to ignore each other. Each, accordingly, pursued his respective plans more vigorously than ever before.

Giddings was the stronger of the two. While Chase had a devoted following throughout the state and potentially powerful office, Giddings had solid control of one particular region, the Reserve. Unified conventions and party harmony were easier to create there, in that one compact area, than in the whole state, so that what Giddings wanted on the Reserve he generally got. Chase, on the other hand, had to muster forces over a wide area, besides winning the approval of the Reserve. This he could do effectively only in the state legislature, when the stakes were high and compromise inevitable. With both Senate seats filled, Chase had lost his most important tactical advantage, and Giddings knew it.

Shortly after Wade's election Giddings began to pull his party toward complete independence. He ignored pleas that Free Soil coalesce with the Whigs. That Free Soilers had helped elect Wade, he argued, did not mean that the party had changed into "a sort of semi-free-soil Sewardism." Nor would he hear any further talk from Chase about cooperating with the Democrats, "no matter how *democratic*" their principles might be. "Our objection to uniting with the democrats is in truth that they have no principles."[12]

Giddings put this talk into action in April, 1851, by calling a Free

Soil convention at Ravenna, on the Reserve, for late June. With Chase sitting on the platform beside him, Giddings pushed through a series of resolutions that applauded most of the new state constitution, condemned its failure to provide black suffrage, denounced the Clay compromise, and entirely omitted any reference to coalitions. The meeting also, to Chase's disgust, called for two other conventions— one in August to make independent state nominations, and one at Cleveland in September to consider the prospects for the presidential race in 1852. Giddings had surgically knifed Chase in all this. The Ravenna meeting was a mass gathering, with no formal delegates, and since it was held on the Reserve, most of those attending were fully behind Giddings.[13]

Chase was steaming. For months he had tried to convince Free Soilers not to make separate nominations for fear of offending the Democrats. Now Giddings had not only insured that there would be state nominations, but had opened the lid on the presidential question a full year in advance. In response, Chase toyed with the idea of opening a new Free Soil paper, either at Columbus or on the Reserve in order to offset the influence of the *True Democrat* and *Sentinel.* Failing at that, he worked hard to prevent the August convention from nominating a candidate for governor. He did not succeed.[14]

There were only two courses left to Chase. Either he could abandon his plans for a coalition, join hands with Giddings, and help lead an independent Free Soil party, or he could support the Democratic nominee. The latter course was a risk calculated to make Giddings back down, and the only action consistent with Chase's own beliefs. He chose the latter. In early September he released a long letter explaining that he would support the Democratic candidate.[15]

Many Free Soilers applauded his decision; many did not. Most were simply sorry that affairs had come to such an impasse. John C. Vaughan of Cleveland remarked sadly of the "coldness" between the two groups of Free Soilers, and regretted that Chase had done what he did. "I would have had you independent," Vaughan argued, "a very champion on the part of freedom." Others were less charitable. Joseph Root and Isaac Parrish, both friends of Giddings, "excommunicated" Chase, Townshend, and anyone else who did not support the Free Soil ticket entirely. Giddings himself remained studiously quiet. Chase's gambit had failed.[16]

Chase should have known that it would; yet he reacted with an uncharacteristic burst of adolescent self-pity. "Not a word of confidence—not a word of respect," he complained, "all remembrance of ten years of devoted service to the cause of human liberty and all appreciation of my present position as resolved and as true to the same cause as ever—all vanished. So be it."[17] Nonetheless, when the Cleveland convention met on September 24, Chase was there, trying to rebuild his influence. He was a man of remarkable resiliency.

The meeting at Cleveland was a prelude to 1852. Giddings had forsaken his friends among the Whigs entirely and was now, in his new drive for independence, turning his eyes toward men whom three years before he would have dismissed as fatuous dreamers. He invited Lewis Tappan, William Goodell, and, interestingly, Gerrit Smith, the paragon of radical politics. Giddings asked for, but did not receive, the attendance of Free Soilers from Massachusetts and New Hampshire—states where coalitions had been at least temporarily successful. Sumner, for instance, wished him well, but noted that he did not think such conventions were necessary. Chase was thus the only prominent coalitionist there, and his influence was at best slight. The delegates drew up resolutions that went far beyond the non-extensionism of 1848 but did not, however, call for outright abolition. That was the only concession not made to Lewis Tappan.[18]

In short, Free Soil was being transformed in Ohio. With Chase in disfavor and Giddings in control, the party was returning to the stance of the defunct Liberty party. This change had national implications, because only Ohio, and in particular only the Western Reserve, was adequately united to form a strong bloc in the convention of 1852. The rest of the party was so split that no other state would have as much power. Moreover, the coalitionists were letting their party move toward radicalism by default. Caught up in the problems of building and maintaining alliances, men such as Sumner and Chase were not inclined to step in and dominate independent Free Soil meetings for fear of offending their allies. Men who were under no such exigencies, such as Giddings with his invincible seat in Congress, quickly filled the void.

By the spring of 1851 there was very little left of the Free Soil party in New York. Field's "cornerstone" resolution had come down from the masthead of the *Atlas* in April, a symbolic gesture that the revolt of 1847 was over. The Van Burens worked hard to cement their new alliance with Marcy and Seymour, and both groups shared a warm distrust for Dickinson and Croswell. As the Barnburners merged with Marcy's Hunkers and became "Softs"—opponents of Dickinson's "Hards"—their leadership changed. Martin Van Buren and Flagg were growing old, abandoning politics for gentler pursuits. John Van

Buren, certain that the revolt had succeeded and that his father's honor had been vindicated, slackened his efforts and returned to his legal practice. King worked diligently in Washington, powerful only in his own district.

Still, a strong streak of antislavery remained. While the compromise of 1850 had temporarily muted the territorial question, the fugitive slave law remained odious. Both the *Post* and the *Atlas* attacked the law fearlessly, for it was massively unpopular in New York. Because the fugitive act did not concern territorial questions, the editors freely changed their arguments from those based on free labor to one grounded in the more radical doctrines of natural rights and the higher law. Denying a jury trial to a runaway, the *Post* declared, clashed with "those doctrines of liberty and equal rights, forming the basis of the democratic party. To deprive a citizen of the right of trial by jury merely because someone charges him with being a slave and pretends to be his owner," Bryant added dryly, "is allowed on all hands not to be very democratic." The *Atlas* even ventured on the thin ice of disunionism. "We certainly know," Cassidy wrote, "that we speak the deliberate judgment . . . of multitudes at the North—who have no sympathy whatever with Mr. Garrison and his followers . . . when we say that they would rather, a hundred times, see the Union dissolved than this law executed."[19]

These were strong words, but they served little purpose in the rebuilding of the New York Democracy. Since no single faction yet controlled the party, Barnburners still depended upon the cooperation of Marcy and Seymour for any influence they might have in drafting platforms at state conventions. At the convention of 1850 this had resulted in a gauzy resolution which applauded the "settlement" of the slavery issue worked out in Congress—but which left New York Democrats free to express their own opinions. The same happened in the convention of 1851. Once again neither an outright condemnation of the compromise nor an unequivocal endorsement could pass through Marcy's skilled hands, and the resolution of 1850 was ratified again.[20]

Barnburners, caught between the conflicting desires of reuniting the party and committing it to antislavery, tiredly agreed. They considered themselves perfectly free to denounce slavery and the compromise in their speeches and newspapers, as they in fact were, but they could not hope to write their beliefs into an official platform. With this gentlemen's agreement in hand they turned—Democrats—to the presidential race before them.[21]

Looking at the wreck of his party in Ohio, New York, and his home state, Sumner grimly concluded that the prospects for 1852 were bleak. "The tendency of both the old parties at present is to national conventions," he observed,

and in both of these our cause will perish. The material for a separate organization, by which to sustain our principles, seems to exist nowhere except in Massachusetts. Had the Barnburners kept aloof from the Hunkers in 1849, the Democratic split would have been complete throughout the free States, and it would have sympathetically affected the Whig party. A new order of things would have appeared, and the beginning of the end would have been at hand.

He was being overly simplistic; he never completely understood the Barnburner movement, and he grossly exaggerated antislavery sentiment among Whigs. But on one point he was correct: "The work in some way is to be done over."[22]

The compromise compounded the Free Soilers' problems. Virtually every member of the party in 1850 predicted that the omnibus bill would settle nothing, that its pro-southern measures—especially the fugitive bill—would only further agitate the North. Even the coarsest Whig or Democrat, they reasoned, would never consent to kidnaping. "In enacting that law," Sumner gloated, "the slave power . . . has given to the free States a sphere of discussion which they would otherwise have missed. No other form of slavery question, not even the Wilmot Proviso, would have afforded equal advantages." His logic was simple: the Wilmot Proviso was essentially an abstract question concerning the future of the territories. The fugitive act brought the slavery issue into the streets. Confident that slavery was now more vulnerable than ever before, Free Soilers waited expectantly for the first case to arise.[23]

It came quickly. Within a few weeks after the passage of the compromise, a runaway was seized in New York City and secretly hurried off to the South before any protests could be raised. Other incidents followed in Pennsylvania and in upstate New York. Then, in February, 1851, a fugitive named Shadrach was captured in Boston. Angry townsmen there wanted no part in enforcing the law, and protests of discontent swelled as a crowd milled in and around the courthouse where the frightened man was being held. Suddenly the mood changed from talk to action. In an instant, Richard Henry Dana later recalled, two huge blacks grabbed the fugitive, spirited him out the door and "hurried . . . toward Cambridge, like a black squall, the crowd driving along with them & cheering as they went." Shadrach escaped to Canada. It was just the sort of incident that Free Soilers hoped would rally thousands to their party.[24]

But Free Soilers found themselves unable to capitalize on the situation. Their outrage was shared and supplanted by the other parties. No prudent politician in Massachusetts, the Western Reserve, or upstate New York dared to endorse the law openly; to have done so would have meant political suicide. Even the Whig state convention of Massachusetts publicly condemned the law. Moreover, outside the few districts in which antislavery was strong, the fugitive act was generally accepted. Clergymen, businessmen, and politicians throughout the North begged the voters to set aside their reservations and to accept it as a reasonable concession to the South. There was no sense, they pointed out, in disrupting the Union over the fate of a few slaves. Northerners generally accepted this advice. While events such as the Shadrach rescue were good newspaper fare, far more common was the willingness of the North to aid in capturing fugitives. Between 1850 and 1854 the vast majority of runaways seized under the law were quietly returned.[25]

The success of the fugitive law mirrored that of the rest of the compromise. For six long years the country had grappled with the slavery question, and threats of secession in 1850 had persuaded many northerners and southerners alike that the Union would collapse unless an answer was found. The compromise, as unsatisfactory as it may have been in its parts, appeared to be workable on the whole, and prominent Whigs and Democrats moved to its support. Leaders of both major parties sensed the potential harm in the slavery problem; both sincerely wished to remove it from the political arena. Behind them were the voters, equally uncomfortable with the slavery issue and equally ready to turn to other topics. The mood was toxic to Free Soil. Without an active, open debate over slavery, the party would suffocate.

The Whig and Democratic conventions mirrored the success of the compromise. Both parties were determined to bury the slavery issue by ignoring it wherever possible and by simply pointing to the compromise where not. The candidates shared this resolve. Among the Democrats the most prominent names were Marcy, Buchanan, William O. Butler, and, off in the shadows, Franklin Pierce of New Hampshire. All these men had endorsed the omnibus. Whigs debated over Webster, Fillmore, and General Winfield Scott. Of these three, Webster and Fillmore had played highly visible roles in enacting the measure. Scott had taken very little interest in the issue at all, but Seward argued strongly that, if the old general did not endorse the compromise openly, he would likely pick up strength in the heavily populated areas of the North where slavery was unpopular. It was quid pro quo: the South had got the compromise; the North should get the candidate.

The separate conventions followed tortuous, and torturing, paths to agreement. Whig delegates had barely settled into their seats when it was proposed that they endorse the compromise as a "finality." To no one's surprise, the motion passed easily. Then balloting began, with Scott and Fillmore locked in a near-tie and the Webster men holding a crucial balance. It seemed logical that either Webster or the President would relent, give the other his votes, and block Scott, but sentiment among Webster's friends and stubbornness among Fillmore's prevented any such agreement. Through four days and nights and fifty-four exhausting roll calls Scott's forces waited patiently until a break came. It happened at last, and Scott was the nominee.[26]

To some, including Horace Mann, Scott's nomination was a signal that the Whigs were finally prepared to discard their southern wing and oppose slavery. Although Scott lacked antislavery zeal, Mann observed, he was infinitely preferable to Pierce. "There may be all the difference between life and death, in two pilots tho' both profess to steer by the same chart. One may wreck you, while the other may get you safely into port." Other Free Soilers agreed and began to weigh seriously the possibility of voting for Scott.[27]

For the Democrats the only real question was the nominee, and they took forty-nine dreary ballots to decide upon Pierce, the least known and least objectionable man presented to them. Then, after many northern delegates had left for home, they rushed through a resolution declaring that the compromise had ended the need for any more talk about slavery.

Barnburners reacted to the convention with tired optimism. Pierce, being from New England, would be sound against slavery extension, King hoped, while the *Post* lamely dismissed the platform as irrelevant. No Democrat needed to support it to remain a Democrat. "For our own part," Bryant concluded, "we do not mean to recognize any termination to the discussion of . . . slavery as long as there is anything left to discuss." Martin Van Buren, meanwhile, was joyous. The convention had done well, "extremely well & the result will be the restoration of the guidance of the Party to honest leaders, at no distant day." Van Buren's Radicals generally accepted his advice, and as the day for election approached they entered the contest solid for Pierce.[28]

For Chase, however, the selection of Pierce was a stunning blow.

He had hoped that the Democrats would see the desirability of uniting with the Free Soilers, and when they did not he became disheartened and confused. "I cannot consistently sustain, Pierce, [William R.] King, and the Slavery Platform of Baltimore," he advised Hamlin. But he did not know where else to go. "What is to be done beyond I am not so clear about," he continued. "If we could have an Independent Democratic Rally, thoroughly democratic in name & fact . . . I should support it cheerfully. But a *mere free-soil* rally will simply elect Pierce and, I fear, ensure the indefinite extension of slavery."[29]

Had Chase fully realized what was happening to the poltical antislavery movement during 1852, he might have been content with mere Free Soil. Giddings's Cleveland convention had opened the door for abolitionists and radical Liberty men to enter the party. By June, 1852, Tappan and others were actively working to pull Free Soil away from the non-extensionism of the 1848 campaign. "The *Buffalo Platform* is defunct," Tappan insisted. ". . . It has gone to the tomb of the Capulets." The Free Soil party of 1848 had been too willing to compromise, he explained, too ready to settle for partial gains. "It is natural enough that such men as Van Buren & Stanton should vault from the Platform," Tappan cried, "but when we see such men as P King, Mann, Cleveland, Tuck, etc. meditating voting for a Compromise Candidate it behooves the friends of Liberty to summon high principles, not only against the *extension* but the *existence* of Slavery."[30]

Giddings concurred. Hurt by his failure to become senator and depressed at the apparent success of the compromise, he concluded that neither major party would ever be brought to the support of antislavery. The Whigs had seemingly rejected it; the Democrats were beyond hope. The only thing left to do was to form a committed phalanx of abolitionists and antislavery men and wait for the North to fall in line.

Too late Chase recognized the Free Soilers' drift toward radicalism, but there was little he could do to stop it. With the national convention scheduled to meet at Pittsburgh in August, he urged his supporters to be there in force to head off Tappan and Giddings. He advised Hamlin:

The present duty seems to be that of putting the Pittsburgh Convention on the right ground and under the right name—then getting the right candidates and then giving the largest possible vote. My judgment is that it should assume the name of the Independent Democracy—adopt the Buffalo Platform modified by the introduction of judicious Land Reform & European Freedom Resolutions—and nominate Hale for President. . . .

Gamaliel Bailey of the *National Era* agreed. "The old Buffalo Platform is still in good condition—a plank or two less, a plank or two more, and we shall have a sound, broad basis, Constitutional, Democratic, American."[31]

The Pittsburgh convention was a celebration of ill will. Although the delegates were enthusiastic and more united in their hatred of slavery than those in 1848, their leaders moved in an atmosphere of suspicion and mutual distrust. Prominent coalitionists such as Henry Wilson, who chaired the meeting, shared the same podium with Lewis Tappan, Gerrit Smith, and Joshua Giddings. Moreover, neither of the two likely nominees, Chase and Hale, wanted the thankless role of sacrificial lamb and sent letters to the convention saying so. Giddings headed the crucial resolutions committee—a fact which chilled any Free Soiler with Democratic leanings. On the other hand, the delegates chose to abandon "Free Soil" and call themselves Free Democrats, a name that rested uneasily with former Whigs or Liberty men.[32]

Hale was nominated on the first ballot. Chase had never had much chance to be the nominee; his letter to the convention and his near-defection to the Democrats in 1851 had insured that. But the ease and speed with which the delegates passed him by made him later wonder aloud if he had been the victim of a conspiracy. He was not, of course. Though Hale took weeks to decide to accept the nomination, he at length consented and waded vigorously into the campaign. He offered hope to all factions. His Democratic background appealed to men such as Chase, but he had formed his New Hampshire coalition with Whigs. If he was not acceptable to radical abolitionists such as Gerrit Smith, he was attractive to Lewis Tappan, who had supported him in 1847. Hale, in short, was an eminent compromise.[33]

So was George W. Julian, the nominee for vice president. Julian was a freshman congressman from Indiana who had quartered with Giddings in Washington and who would, a few years later, marry the Ohioan's daughter. He was young and had not formed any notable attachments to either of the major parties, although he had been a Whig in the early 1840s. Perhaps his strongest recommendation was that everyone liked him but few knew him apart from his attacks on the compromise in Congress. While he did not engender great devotion, he was a thoroughly respectable candidate.[34]

With that out of the way, the delegates turned to the all-important resolutions. Heretofore the convention had moved gingerly and amiably with a genuine desire to act harmoniously. In general, the coalitionists had been treated rather well. The resolutions committee, however, showed Giddings's increasing influence. The committee was an amalgam of anti-coalitionists, such as Giddings and Adams, and abolitionists such as Gerrit Smith. Smith naturally wanted to commit the party to immediate and direct abolition. This Giddings and Adams wisely refused, for the party would have shrunk drastically in size. Besides, most Free Soilers were not willing to go that far. But the committee did take pains to separate Free Soilers once and for all from the designs of the coalitionists.[35]

The final document was far closer to the Liberty platform of 1844 than the Free Soil resolutions of 1848. Most of the resolutions dealt with severing the federal government from all ties with slavery and placing "the exercise of its legitimate and constitutional influence on the side of freedom." All that was acceptable to the moderates, but four planks were decidedly radical. One called for recognizing the government of Haiti—a political grenade to all but abolitionists. Another stated, in terms reminiscent of the abolitionist press, that slavery "is a sin against God and a crime against man . . . , and that Christianity, humanity, and patriotism, alike demand its abolition." In a blast at the compromise the platform declared that "the doctrine that any human law is a finality, and not subject to modification or repeal, is not in accordance with the creed of the founders of our Government, and is dangerous to the liberties of the people." This could be taken two ways: either as a reaffirmation of the "higher law" and a call for continued agitation, or as a veiled threat to resist, legally or not, an act of Congress. Finally, in what must have been a mortifying blow to Chase and Wilson, the committee resolved not to cooperate, under any circumstances, with the Whigs or Democrats. Free Soil was "not organized to aid either the Whig or Democratic wing of the great Slave Compromise party of the nation, but to defeat them both. . . ." The old parties were "hopelessly corrupt, and utterly unworthy of confidence." These resolutions passed with surprising ease, and the delegates went home.[36]

The Pittsburgh convention perfectly reflected the state of Free Soil in 1852. There had been a sincere attempt to appease all factions in the choice of nominees, but the resolutions left little doubt that the independents were in control. Faced with deepening apathy over the slavery issue and a dwindling constituency, the coalitionists had been unable to sustain their plans to form a grand national antislavery alliance. More radical members had taken control and had committed the party to the one course that seemed honorable—independence. It was a move that guaranteed the party would be small, but four years of failure and dissent had effectively destroyed any hopes for anything else. Political antislavery had come full circle: from a small band of reformers it had moved through a diverse conglomerate of optimists and pragmatists, and back again to the small band.

It was not a happy situation for the coalitionists. Chase summed up his feelings in a letter to his friend Hamlin. His "general impression" was that the action of the convention would satisfy only a devoted few. "If they had taken the name Independent Democracy, and had adopted no extreme resolutions," he mourned, "the nominations could have made about a fair balance, and the draft would have been about equal from the old parties." But Chase was not optimistic. "For myself I propose to accept the Platform and support the nomination as on the whole as near to my ideas of what is best, as I could expect, not having had the making of them myself. But I think I shall not sink my individuality in this organization, which it seems to me, must be temporary."[37]

The campaign was lifeless. Scott was an uninspiring man who succeeded only in driving away hordes of southern votes while gathering precious few in the North. Pierce was wisely quiet. He was fully aware that he was running far ahead of Scott, so he said nothing to alienate either Barnburners in New York or extremists in the South. Hale was more lively. Breaking with tradition, he toured the North, making speeches and eating roast beef at Free Democratic rallies. But he had no following of devoted partisans as Van Buren had had, nor did he benefit from the excited optimism that had characterized 1848.[38]

The apathy that dogged Hale gripped the state campaigns also. For all their moral uprightness, Giddings's new allies were terrible organizers. Tappan, having helped set the party on higher grounds, took almost no interest in the campaign. Gerrit Smith busied himself with running for Congress in his own district on a platform that was a good deal more radical than that of the national party. Giddings returned from Pittsburgh to find his district ruthlessly gerrymandered against him; he spent most of the campaign warding off defeat. In Massachusetts Adams convinced Mann to stand for governor, but most Massachusetts Whigs found Scott acceptable. Democrats there, anticipating Pierce's triumph, simply waited for the federal patronage to fall into their hands.[39]

Many Free Soilers were conspicuous by their absence. Sumner did almost nothing for the party; so did Chase. Preston King, the one Barnburner who might have been expected to resist the Baltimore proceedings, quietly supported Pierce while loudly criticizing the

Democratic platform. Active support for Free Soil among the other Barnburners had evaporated, and the few votes Hale received in New York came mostly from former Liberty men. In Pennsylvania, which had never had a strong Free Soil organization, the party all but disappeared. Wilmot, the man who had helped start it all, retired from Congress and politics; most of his followers turned to Pierce. The party was in equally bad shape in the Old Northwest.

The returns confirmed this collapse. In every state, most importantly New York, the Free Soil vote plummeted, and Hale ended his efforts with only 156,000 votes. This was about half Van Buren's total in 1848, although more than twice Birney's in 1844. Plainly, the defection of the Barnburners was the severest blow, but the signs of disintegration were all too apparent everywhere. Giddings did manage to retain his seat, and Edward Wade, surprisingly, joined him from the Western Reserve. But no other Free Democrat was elected to Congress except Gerrit Smith. More importantly, in no state did the Free Soilers hold a balance of power between the major parties. They were left with nothing, literally, with which to bargain.[40]

Only one result brightened the election for the antislavery forces—Scott's overwhelming defeat. The old general won only four states, with Massachusetts and Vermont alone voting for him in the North. Try as they might, the Whigs could not evade the sense of doom that engulfed them. Their party was split, irrevocably, and sensible observers knew that they would never again seriously contend for the presidency. It was a little ironic that Free Soilers, with their new-found independence, nowhere took advantage of the situation and attempted to bargain with the defeated Whigs. Only the Democrats emerged from the contest with a viable party organization, and they swept all before them.

Many Free Soilers dismissed the results. The Ashtabula *Sentinel* had predicted early in the campaign that the party had no chance to make a good showing, but remained sanguine that the high principles and moral appeal of the Free Democracy would bear fruit in time. "We are just now like a man who begins to bail out a sunken boat," the editor commented. "The first few bucketsful offer very little encouragement; but when the boat begins to rise above the surface, he finds every stroke tells with visible effect." Similarly, Bailey observed in the *Era* that the proslavery factions of both major parties were so entirely in control that antislavery Whigs and Democrats would soon have no place to turn except "into the ranks of the Free Democracy." Could he have known what would happen in Kansas two years later, he would have congratulated himself on his prescience.[41]

But for the moment political antislavery was in eclipse. Those who had bid good riddance to the departure of the Barnburners or to the alienation of Chase and the coalitionists missed a critical point: however the party proceeded, it had to obtain votes and offices in order to remain a force for the movement. Reformers and abolitionists had done good work in bringing the slavery issue before the public, but they were powerless in rewriting the law. Changes in the public conscience took time, and time was fast running out. Slavery was expanding, not contracting, in the 1850s, and only concerted political action and a ruthless wielding of the balance of power had any chance of stopping it. For Free Soil to mobilize that action, it had to get and keep voters from all parties, Liberty, Whigs and Democratic. Without a broad base the party had nothing to build on, and was doomed to remain a small minority of stalwarts rather than the great national party of freedom that Sumner had envisioned four years earlier.

During 1853 the party gamely hung on, but with little real success. Chase drifted away from the organization, served out his term in the Senate, and became governor of Ohio in 1855 with the help of nativist Know Nothings. Giddings remained in the House, becoming close friends with Gerrit Smith. In Massachusetts the coalition attempted to revise the state constitution, failed, and broke apart. In 1854, with Wilson's help, all parties in the state fell before the Know Nothings, who captured almost every seat in the state legislature. Sumner, off in Washington, was a man without a party, and Adams had decided to retire from politics altogether. In New York Barnburners jockeyed for influence in Pierce's cabinet, compromising their antislavery even more.[42]

And then in January, 1854, Stephen A. Douglas of Illinois introduced a bill to organize the Kansas and Nebraska territories, with the question of slavery to be handled through popular sovereignty. Anti-extensionism, which had seemed so dead, suddenly rose again, with new allies.

EPILOGUE

NO single factor killed Free Soil; the party succumbed, rather, to a congeries of problems, some within their control, some not. Doubtless part of the blame for the demise of Free Soil lay in weak and often sloppy organization. In every state but New York Free Soilers relied almost solely upon the emotional and moral appeal of their ideology to attract voters. They held mass rallies; they worked their speakers mercilessly; they spread their gospel through newspapers and pamphlets. This method worked reasonably well in the presidential campaign of 1848, when outrage over the extension of slavery was high and when opposition to the major party candidates was widespread. In Massachusetts, Vermont, the Western Reserve, and northern Illinois, where slavery, Cass, and Taylor were all unpopular, the doctrines of Free Soil found a ready and willing audience. But merely sermonizing about the evils of slavery had one major drawback: it tended to confine the party's strength to areas where antislavery sentiment was already strong. In districts where hostility to slave extension was less outspoken, Free Soil gained only a weak foothold.

A significant exception to this pattern was New York. Opposition to slavery was of course deep in New York; the state had long been a center for abolitionists and antislavery reformers and was expected to contribute heavily to the Free Soil vote in 1848. The presence of Martin Van Buren, a native son and leader of the seceding Barnburners, certainly helped. Nonetheless, Van Buren's vote there would likely have been far smaller without the expert and painstaking organizational work of the Barnburners. Unlike Free Soilers in other states, who hoped that their message would be a magnet attracting voters to their side, Barnburners carried the campaign directly and personally to the electorate. Working with a few men in each small school district, they made thorough lists of voters and concentrated on persuading those who were receptive to Free Soil but who had not made a clear decision to join. The Barnburners largely ignored persons who were either already firmly committed to Free Soil or who were adamant Whigs or Democrats. Using information gleaned from these efforts, Barnburners knew precisely which districts needed the additional influence of a mass rally or a party newspaper. It was an effective tactic, for it gave Van Buren at least one-fifth of the vote in all but a few counties in New York—no mean feat in a state so large and diversified. It also gave them a potentially broad basis of popular support for future elections, something which Massachusetts and Ohio Free Soilers did not have.

The Free Soilers' poor organization persisted after the election. After November, 1848, many Free Soilers recognized that winning senatorships and state and local offices would strengthen the party for 1852. Since the party was in a majority in no state, however, Free Soilers needed to form working coalitions with one of the major organizations. The success of such coalitions required tight discipline and utmost cooperation among Free Soilers, discipline and cooperation that were not forthcoming. Not until fully two years after the Buffalo convention were Massachusetts Free Soilers able to put their coalition with the Democrats into effect; even then they were badly divided. Sumner's election should have shown Adams and Palfrey that compromise and coalition could bear fruit to the cause. They chose to interpret it as a corruption of principle. The same situation existed in Ohio. Chase, who otherwise was a gifted and bright politician, foolishly neglected to inform Giddings and the Whig Free Soilers of his plan to coalesce with the Democrats in order to win the Senate seat. Giddings, in turn, failed to make his associates understand that Chase had won a major triumph that might form the basis for future Free Soil gains. Ignoring the fact that a coalition with Democrats might be used to place some Whig Free Soiler in the Senate in the future, Giddings and Riddle, along with the *True Democrat,* were either lukewarm or actively hostile to Chase's efforts.

The failures in Ohio and Massachusetts point up an attitude, deeply ingrained in many Free Soilers, that made unity within the party difficult. Free Soil was an amalgam of men who had formerly been members of one or the other of the two major parties. While all Free

Soilers considered ending the extension of slavery to be their prime political goal, they found it hard to give up their past party loyalties. Palfrey, for example, frankly expected Free Soil to find its strength among the Whigs; even when threatened with defeat in his district, he neglected to appeal to the Democrats for aid. Giddings and Riddle looked instinctively to the Whig party when talking of coalition. Chase, on the other hand, had courted the Democrats for years. He resisted all suggestions that Free Soil combine with the Whigs, and he proposed that the party be renamed the "Independent Democracy." None of these men learned from Hale's example in New Hampshire. Hale, an antislavery Democrat, was perfectly willing to merge with the Whigs if such a course suited his political needs and thereby succeeded not only in capturing a Senate seat but also in retaining control of antislavery forces in New Hampshire for six full years after 1846. It was ironic that men who committed themselves to breaking the power of the major parties should let past party prejudices trip them. Their attitudes undermined many of their best efforts.

Other Free Soilers were simply reluctant to enter fully into the game of party politics. By 1848 most Americans had accepted parties as necessary and even desirable; some had not. Of the latter, men such as Lewis Tappan considered parties inherently corrupt. Tappan, like Birney, insisted that any antislavery party be kept small and free from all coalitions. Tappan of course was a minor figure in the Free Soil movement. Significantly, however, his views were adopted by major figures in the party such as Giddings. When a major architect of the Free Soil party demanded that the organization be limited to antislavery stalwarts, the chances for a mutual division of the spoils with either the Whigs or the Democrats were vastly reduced.

In fairness to those who wished to keep Free Soil independent, it must be noted that they had ample reason to distrust the major parties. Neither Whigs nor Democrats had ever shown any willingness to meet the slavery problem except by compromise, and compromise was incompatible with the Free Soil ideology. The defection of the Barnburners in 1849 and 1850 made other Free Soilers, especially former Whigs, more skeptical of placing any faith in the other parties. Passage of the Compromise of 1850 heightened this feeling. It was, then, perhaps inevitable that opposition to all coalitions was so strong among Free Soilers by 1852.

Nor was winning elections the only goal of Free Soilers. Chase and Sumner certainly longed for the day when the antislavery forces would be welded into a major, dominant national party, and they pursued coalitions for that end. But others, notably the Barnburners, never really expected Free Soil to become a permanent political organization. They joined Free Soil partly for political revenge and partly to teach the Democracy that the North would never tolerate the extension of slavery. The smashing defeat of Cass and the passage of the Compromise of 1850 apparently convinced them that they had succeeded in their plans, and so they rejoined their old party. Similarly, Adams, Giddings (after 1850), and Tappan regarded Free Soil as an educational tool designed to awaken the other parties to the political power and moral correctness of the antislavery forces. For them independence from the other organizations was the only way to preserve the impact of Free Soil.

Even had the Free Soilers been flawlessly professional politicians, however, they would have still encountered almost insurmountable obstacles in the structure of the American political system. In the tenth number of the *Federalist Papers,* James Madison correctly assumed that the rise of political factions was inescapable in so large a nation as the United States. He pointed out, however, that the Constitution severely hampered the ability of any one faction to control the government. There was, for instance, the sheer number of elected offices to be won. In order to rule, a faction needed to win a majority in the House and the Senate, plus the presidency. Doing that, in turn, required the faction to win broad support in every section of an enormously large and diversified country.

Against these checks and balances, Free Soil was doomed. It was essentially a faction, a sectional party revolving around one highly explosive issue. While it might win large numbers of popular votes, it was confined to a few areas of antislavery sentiment. Consequently its chances of winning a majority of elective offices were slim. Even if Free Soilers had carried New York, Ohio, and Massachusetts—a feat that would have given them an impressive popular total—they still would have gained only a few congressional seats. Nor would they have won enough electoral votes to secure the presidency. Van Buren's 100,000 votes in New York may have destroyed Cass there, but it won him no ballots in the Electoral College.

For all his talk of curbing the power of factions, Madison did not foresee the rise of the two-party system, a further barrier to the success of Free Soil. By the 1840s the Whigs and the Democrats had emerged into two large conglomerates of groups from every section loosely knit by vague and often undefined ideologies. The major parties were broad and flexible enough to enjoy massive popular support, and they were approximately equal in strength. Partisanship was thus fierce and intense. Newspapers existed less to report the news than to justify a candidate, and voters and congressmen alike clung to their parties with spirited devotion. Ticket splitting was rare; once a man chose a party, he was likely to remain with it until either he or the party died.

The issues that divided Whigs and Democrats facilitated this loyalty. Banks, internal improvements, and tariffs may puzzle and bore later generations; Jacksonian Americans debated them with religious fervor. To men living in an expanding country on the verge of industrialization, these issues were matters of the highest urgency. Neither party was totally unified on any of these subjects. Western Democrats, mired in bad roads, tended to favor internal improvements more than their counterparts in the East; Massachusetts Whigs, with their strong state banking system, were less upset by the collapse of the Bank of the United States than were Whigs from other regions. Regardless of these differences, the party system functioned well as a forum for discussion.

Sectionalism was largely absent from this picture. Tariffs, banks, internal improvements, even temperance, all found supporters and detractors on both sides of the Potomac, and, as long as they were the only issues being debated the party system worked well. Leaders of both parties recognized, however, that the slavery question would polarize politics along sectional lines, and they resisted all attempts to bring slavery into the political field. Winthrop, Greeley, and Webster, all of whom detested slavery, elected to work to end it through compromise and adjustment in order to preserve their party. Their caution was real; their pleas to the Free Soilers to desist were sincere. This reluctance to upset the system was widely shared in the North and provided one more stumbling block to Free Soil.

The Compromise of 1850 demonstrated the power of the two-party system. Realizing the danger not only to the parties but to the Union, Whigs and Democrats combined to pass measures that were remarkably effective in muting sectional tensions. Democrats like Douglas joined with Whigs like Clay to force the measures through Congress and defeat the efforts of Free Soilers to make the legislation more antislavery. When the Compromise was presented to the voters as the handiwork of both parties, it was accepted overwhelmingly.

The success of the Compromise also uncovered basic inadequacies in the Free Soil appeal. Those who joined Free Soil did so from no one motivation. Some feared southern power and influence; some considered slavery a drag on national progress and development; others mourned its degrading effect upon the white and saw it as a blot on the national honor. No doubt all Free Soilers shared these views to some extent, yet when they met to draw up a platform the only sure common ground among them was simply preventing the extension of slavery. It was essentially a negative position, one that depended intensely on the threat of slave expansion. When the Compromise apparently removed that threat, there was little that Free Soil could continue to build on, and the movement began to fold. By 1852 the only course left was either coalition, which Chase proposed, or a reversion to the Liberty concept of a party that educated voters to high ideals. Either way, the power of the party's appeal was spent.

The inability of the Free Soilers to maintain their ideological force may seem puzzling since only a few years later the Republican party so effectively used a similar issue to create a new permanent national political organization. At first glance the struggles over the annexation of Texas and the Wilmot Proviso closely resemble those over Kansas and Nebraska. There is a crucial difference. Almost everyone considered the admission of Texas to be inevitable, but few seriously believed it could be kept free. Similarly, few realistic southerners expected California to become a slave state. Kansas was a different matter. No one in the North conceded it to slavery; when southerners demanded the right to take their slaves there, northerners were furious. The war to extend slavery had come home to a territory that they had accepted as free. With the Whig party dead and the party system in flux, the Free Soil ideology was resurrected to a power it had not been able to enjoy in 1848.

Free Soil was not a total failure. Its legacy of future leaders in national affairs, for instance, was remarkable. Chase, for all his bottomless ambition, was a gifted man who went on to serve well as Lincoln's Secretary of the Treasury; he later became Chief Justice of the United States during the critical Reconstruction period. Sumner remained in the Senate until his death in 1874, arguing persuasively with Lincoln on the need for emancipation and for the absolute necessity of securing equal rights to the freedmen after the war. He was, moreover, unquestionably the most powerful member of the Senate Foreign Relations Committee at a time when British intervention might have scotched the North's hopes for victory. Adams was minister to England during the same period. Wilson joined Sumner in the Senate and later became Vice President. Hannibal Hamlin of Maine was also a senator and Vice President. Giddings and Hale both became diplomats. Tilden was governor of New York when he narrowly missed becoming president in 1877.

Much of the ideology of Free Soil survived also. Neither the 1856 nor the 1860 Republican platforms specifically mentioned the slave power by name, but the implication was clear when the Buchanan administration was denounced as subservient to the "exactions of a sectional interest." Republicans also demanded an end to the extension of slavery into the territories, although of course they did not speak of the Wilmot Proviso. In demanding that Kansas be left free, they used Chase's old argument that the national government do nothing positive to encourage or support slavery. Moreover, they extolled the virtues of Free labor in language reminiscent of the Barnburners; they called for a homesteading act just as the Free Soilers had asked for land reform. There were similarities in what the two parties omitted from their platforms, too. Neither, for example, advocated full equal rights for the blacks.

Perhaps the fairest estimation of the impact of Free Soil is that it was a necessary wedge that opened a crack in the political system through which the Republican party later emerged. Doomed from the start by constitutional obstacles and the presence of the two-party system, crippled by its own blunders, and undercut by the Compromise of 1850, Free Soil never had the opportunity or the means to become the national party of freedom that its supporters hoped. Yet Free Soil performed an essential function. It helped open the slavery question, forced it before the nation in political debate, and thus laid the basis for future northern politicians to form a broad antislavery party. Once the Whig party was gone and the slavery issue appeared again, the antislavery forces were ready to begin anew.

STATISTICAL APPENDIX AND MAPS

NOTES ON METHODS

The statistical analysis in this work rests upon comparison of voting returns, on a county-by-county or town-by-town basis, with various indices of wealth, ethnicity, and social status. Relationships between variables have been measured through coefficients of correlation using the Pearson product-moment method. A coefficient of +1.00 would indicate a perfect positive relationship between variables (e.g., that the number of votes for Van Buren in each county was directly proportional to the number of, say, Baptists); a coefficient of -1.00 would indicate a perfect negative relationship (e.g., the more Irish voters there were in a county, the fewer Free Soil votes); and a coefficient of 0.00 would indicate no statistical relationship at all. In general, coefficients of correlation between +.50 and -.50 are statistically insignificant. I have not always followed this rule, for reasons that should be apparent from the analysis that follows. In dealing with the relationships among a number of variables over several years, one may and often does find that the coefficient among, for instance, Van Buren's vote and that of several Whig candidates may start at a meaningless level of, say, .05, then progress to -.30. The latter figure is, strictly speaking, probably not significant, yet the shift is.

I must stress that these coefficients of correlation in no way prove that meaningful relationships exist. The technique is useful, however, in suggesting possible factors involved in voting behavior that other, non-statistical methods might overlook. Also, it is helpful in reinforcing conclusions gained from other sources.

For good discussions of statistical methods see V. O. Key, Jr., *A Primer of Statistics for Political Scientists* (New York: Thomas Y. Crowell, 1954);

Charles M. Dollar and Richard H. Jensen, *Historian's Guide to Statistics: Quantitative Analysis and Historical Research* (New York: Holt, Rinehart, and Winston, 1971); Frederick Williams, *Reasoning with Statistics: Simplified Examples in Communications Research* (New York: Holt, Rinehart and Winston, 1968), esp. ch. 10.

STATISTICAL SUMMARY

In the three key states under consideration, one can make the following generalizations based upon correlations among votes, by county:

Massachusetts (excluding Boston-Suffolk County)

The election of 1848 seriously disrupted both major parties in Massachusetts, but the effect was greatest among Democrats. As the correlations in Table 1 suggest, Democratic solidarity collapsed between 1844 and 1852. A weak, poorly-organized party, Democrats suffered more than Whigs from defections to Free Soil in 1848 and never recovered their unity. The bitter contest for Senator in 1851 produced a major realignment of the party by 1852.

Table 1:
Correlation of Democratic Presidential Vote, Massachusetts, 1844-52

	Polk (1844)	Cass (1848)	Pierce (1852)
Polk	1.0	.76	.02
Cass	----	1.0	-.19
Pierce	----	---	1.0

Whigs were hurt also, but in a different way. Table 2 indicates a deterioration in Whig unity for the same period although not so badly as for Democrats. The comparison between Clay's vote and Scott's suggests that the Whig party of 1852 was different from that of 1844, but the stronger correlation between the Whig vote in 1848 and that in 1852 indicates a greater similarity in party support during the latter two elections.

Table 2:
Correlation of Whig Presidential Vote, Massachusetts, 1844-52

	Clay (1844)	Taylor (1848)	Scott (1852)
Clay	1.0	.66	.20
Taylor	----	1.0	.49
Scott	----	----	1.0

Despite the impact of Free Soil upon Democrats, Table 3 suggests that in 1848—the key election—Van Buren ran best where Whigs were weakest and that this pattern persisted through 1852. The implication here is that Free Soil was a combined protest against slavery and the domination of the Whig party. It created a permanent exodus of antislavery partisans and carried with it those quondam Democrats who had never completely identified with their parent party and who stayed away from it in 1852.

Table 3:
Correlation of Free Soil Vote, 1848, and Major Parties, 1844-52

	Clay	Polk	Taylor	Cass	Scott	Pierce
Van Buren (1848)	-.31	-.16	-.70	-.22	-.80	-.03

The same degeneration of unity that characterized Whigs and Democrats also affected the antislavery movement. Table 4 suggests that Van Buren's support for 1848 was far more similar to Birney's than to Hale's. Again, the senatorial contest of 1851 appears to have alienated the more radical elements of Free Soil who, by 1852, had abandoned politics altogether.

Table 4:
Correlation of Antislavery Vote, Massachusetts, 1844-52

	Birney (1844)	Van Buren (1848)	Hale (1852)
Birney	1.0	.71	.28
Van Buren	----	1.0	.59
Hale	----	----	1.0

The excellent state censuses of Massachusetts—unsurpassed at the time—provided an opportunity to compare voter preference with a variety of social and economic data on a town-by-town basis. This comparison was done using gubernatorial returns, since presidential records were unavailable on a town basis. With Van Buren's controversial presence thus eliminated, it was hoped that some profile of the ethnic and occupational bases of Free Soil would emerge. No such profile was found, however. Of the various indices of ethnicity and economic identification, the only consistent pattern involved Irish. They tended to support Democratic candidates, and in the gubernatorial election of 1852 in Boston (surveyed on a ward-by-ward basis) they tended not to support Free Soil. All other correlations were negligible.

New York (excluding New York City)

Voting patterns in New York offer few surprises. Despite a strong current of antislavery sentiment among Whigs, few joined Free Soil. Van Buren was unacceptable to New York Whigs regardless of his party label. Thus, the Whig party remained strong and cohesive throughout the period. (See Table 5).

Table 5:
Correlation of Whig Presidential Vote, New York, 1844-52

	Clay (1844)	Taylor (1848)	Scott (1852)
Clay	1.0	.83	.89
Taylor	----	1.0	.78
Scott	----	----	1.0

Democrats clearly fell apart between 1844 and 1848, then regained their unity in 1852 (Table 6). Table 7 indicates that Van Buren took his support in areas that were normally Democratic strongholds.

Table 6:
Correlation of Democratic Presidential Vote, New York, 1844-52

	Polk (1844)	Cass (1848)	Pierce (1852)
Polk	1.0	.24	.87
Cass	----	1.0	.48
Pierce	----	----	1.0

Table 7:
Correlation of Free Soil Vote, 1848, and Major Parties, 1844-52

	Clay	Polk	Taylor	Cass	Scott	Pierce
Van Buren (1848)	-.33	-.02	-.54	-.79	-.26	-.30

Table 8 suggests that third-party antislavery sentiment in New York was more consistent than in Massachusetts. The correlation between Birney's vote and Van Buren's is high, considering the disparity between the number of votes cast for each man. But the correlation between Birney and Hale is even higher—a fact that suggests Free Soil support in 1852 was very similar to that of the Liberty party in 1844.

Table 8:
Correlation of Antislavery Vote, New York, 1844-52

	Birney (1844)	Van Buren (1848)	Hale (1852)
Birney	1.0	.58	.89
Van Buren	---	1.0	.69
Hale	---	----	1.0

Ohio

The raw vote in Ohio suggests that Free Soil hurt Whigs more than Democrats. Correlations of voting patterns tend to confirm this, although not conclusively. Table 9 indicates near perfect unity among Democrats between 1844 and 1852, while Table 10 suggests an erosion in Whig solidarity during the same period.

Table 9:
Correlation of Democratic Presidential Vote, Ohio, 1844-52

	Polk (1844)	Cass (1848)	Pierce (1852)
Polk	1.0	.97	.94
Cass	----	1.0	.95
Pierce	----	----	1.0

Table 10:
Correlation of Whig Presidential Vote, Ohio, 1844-52

	Clay (1844)	Taylor (1848)	Scott (1852)
Clay	1.0	.55	.73
Taylor	----	1.0	.92
Scott	----	----	1.0

Table 11 is somewhat puzzling, then, because it indicates that Van Buren ran well in areas where both Democrats and Whigs were weak. The implication is that Free Soil hurt both parties about the same.

Table 11:
Correlation of Free Soil Vote, 1848, and Major Parties, 1844-52

	Clay	Polk	Taylor	Cass	Scott	Pierce
Van Buren (1848)	.36	-.53	-.54	-.60	-.26	-.65

Yet it should be remembered that the antislavery vote in Ohio was concentrated in a particular area, the Western Reserve. There, antislavery dominated both major parties while having little impact elsewhere. This support was consistent across time, regardless of candidates and party labels. Table 12 shows excellent unity between 1844 and 1852 in the antislavery vote. Giddings's antislavery Whigs joined a solid and reliable contingent of Liberty men.

Table 12:
Correlation of Antislavery Vote, Ohio, 1844-52

	Birney (1844)	Van Buren (1848)	Hale (1852)
Birney	1.0	.85	.85
Van Buren	----	1.0	.95
Hale	----	----	1.0

Michigan, Wisconsin, and Illinois

The correlations from these states suggest that much the same pattern existed there as in Ohio. The figures from Michigan almost duplicate those from Ohio. In Illinois they are less significant statistically, but generally run in the same direction. In Wisconsin (which was not a state in 1840 and 1844) they are somewhat more pronounced than in Ohio.

Other northern states

I did not sample the correlations from other northern states because the votes in those states for Free Soil were so small that any sort of statistical analysis based on a statewide vote would have been extremely tenuous. It is true that Free Soil did have an impact in certain sections of these states, particularly in Pennsylvania and Maine, but this impact was limited mainly to local races.

Total Votes: (All states)

1844

Polk/Dallas	1,339,368
Clay/Frelinghuysen	1,300,687
Birney/Morris	62,197

1848

Taylor/Fillmore	1,362,101
Cass/W. O. Butler	1,222,674
Van Buren/Adams	291,616
Smith/Foote	2,733

1852

Pierce/Wm. Rufus D. King	1,609,038
Scott/Graham	1,386,629
Hale/Julian	156,297

Source: *Historical Review of Presidential Candidates from 1788 to 1968* (Washington, D.C., Cong. Q Service [1969] pp. 13-14).

Total Votes and Percentage Cast for Free Soil

1848			1852		
Maine			**Maine**		
Taylor	35,125		Scott	32,543	
Cass	39,880		Pierce	41,609	
Van Buren	12,096	= 13.9%	Hale	8,030	= 9.8%
Massachusetts			**Massachusetts**		
Taylor	61,070		Scott	54,163	
Cass	35,231		Pierce	46,967	
Van Buren	38,058	= 28.3%	Hale	28,998	= 22.3%
Rhode Island			**Rhode Island**		
Taylor	6,779		Scott	7,626	
Cass	3,646		Pierce	8,735	
Van Buren	730	= 6.5%	Hale	644	= 3.8%
Vermont			**Vermont**		
Taylor	23,122		Scott	22,173	
Cass	10,948		Pierce	13,044	
Van Buren	14,337	= 29.6%	Hale	8,621	= 19.7%
New Hampshire			**New Hampshire**		
Taylor	14,781		Scott	16,147	
Cass	27,703		Pierce	29,997	
Van Buren	7,560	= 15.1%	Hale	6,695	= 12.7%
Connecticut			**Connecticut**		
Taylor	30,314		Scott	30,359	
Cass	27,046		Pierce	33,249	
Van Buren	5,005	= 8%	Hale	3,160	= 4.7%

	1848			1852	

New York

Taylor	218,540
Cass	114,230
Van Buren	120,515 = 26.6%

New York

Scott	234,882
Pierce	262,083
Hale	25,329 = 4.8%

New Jersey

Taylor	40,015
Cass	36,901
Van Buren	829 = 1%

New Jersey

Scott	38,556
Pierce	44,305
Hale	350 = 0.4%

Pennsylvania

Taylor	185,005
Cass	171,989
Van Buren	11,275 = 3.1%

Pennsylvania

Scott	179,172
Pierce	198,568
Hale	8,524 = 2.2%

Ohio

Taylor	134,598
Cass	146,815
Van Buren	33,662 = 10.7%

Ohio

Scott	155,349
Pierce	169,211
Hale	31,672 = 8.9%

Indiana

Taylor	59,340
Cass	74,340
Van Buren	7,883 = 5.2%

Indiana

Scott	80,901
Pierce	95,340
Hale	6,929 = 3.8%

Illinois

Taylor	52,587
Cass	56,301
Van Buren	15,761 = 12.6%

Illinois

Scott	64,734
Pierce	80,597
Hale	9,966 = 6.4%

Michigan

Taylor	23,440
Cass	30,687
Van Buren	10,389 = 16%

Michigan

Scott	33,859
Pierce	41,842
Hale	7,237 = 8.7%

	1848			1852	
Wisconsin			**Wisconsin**		
Taylor	13,746		Scott	20,843	
Cass	14,892		Pierce	31,673	
Van Buren	10,428	= 26.7%	Hale	8,780	= 14.3%
Iowa			**Iowa**		
Taylor	11,148		Scott	15,856	
Cass	12,094		Pierce	17,763	
Van Buren	1,126	= 4.6%	Hale	7,237	= 4.6%
Total northern vote			**Total northern vote**		
Taylor	919,660		Scott	987,163	
Cass	802,703		Pierce	1,114,983	
Van Buren	289,654	= 14.4%	Hale	156,539	= 6.9%
	2,012,017			2,258,685	

Note: *The Whig Almanac . . . 1849* notes (p. 59) that "in several instances the official aggregate does not correspond with the details as given in the authorities quoted. In such cases [the compiler] has assumed that the official or other additions were correct, and entered them accordingly." For this reason my totals differ from those of the *Almanac*.

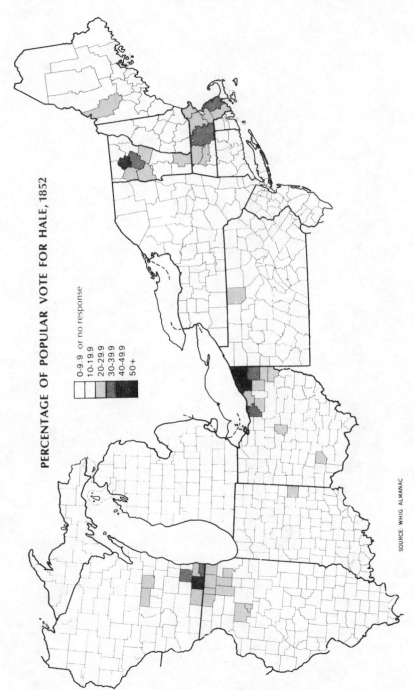

PERCENTAGE OF POPULAR VOTE FOR HALE, 1852

0-9.9 or no response
10-19.9
20-29.9
30-39.9
40-49.9
50+

SOURCE: WHIG ALMANAC

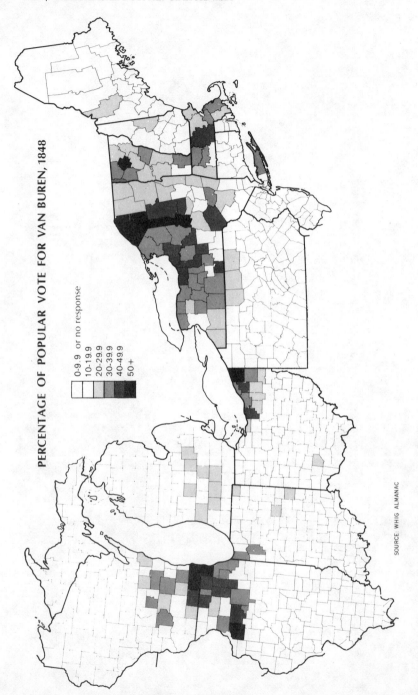

PERCENTAGE OF POPULAR VOTE FOR VAN BUREN, 1848

0-9.9 or no response
10-19.9
20-29.9
30-39.9
40-49.9
50+

SOURCE: WHIG ALMANAC

NOTES

ABBREVIATIONS FREQUENTLY USED

Manuscript collections, libraries, and historical societies

AFP-MHS	Adams Family Papers, Massachusetts Historical Society
BFP-LC	Blair Family Papers, Library of Congress
SPC-HSP	Salmon P. Chase Papers, Historical Society of Pennsylvania
SPC-LC	Salmon P. Chase Papers, Library of Congress
JAD-CU	John A. Dix Papers, Special Collections, Columbia University
ACF-CU	Azariah C. Flagg Papers, Special Collections, Columbia University
ACF-NYPL	Azariah C. Flagg Papers, New York Public Library
JRG-OHS	Joshua R. Giddings Papers, Ohio Historical Society
GJP-LC	Giddings-Julian Papers, Library of Congress
JPH-NHHS	John P. Hale Papers, New Hampshire Historical Society
WLM-LC	William L. Marcy Papers, Library of Congress
JKP-LC	James K. Polk Papers, Library of Congress
CS-HL	Charles Sumner Papers, Houghton Library, Harvard University
MVB-LC	Martin Van Buren Papers, Library of Congress
RCW-MHS	Robert C. Winthrop Papers, Massachusetts Historical Society
WBC-NYPL	Wright-Butler Correspondence, New York Public Library
CHS	Chicago Historical Society
WHRS	Western Reserve Historical Society

Journals

AHR	*American Historical Review*
JAH	*Journal of American History*
JSH	*Journal of Southern History*
MVHR	*Mississippi Valley Historical Review*

INTRODUCTION

1. Greeley to S. Colfax, Sept. 15, 1848, Greeley-Colfax corr., NYPL; Garrison to H. Garrison, July 26, 1848 Garrison Papers, Boston Public Library.
2. *Political Recollections* (1883), p. 131.
3. See Eric Foner, *Free Soil, Free Labor, Free Men: The Ideology of the Republican Party before the Civil War* (1970); Bernard Bailyn, *The Ideological Origins of the American Revolution* (1967); Marvin Meyers, *The Jacksonian Persuasion: Politics and Beliefs* (1957). For the contrary view, that American politics functions independently of ideology, see Maurice Duverger, *Political Parties* (1951, 1955), p. 210. A modified view of Duverger's analysis is Richard P. McCormick, *The Second American Party System* (1966).
4. On concepts of ideology, see Foner, introduction; Ronald G. Walters, *The Antislavery Appeal: American Abolitionism after 1830* (1976), introduction; Clifford Geertz, "Ideology as a Cultural System," and David Apter, "Ideology and Discontent," in Apter, ed., *Ideology and Discontent* (1964), pp. 15-77. On the disparity between formal theory and cultural perspective, see Robert Conquest, "The Role of the Intellectual in International Misunderstanding," *Encounter* 51 (Aug., 1978): 29-42.

1. THE BARNBURNERS

1. On Tyler and the politics of annexation, see Robert Seager II, *And Tyler Too* (1963); Charles M. Wiltse, *John C. Calhoun: Sectionalist, 1840-1850* (1951); Charles G. Sellers, *James K. Polk: Continentalist, 1843-1846* (1966); and the works in n. 25 below.
2. See Herbert D. A. Donovan, *The Barnburners* (1925); Walter L. Ferree, "The New York Democracy: Division and Reunion, 1847-1852" (Ph.D. diss., University of Pennsylvania, 1957); Robert V. Remini, "The Albany Regency," *New York History* 39 (1958): 341-55; Jabez Hammond, *Political Parties in the State of New York* (2 vols., 1844); and the biographies in n. 3 below.
3. Harriet A. Weed, ed., *Autobiography of Thurlow Weed* (1884), p. 103. See Remini, *Martin Van Buren and the Making of the Democratic Party* (1959); John A. Garraty, *Silas Wright* (1949); Ivor D. Spencer, *The Victor and the Spoils: A Life of William L. Marcy* (1959); Ernest P. Muller, "Preston King: A Political Biography" (Ph.D. diss., Columbia University, 1959); Martin Lichterman, "John Adams Dix, 1798-1897" (Ph.D. diss., Columbia University, 1952).
4. See James C. Curtis, *The Fox at Bay: Martin Van Buren and the Presidency* (1970); Gordon E. Park, "Martin Van Buren and the Reorganization of the Democratic Party, 1841-1844" (Ph.D. diss., University of Wisconsin, 1965).
5. See A. Kendall to Van Buren, April 19, 1844, MVB-LC; S. Wright to W. L. Marcy, Jan. 28, 1844, WLM-LC.
6. Martin Van Buren, *Inquiry into the Origin and Course of Political Parties in the United States* (1867), p. 309. This rambling work is the nearest Van Buren ever came to a full statement of his political beliefs. See also Meyers, *The Jacksonian Persuasion*, ch. 7 and appendix B; Max M. Mintz, "The Political Ideas of Martin Van Buren" *New York History* 30 (1949): 422-48.
7. The best examination of the ideology of Jeffersonian Republicanism is Lance Banning, *The Jeffersonian Persuasion: Evolution of a Party Ideology* (1978). It should be read in conjunction with Gordon S. Wood, *The Creation of the American Republic* (1969); Bailyn, *Ideological Origins*; Richard Buel, Jr., *Securing the Revolution: Ideology in American Politics, 1789-1815* (1972).
8. Jefferson to Madison, Oct. 28, 1785, in Julian B. Boyd et al., eds., *The Papers of Thomas Jefferson* (19 vols. to date, 1950-74), 8:682; Jefferson to Adams, Oct. 28, 1813, in Lester J. Cappon, ed. *The Adams-Jefferson Letters* (2 vols., 1959), 2:388-89.
9. *Adams-Jefferson Letters*, 2:389; John Taylor, *Arator* (1818), p. 189.

10. Jefferson, *Notes on the State of Virginia*, ed. William Peden (1955), p. 120; Taylor, p. 193.
11. Jefferson, p. 121.
12. John L. O'Sullivan, "The Democratic Principle," *United States Magazine and Democratic Review* 1 (Oct., 1937): 1. The article on the Panic was suggestively titled "The Moral of the Crisis," ibid., pp. 108-22.
13. O'Sullivan, "The Democratic Principle," pp. 2, 7.
14. Ibid., p. 4.
15. Ibid., p. 6; Theodore Sedgwick, Jr., ed., *A Collection of the Political Writings of William Leggett* (2 vols., 1840), 1:85.
16. O'Sullivan, "The Moral of the Crisis," pp. 112-14; *Political Writings of Leggett*, 1:80.
17. For a superb analysis, see Michael Wallace, "Changing Concepts of Party in the United States: New York, 1815-1828," *AHR* 74 (1968): 453-91; also Hammond, *Political Parties*, 1, ch. 7.
18. John C. Fitzpatrick, ed., *The Autobiography of Martin Van Buren* (1969), p. 125 (originally issued as vol. 2 of *Annual Report of the American Historical Association* [1918]).
19. Charles Z. Lincoln, ed., *Messages from the Governors of the State of New York* (10 vols., 1909) 3:274.
20. Ibid., 3:275; Van Buren, *Autobiography*, p. 125.
21. O'Sullivan, "The Democratic Principle," p. 2; *Messages from the Governors*, 3:278.
22. Hammond, *Political Parties*, 1:487, 193. See also Banning, p. 51.
23. *Messages from the Governors*, 3:275. See Wallace, p. 478.
24. *Messages from the Governors*, 3:277; O'Sullivan, "The Democratic Principle," p. 2; Van Buren, *Autobiography*, p. 124; Van Buren to F. P. Blair, Sr., Feb. 4, 1856, BFP-LC.
25. Blair to Van Buren, March 18, 1844, MVB-LC; New York *Morning News*, Dec. 27, 1845. Three excellent works on the background and articulation of the concept of manifest destiny are: Frederick Merk, *Manifest Destiny and Mission in American History* (1963); A. K. Weinberg, *Manifest Destiny: A Study of Nationalist Expansionism in American History* (1935); Norman A. Graebner, *Empire on the Pacific: A Study in American Continental Expansion* (1955).
26. Wright to B. F. Butler, May 20, 1844, WBC-NYPL; also New York *Evening Post*, May 18, 1844.
27. New York *Evening Post*, April 6, 1844; see also B. F. Butler to Van Buren, April 6, 1844, MVB-LC.
28. New York *Evening Post*, April 13, 1844.
29. Ibid., April 6, 1844.
30. Ibid., Sept. 8, 1851. See also New York *Morning News*, March 21, 1846; Eric Foner, "Racial Attitudes of the Free Soil Party in New York," *New York History* 46 (1965): 311-29.
31. Albany *Atlas*, April 22, 1848; also Aug. 12, 1847.
32. Ibid., Feb. 3, 1847; New York *Evening Post*, May 28, 1847.
33. James D. Richardson, ed., *A Compilation of the Messages and Papers of the Presidents, 1789-1902* (11 vols., 1907) 3:318; J. Hammond to Van Buren, April 7, 1844, MVB-LC.
34. New York *Evening Post*, April 20, 1844; see also New York *Morning News*, Jan. 28, 1845.
35. New York *Evening Post*, April 20, 1844.
36. New York *Morning News*, Dec. 17, 1844; New York *Evening Post*, March 23, 1844.
37. New York *Evening Post*, March 23, 1844.
38. P. King to Van Buren, Feb. 14, 1845, MVB-LC; New York *Morning News*, Jan. 28, 1845.

39. Wright to Van Buren, April 8, 1844; Van Buren to Blair, Sept. 12, 1842, BFP-LC; Hammond to Van Buren, April 7, 1844, MVB-LC.
40. Both Van Buren's and Clay's letters are in *Niles' Register*, 66 (1844): 154-57 (quotation on p. 156).
41. Flagg to O. Hungerford, May 9, 1844, ACF-NYPL.
42. Good accounts of the convention are in O'Sullivan to Van Buren, May 27, 28, 29, 1844, MVB-LC. Better and less biased is Sellers, pp. 88-105.
43. B. F. Butler to Van Buren, May 31, 1844, MVB-LC.
44. Jabez Hammond, *Political History of the State of New York . . . Including the Life of Silas Wright* (1849), pp. 442, 445.
45. T. Sedgwick, Sr. to C. Sumner, June 9, 1844, CS-HU.
46. New York *Evening Post*, Oct. 7, 1847. On the Hunkers, see Donovan, pp. 14-34; Spencer, chs. 8-11; Ferree, passim.
47. New York *Morning News*, Sept. 6, 1844. See also Wright to J. Fine, n.d., in Hammond, *Wright*, p. 489; Wright to Dix, Aug. 6, 1844, JAD-CU.
48. O'Sullivan to Van Buren, Oct. 28, 1844, MVB-LC; Van Buren to O'Sullivan, in New York *Morning News*, Nov. 2, 1844. There is no conclusive evidence to suggest that Polk was deliberately snubbed by New York Democrats. Wright's personal popularity and hostility to annexation were the probable causes of the discrepancy in votes (see New York *Evening Post*, Nov. 14, 26, 1844, and statistical appendix).
49. B. F. Butler to Van Buren, Dec. 9, 1844, MVB-LC.
50. Milo M. Quaife, ed., *The Diary of James K. Polk* (4 vols., 1910), 1:104; also quoted in Sellers, p. 164. Ch. 5 of the latter work contains the best analysis of Polk's cabinet dilemma; see also Norman A. Graebner, "James K. Polk: A Study in Federal Patronage," *MVHR* 38 (1952): 613-52.
51. See Polk to Wright, Dec. 7, 1844, Wright to Polk, Dec. 20, 1844, in Ransom H. Gillet, *The Life and Times of Silas Wright* (2 vols., 1874), 2:1631-39.
52. Polk to B. F. Butler, Feb. 25, 1845, B. F. Butler to Polk, Feb. 27, 1845, JKP-LC; Polk to Marcy, March 1, 1845, WLM-LC; also Polk to Van Buren, March 1, 1845, MVB-LC.
53. Van Buren and Wright to O'Sullivan, March 14, 1845, MVB-LC; Wright to Polk, July 21, 1845, in Gillet, 2:1648-53. See also Hammond, *Wright*, ch. 17.
54. Ibid., p. 534.
55. See Garraty's excellent analysis, pp. 336-339.
56. Greeley to Schuyler Colfax, Jan. 22, 1846, Greeley-Colfax corr., NYPL. See also New York *Morning News*, Jan. 23, May 15, 22, 1845; Albany *Atlas*, Jan., Feb., 1846, passim; Albany *Argus*, May 6, 8, 9, 19, 1845; Donovan, pp. 67-70; Hammond, *Wright*, chs. 18-20.
57. Dix to Van Buren, March 27, 1846, MVB-LC; New York *Morning News*, May 22, 1845.
58. See Garraty, pp. 362-388.
59. Wright to Dix, Nov. 2, 1846, in Gillet, 2: 1721-1723. See also Hammond, *Wright*, ch. 22.
60. Albany *Atlas*, Dec. 8, 1846; Dix to A. C. Flagg, Nov. 9, 1846, ACF-NYPL. A county-by-county statistical correlation of the gubernatorial returns for 1844 and 1846 suggests extensive cross voting in the latter year, with neither Whigs nor Democrats maintaining their traditional areas of support. The coefficient of correlation (see statistical appendix) between Wright's 1844 and 1846 votes is only +.49. Normally, when party unity remains strong from election to election, one can reasonably expect a coefficient of +.80 or more. Sample counties indicate that the Whigs benefited most from this breakdown in Democratic solidarity.
61. The quotations are from Albany *Atlas*, Dec. 8, 1846. The articles ran from Dec. 4 to Dec. 10, 1846, and were reissued as a pamphlet (see copy in MVB-LC). See also Albany *Argus*, Nov. 19, 1846.

2. THE CONSCIENCE WHIGS

1. Quoted in Robert F. Dalzell, Jr., *Daniel Webster and the Trial of American Nationalism, 1843-1852* (1973), p. 85. Chs. 3 and 4 of this work contain excellent analyses of the Whig dilemma over annexation, as does Kinley J. Brauer's *Cotton versus Conscience: Massachusetts Whig Politics and Southwestern Expansion, 1843-1848* (1967).

2. For an introduction to this rich field, see Lois K. Mathews, *The Expansion of New England: The Spread of New England Settlements and Institutions to the Mississippi River* (1909); Harlan Hatcher, *The Western Reserve: The Story of New Connecticut in Ohio* (1966); and the various special political and intellectual studies cited below.

3. John L. Thomas applied this term specifically to nineteenth-century Republicans in Bernard Bailyn et al., *The Great Republic: A History of the American People* (2 vols., 1977), 2:867, 876. Many of its central concepts are found in Thomas's "Romantic Reform in America, 1815-1865," *American Quarterly* 17 (1965): 656-81.

4. See Alice Felt Tyler, *Freedom's Ferment: Phases of American Social History to 1860* (1944); David Brion Davis, "Some Themes of Counter-Subversion: An Analysis of Anti-Masonic, Anti-Catholic, and Anti-Mormon Literature," *MVHR* 47 (1960): 205-24. Unfortunately, no modern analysis of anti-Masonry is available.

5. See Boston *Courier*, Jan. 30, 31, 1845; Boston *Daily Advertiser*, Jan. 30, 31, 1845.

6. See Martin Duberman, *Charles Francis Adams, 1807-1886* (1961); David Donald, *Charles Sumner and the Coming of the Civil War* (1960); Frank Otto Gatell, *John Gorham Palfrey and the New England Conscience* (1963); Moorfield Storey and Edward Waldo Emerson, *Ebenezer Rockwood Hoar: A Memoir* (1911); Henry Wilson, *History of the Rise and Fall of the Slave Power in America* (3 vols., 1872-77), vol. 2; Ernest McKay, *Henry Wilson: Practical Radical* (1971).

7. R. C. Winthrop, quoted in Edward L. Pierce, *Memoirs and Letters of Charles Sumner* (4 vols., 1877-94), 2:356; C. F. Adams, diary, Sept. 24, 1845, AFP-MHS.

8. N. Appleton to C. F. Adams et al., Nov. 10, 1845, Appleton Papers, MHS; A. Lawrence to Adams, Nov. 14, 1845, in Adams, diary, Nov. 17, 1845, AFP-MHS.

9. C. F. Adams, diary, Nov. 17, 1845, AFP-MHS; Storey and Emerson, p. 43; Wilson, 2:115-18.

10. The best biography of Giddings is James B. Stewart, *Joshua R. Giddings and the Tactics of Radical Politics* (1970); see also George W. Julian, *The Life of Joshua R. Giddings* (1892).

11. See Albert G. Riddle, "The Rise of Antislavery Sentiment on the Western Reserve," *Magazine of Western History* 6 (1887): 145-56; John L. Hammond, "Revival Religion and Antislavery Politics," *American Sociological Review* 39 (1974): 175-86; Edgar A. Holt, "Party Politics in Ohio, 1840-1850," *Ohio Archaeological and Historical Publications* 37 (1928): 439-591, 38 (1929): 47-182, 260-402.

12. Holt, 38: 135-136; also A. Kellogg to J. R. Giddings, Jan. 12, 1844, JRG-OHS.

13. S. M. Gates to Giddings, Oct. 2, 1844, JRG-OHS; also E. Wade to Giddings, July 7, 1842, ibid.

14. Cleveland *Herald*, July 31, 1845.

15. Ashtabula *Sentinel*, Nov. 16, 1844.

16. Giddings to L. W. Giddings, May 10, 1846, GJP-LC.

17. See Glyndon G. Van Deusen, "Aspects of Whig Thought in the Jacksonian Period," *AHR* 64 (1958): 305-22; Richard N. Current, *Daniel Webster and the Rise of National Conservatism* (1955); Lynn L. Marshall, "The Strange Stillbirth of the Whig Party," *AHR* 72 (1967): 445-68; Paul Goodman, "Ethics and Enterprise: The Values of the Boston Elite, 1800-1860," *American Quarterly* 18 (1966): 437-51; Meyers, pp. 235ff.

18. *Messages and Papers of the Presidents*, 2:311.
19. Daniel Webster, *The Writings and Speeches of Daniel Webster* (18 vols., 1903), 4:116; Edward Everett, "Fourth of July at Lowell, 1830," in Daniel Walker Howe, ed., *The American Whigs* (1973), p. 26; Cleveland *Herald*, July 14, 1846. On progress, see Arthur A. Ekirch, Jr., *The Idea of Progress in America, 1815-1860* (1944); Goodman, "Ethics and Enterprise."
20. See Richard D. Brown, *Modernization: The Transformation of American Life, 1600-1865* (1976).
21. The literature on this concept is vast, but in general one should look at Perry Miller, *The Life of the Mind in America from the Revolution to the Civil War* (1965); John Reinhardt, "The Evolution of William Ellery Channing's Sociopolitical Ideas," *American Literature* 26 (1954): 157-65; Timothy L. Smith, *Revivalism and Social Reform: American Protestantism on the Eve of the Civil War* (1957); also see n. 22 below.
22. Springfield *Republican*, Nov. 28, 1846; Horace Mann, "The Necessity of Education in a Republican Government," in Howe, pp. 151, 149. The duality in the New England concept of man has been brilliantly suggested in Howe, *The Unitarian Conscience: Harvard Moral Philosophy, 1805-1861* (1970); see also Miller, "From Edwards to Emerson," in *Errand into the Wilderness* (1956), pp. 184-203.
23. Edward W. Emerson and Waldo E. Forbes, eds., *Journals of Ralph Waldo Emerson* (10 vols., 1909-14), 8:311, 7:12.
24. Adams, diary, Jan. 24, 1845, AFP-MHS; Sumner to Lord Morpeth, Jan. 1, 1844, in *Memoirs and Letters of Sumner*, 2:297.
25. John Gorham Palfrey, *Papers on the Slave Power* (1846), p. 29.
26. Charles Sumner, *Complete Works* (20 vols., 1890), 3:65, 81.
27. Ibid., p. 81; Ashtabula *Sentinel*, April 26, 1851 (also May 17, 1851).
28. Ashtabula *Sentinel*, Oct. 12, 1846.
29. Boston *Whig*, May 11, 1847.
30. Ibid., May 20, July 3, 1847.
31. S. C. Phillips, *An Address on the Annexation of Texas, and the Aspect of Slavery in the United States* (1845), p. 34; Palfrey, pp. 29, 3.
32. Ashtabula *Sentinel*, June 21, 1851.
33. Phillips, p. 35; see also Palfrey, p. 5; C. F. Adams, *Texas and the Massachusetts Resolutions* (1844), p. 6.
34. Adams et al., to S. P. Chase, June 25, 1845, SPC-LC; Adams, *Texas*, p. 46; Giddings to M. Giddings, June 19, 1842, GJP-LC.
35. Adams, diary, Feb. 2, 1844 (newspaper clipping), AFP-MHS; Palfrey to ministers of Massachusetts (clipping), ibid., Nov. 3, 1845; Wilson, 2:115.
36. Giddings to Calhoun, Dec. 2, 1842, JRG-OHS; Sumner, 1:157.
37. Jefferson to John Adams, Oct. 28, 1813, *Adams-Jefferson Letters* 2:389. See also Robert Rich, "A Wilderness of Whigs: The Wealthy Men of Boston," *Journal of Social History* 4 (1971): 263-76; Thomas H. O'Connor, *Lords of the Loom: The Cotton Whigs and the Coming of the Civil War* (1968); and the works in n. 1 and n. 17 above.
38. See Arthur B. Darling, *Political Changes in Massachusetts, 1824-1848* (1925).
39. See ibid.; Arthur M. Schlesinger, Jr., *The Age of Jackson* (1945), chs. 12, 13.
40. Sumner, 1:159; Adams, *Texas*, p. 47.
41. C. F. Adams, quoted in Charles F. Adams, Jr., *Richard Henry Dana* (2 vols., 1890), 2:68.
42. *Congressional Globe*, 29 Cong., 1 Sess., 15, Appendix: 643 (May 12, 1846).
43. Ashtabula *Sentinel*, July 13, 1846.
44. Ibid., March 22, 1847.
45. Cleveland *Herald*, July 16, 1846; A. G. Riddle to Giddings, July 4, 1846, JRG-OHS.
46. Chase to Giddings, Sept. 23, 1846, SPC-LC.
47. E. Wade, P. Hale, Dec. 13, 1847, JPH-NHHS.

48. Giddings to Greeley, Dec. 24, 1846, GJP-LC.
49. Adams, diary, July 3, 1846, AFP-MHS.
50. R. C. Winthrop to J. H. Clifford, May 14, 1846, RCW-MHS.
51. Boston *Whig*, July 16, 1846; *Memoirs and Letters of Sumner*, 3: 116-17.
52. Hayden to Winthrop, July 23, 1846, RCW-MHS; Winthrop to Sumner, Aug. 17, 1846, CS-HL. The episode is admirably treated in Donald, pp. 143-46.
53. Winthrop to Clifford, Sept. 9, 1846, RCW-MHS.
54. Boston *Courier*, Sept. 25, 1846; Adams, diary, Sept. 19, 1846, AFP-MHS.
55. See accounts of the convention in Boston *Courier*, Sept. 24, 25, 1846; Boston *Daily Advertiser*, Sept. 25, 29, 1846; Springfield *Weekly Republican*, Sept. 26, 1846; also, Donald, pp. 146-49.
56. Boston *Atlas*, Oct. 31, 1846; Adams, diary, Nov. 10, 1846, AFP-MHS.
57. Adams to Giddings, Dec. 16, 1846, JRG-OHS; Sumner to Lord Morpeth, Jan. 31, 1847, in *Memoirs and Letters of Sumner*, 3:139.

3. THE LIBERTY PARTY

1. The literature on abolitionism and its various facets is too vast for a thorough citation of sources. Of the more recent works, the best survey is James B. Stewart, *Holy Warriors: The Abolitionists and American Society* (1976), which contains an extensive bibliography. Good interpretive works which illuminate the philosophical and tactical divisions among abolitionists are Aileen Kraditor, *Means and Ends in American Abolitionism: Garrison and His Critics on Strategy and Tactics, 1834-1850* (1967); Ronald G. Walters, *The Antislavery Appeal: American Abolitionism after 1830* (1976); Lewis Perry, *Radical Abolitionism: Anarchy and the Government of God in Antislavery Thought* (1973); Richard H. Sewell, *Ballots for Freedom: Antislavery Politics in the United States, 1837-1860* (1976), chs. 1-4.
2. See Jane H. and William H. Pease, *Bound with Them in Chains: A Biographical History of the Antislavery Movement* (1972); Betty Fladeland, *James Gillespie Birney: Slaveholder to Abolitionist* (1955); Bertram Wyatt-Brown, *Lewis Tappan and the Evangelical War against Slavery* (1969); Ralph V. Harlow, *Gerrit Smith, Philanthropist and Reformer* (1939); Benjamin P. Thomas, *Theodore Weld: Crusader for Freedom* (1950).
3. J. G. Birney et al. to B. Green, July 11, 1838, Elizur Wright Papers, LC; E. Wright to Birney, Feb. 6, 1844, in Dwight L. Dumond, ed., *Letters of James Gillespie Birney, 1831-1857* (2 vols., 1938), 2:778.
4. T. D. Weld to Garrison, Jan. 2, 1833, in Gilbert H. Barnes and Dwight L. Dumond, eds., *Letters of Theodore Dwight Weld, Angelina Grimke Weld, and Sarah Grimke* (2 vols., 1934), 1:98; Amos A. Phelps, *Lectures on Slavery and Its Remedy* (1834), p. 154.
5. See Walters, ch. 1; David Brion Davis, "The Emergence of Immediatism in British and American Antislavery Thought," *MVHR* 49 (1962): 209-30; Stewart, *Holy Warriors*, chs. 2 and 3.
6. See Walters, pp. 5, 22; Stewart, *Holy Warriors*, ch. 4.
7. Chicago *Western Citizen*, July 21, 1846; L. Tappan to Birney, Tappan Papers, LC.
8. "Debate on Slavery," *Journal of the American Baptist Antislavery Convention*, 1 (1841): 76; E. Peabody to Hale, Jan. 15, 1845, JPH-NHHS. See also Wyatt-Brown, "Prelude to Abolitionism: Sabbatarian Politics and the Rise of the Second Party System," *JAH* 58 (1971): 316-41; Ronald P. Formisano, "Political Character, Antipartyism, and the Second Party System," *American Quarterly* 21 (1969): 683-709.
9. Birney et al. to Green, July 11, 1838, Elizur Wright Papers, LC.
10. Garrison, quoted in Walters, p. 13; see also Kraditor, pp. 158-159.
11. Kirk H. Porter and Donald B. Johnson, eds., *National Party Platforms, 1840-1860* (1961), pp. 4-8.

12. Cincinnati *Philanthropist*, May 8, 1844; Birney to W. E. Austin et al., Feb. 23, 1844, in *Birney Letters*, 2:790.
13. Birney, diary, April 19, 1842, Birney Papers, LC.
14. No modern critical biography of Chase exists; most works on him deal with the period after 1860. See Jacob Schuckers, *The Life and Public Services of Salmon P. Chase* (1874); Reinhard Luthin, "Salmon P. Chase: Political Career before the Civil War," *MVHR* 29 (1943): 517-40.
15. See Chase, diary, Feb. 13, 1844, Chase to L. Tappan, May 26, 1842, SPC-LC; Joseph G. Rayback, "The Liberty Leaders of Ohio: Exponents of Antislavery Coalition," *Ohio State Archaeological and Historical Quarterly* 57 (1948): 165-78.
16. Chase to [Giddings], Aug. 14, 1846, SPC-LC; Chase to Giddings, Feb. 9, 1843, GJP-LC; also Cincinnati *Philanthropist*, May 29, 1844.
17. Chase to Giddings, Jan. 21, 1842, JRG-OHS; Chase to L. Tappan, Sept. 24, 1842, SPC-LC; Bailey to Birney, March 31, 1843, in *Birney Letters*, 2:726.
18. Cincinnati *Philanthropist*, Dec. 25, 1844; circular, April 19, 1845, in SPC-LC; see also Boston *Emancipator*, July 2, 1845.
19. L. Tappan to B. Tappan, Jan. 4, 1845, L. Tappan Papers, LC; Birney, diary, April 19, 1842, Birney Papers, LC; also Boston *Emancipator*, May 14, 1846.
20. Analytical studies on the Constitution and slavery include Allan Nevins, "The Constitution, Slavery, and the Territories," *The Gaspar Bacon Lectures on the Constitution of the United States, 1940-1950* (1953), pp. 95-141; Jacobus ten Broek, *Antislavery Origins of the Fourteenth Amendment* (1951); Howard Jay Graham, *Everyman's Constitution* (1968), chs. 5-7; Mark DeWolfe Howe, "Federalism and Civil Rights," *Massachusetts Historical Society Proceedings* 77 (1965): 15-27; Robert Russel, "Constitutional Doctrines with Regard to Slavery in the Territories," *JSH* 32 (1966): 466-86; Arthur Bestor, "State Sovereignty and Slavery: A Reinterpretation of Proslavery Constitutional Doctrine, 1846-1860," *Journal of the Illinois State Historical Society* 54 (1961): 117-80.
21. William Goodell *Views of American Constitutional Law, in Its Bearing upon American Slavery* (1844), pp. 10-11.
22. Ibid., p. 12.
23. Ibid., p. 46.
24. Ibid., pp. 41, 49. On Article 4, see William M. Wiecek, *The Guarantee Clause of the U.S. Constitution* (1972).
25. Goodell, pp. 61, 59.
26. Ibid., pp. 84, 154, 152. See also Birney to J. Leavitt, et al., Jan. 10, 1842, in *Birney Letters*, 2: 645-56.
27. Cincinnati *Philanthropist*, April 23, 1845; See also Chase to L. Tappan, May 26, 1842, SPC-LC.
28. Salmon P. Chase, *An Argument for the Defendent, Submitted to the Supreme Court of the United States, at the December Term, 1845, in the Case of Wharton Jones vs. John Vanzandt* (1847); "Address to the Southern and Western Liberty Convention," in S. P. Chase and C. D. Cleveland, *Anti-Slavery Addresses of 1844 and 1845* (reprint, 1969), p. 81.
29. Chase's coworker in the case was William Henry Seward of New York. There is no evidence that the two collaborated in the drafting of Chase's appeal.
30. Chase, *Vanzandt*, pp. 93-94.
31. Ibid., pp. 83, 79.
32. Cincinnati *Philanthropist*, April 23, 1845.
33. Chase, *Vanzandt*, p. 84.
34. Ibid., p. 84.
35. Ibid., pp. 99-100.
36. Cincinnati *Philanthropist*, Jan. 22, 1845.
37. U. Seeley to Chase, Dec. 2, 1845, SPC-LC; W. Slade to Giddings, April 27, 1846, JRG-OHS; R. McMurdee to Chase, June 6, 1845, SPC-LC.
38. Q. F. Atkins to Chase, June 28, 1845, R. Errett to Chase, May 9, 1846, SPC-LC.

39.   Hale's life and politics are ably treated in Richard H. Sewell, *John P. Hale and the Politics of Abolition* (1965).
40.   G. W. Julian to I. Julian, Jan. 25, 1850, GJP-LC.
41.   A. Tuck to Hale, Jan. 15, 1845, JPH-NHHS. See also S. K. Lathrop to Hale, Jan. 16, 1845, J. A. Wiggins to Hale, Jan. 17, 1845, Jacob Ela to Hale, Feb. 3, 1845, ibid.
42.   See Joseph G. Rayback, *Free Soil: The Election of 1848* (1970), pp. 57-59; also Hale to Chase, April 3, 1846, SPC-HSP.
43.   Hale to J. L. Carlton, March 15, 1847, JPH-NHHS.
44.   Chase to Hale, Jan. 30, 1846, E. Loring to Hale, Sept. 9, 1846, ibid.
45.   T. Foster to Birney, Aug. 1, 1846, in *Birney Letters*, 2:1025; "Address of the Liberty State Convention," in Boston *Emancipator*, Aug. 12, 1846; Birney to T. Foster, March 27, 1847, in *Birney Letters*, 2:1041.
46.   See Kraditor, pp. 149-54.

4. THE WILMOT PROVISO

1.   *Congressional Globe*, 29 Cong., 1 Sess., 15:1217 (Aug. 8, 1846). See also Charles B. Going, *David Wilmot, Free Soiler* (1924). Brinkerhoff claimed coauthorship (Cincinnati *Philanthropist*, Oct. 14, 1846), although Going disputes this. See also Richard R. Stenberg, "Motivations of the Wilmot Proviso," *MVHR* 18 (1932): 535-41.
2.   See Chaplain W. Morrison, *Democratic Politics and Sectionalism: The Wilmot Proviso Controversy* (1967) for a detailed account of the congressional history of the Proviso, and a good analysis of the political problems it caused.
3.   King to Flagg, Jan. 18, 1847, ACF-NYPL; Quaife, *Polk Diary*, 2:75. See also Muller, "Preston King," ch. 14.
4.   Albany *Atlas*, Feb. 3, 1847; also Sept. 6, 1847.
5.   Wright to Dix, Jan. 19, 1847, in Gillet, 2:1915-21; also Wright to Dix, March 22, 1847, ibid., 2:1922-25.
6.   New York *Evening Post*, Nov. 8, 1847.
7.   Ibid., Aug. 6, 1847; Albany *Atlas*, Feb. 3, 1847. The free labor concept has been expertly handled in Foner, *Free Soil*, ch. 1.
8.   New York *Evening Post*, April 20, 1844, Aug. 6, 1847. See also Foner, "Racial Attitudes," and compare Eugene F. Berwanger, *The Frontier Against Slavery: Western Anti-Negro Prejudice and the Slavery Extension Controversy* (1967); James A. Rawley, *Race and Politics: "Bleeding Kansas" and the Coming of the Civil War* (1969).
9.   Chase, *Vanzandt*, p. 62.
10.   Ibid., pp. 63-67; see also Cincinnati *Philanthropist*, Oct. 14, 1846.
11.   Chase to [?], Feb. 15, 1847, SPC-LC. Barnburners shared these feelings; see Albany *Atlas*, Aug. 2, 11, 1847.
12.   See Cleveland *Herald*, April 28, 1847; Springfield *Republican*, Sept. 28, 1847.
13.   Sumner to T. Corwin, Sept. 7, 1847, CS-HL. See Dalzell, *Webster*, ch. 4.
14.   King to Flagg, Sept. 14, 1847, ACF-NYPL.
15.   Chase to Giddings, Oct. 20, 1846, SPC-LC.
16.   Boston *Emancipator*, June 16, 1847; Wade to Chase, July 7, 1847, SPC-LC; L. Tappan to Chase, June 23, 1847, L. Tappan Papers, LC.
17.   A. Jewett to Chase, June 7, 1847, SPC-LC; Chicago *Western Citizen*, May 11, 1847; Cincinnati *National Press*, June 30, 1847; Chase to Wade, June 23, 1847, SPC-LC.
18.   Z. Eastman to Hale, May 25, 1847, JPH-NHHS; Boston *Emancipator*, March 31, 1847.
19.   Boston *Emancipator*, June 16, 1847. See also Leavitt to Chase, June 5, Sept. 27, 1847, SPC-HSP; Cincinnati *National Press*, July 28, 1847.
20.   H. B. Stanton to Hale, July 6, 1847, JPH-NHHS.

21. Tuck to Hale, Aug. 2, 1847, Hale to L. Tappan, Oct. 12, 1847, ibid.; also Tuck to Hale, Sept. 10, 1847; Stanton to Chase, Aug. 6, 1847, SPC-LC.
22. In *Birney Letters*, 2:1047-57; see also Kraditor, *Means and Ends*, pp. 153-57.
23. Chicago *Western Citizen*, May 25, 1847.
24. See Stanton to Chase, July 17, Oct. 6, 1847, SPC-HSP; Stanton's article in Boston *Emancipator*, Sept. 1, 1847.
25. Boston *Emancipator*, Oct. 27, 1847. Full convention proceedings are in *National Era*, Nov. 4, 11, 1847.
26. *National Era*, Nov. 4, 1847; Bailey to Chase, Sept. 14, 1847, SPC-HSP.
27. See Rayback, *Free Soil*, ch. 3; Holman Hamilton, *Zachary Taylor: Soldier in the White House* (1951), ch. 5.
28. Cleveland *True Democrat*, Jan. 10, 1848. See also H. Wilson to Giddings, April 10, 1847, JRG-OHS.
29. See J. McLean to Chase, Dec. 22, 1847, SPC-HSP; Francis P. Weisenburger, *The Life of John McLean: A Politician on the United States Supreme Court* (1937).
30. *Congressional Globe*, 29 Cong., 2 Sess., 15, appendix: 237-46 (Feb. 11, 1847).
31. Adams to Giddings, Feb. 27, 1847, Wilson to Giddings, Feb. 24, 1847, Sumner to Giddings, July 28, 1847, JRG-OHS; Giddings to Greeley, April 16, 1847, GJP-LC.
32. Greeley to Giddings, April 24, 1847, JRG-OHS; Corwin to Sumner, Sept. 20, 1847, CS-HL; Corwin to Giddings, Aug. 18, 1847, Adams to Giddings, Nov. 2, 1847, JRG-OHS. See Norman A. Graebner, "Thomas Corwin and the Election of 1848: A Study in Conservative Politics," *JSH* 17 (1951): 162-80.
33. See Donald, *Sumner*, pp. 156-57; Kinley J. Brauer, "The Webster-Lawrence Feud: A Study in Politics and Ambitions," *The Historian* 29 (1966): 34-59.
34. Accounts of the convention are in Boston *Daily Advertiser*, Sept. 30, 1847; Springfield *Republican*, Sept. 30, 1847. See also Boston *Whig*, Sept. 29, 1846; Donald, pp. 157-59; Duberman, *Adams*, pp. 126-27.
35. Adams, diary, Sept. 29, 1847, AFP-MHS; see Boston *Whig*, Oct. 6, 9, 13, 16.
36. Wright to Dix, Jan. 19, 1847, in Gillet, *Wright*, 2:1915-21.
37. Albany *Atlas*, Feb. 3, 1847; also April 2, 1847.
38. Albany *Argus*, Jan. 22, Aug. 26, March 6, Aug. 27, 1847.
39. Wright to J. H. Titus, April 15, 1847, in Gillet, 2:1874-76.
40. See Rayback, pp. 15-18, 116-17; Frank B. Woodford, *Lewis Cass, The Last Jeffersonian* (1950), ch. 13.
41. See Garraty, *Wright*, ch. 17; J. L. Russell to Flagg, Aug. 27, 1847, ACF-NYPL; Albany *Argus*, Aug. 31, 1847.
42. Albany *Atlas*, Aug. 28, 1847; Flagg to Dix, Aug. 31, 1847, JAD-CU; Dix to Flagg, Aug. 30, 1847, ACF-NYPL.
43. Wright to T. M. Burt (copy), Aug. 22, 1847, ACF-NYPL.
44. See Albany *Atlas*, May 1, 3, 6, 14, 17, 20, June 2, 1847; King to Flagg, Sept. 14, 24, 1847, ACF-NYPL.
45. Albany *Atlas*, Sept. 2, 1847; also Sept. 11, 21, 1847; Albany *Argus*, Sept. 8, 1847.
46. Accounts of the convention are in Albany *Atlas*, Sept. 30, Oct. 1, 2, 1847. See also Ferree, "New York Democracy," pp. 60-83.
47. See Albany *Argus*, Oct. 1, 2, 4, 11, 1847, for justifications of this action.
48. Albany *Atlas*, Oct. 2, 1847; New York *Evening Post*, Oct. 8, 1847.
49. Flagg to Van Buren, Oct. 13, 1847, Van Buren to Flagg, Oct. 12, 1847, MVB-LC.
50. To Van Buren, Nov. 13, 1847, ibid.
51. Oct. 28, 1847; see also Albany *Atlas*, Oct. 12, 16, 27, 1847.

5. 1848

1. Cleveland *True Democrat*, March 1, 1848.
2. See Chase to Hale; April 29, June 20, 1848, JPH-NHHS.
3. See Chase to Giddings, Feb. 29, March 10, 1848, JRG-OHS.
4. Giddings to Chase, April 7, 1848, SPC-HSP. See also J. Brinkerhoff to Chase, March 28, 1848, ibid.; S. Lewis to Hale, March 29, 1848, JPH-NHHS.
5. See Stewart, *Giddings*, ch. 8; Donald, *Sumner*, pp. 160-62; Boston *Whig*, Dec. 16, 23, 29, 30, 31, 1847; Gatell, *Palfrey*, pp. 143-47.
6. Boston *Atlas*, Jan. 27, March 17, 1848; also *Memoirs and Letters of Sumner*, 3:148-49.
7. See Sumner to Giddings, Feb. 1, 3, 10, 11, 1848, Giddings to J. A. Giddings, Jan. 13, 1848, JRG-OHS; Boston *Whig*, Dec. 16, 23, 1847.
8. Sumner to Giddings, Feb. 3, 1848, Giddings to L. W. Giddings, Jan. 30, 1848, JRG-OHS.
9. Giddings to J. A. Giddings, May 7, 1848, ibid.
10. See Giddings to [?], April 5, 1848, ibid.
11. Adams to Giddings, Feb. 10, 1848, ibid.
12. See Ferree, "New York Democracy," ch. 3; Albany *Atlas*, Nov. 18, 22, Dec. 17, 18, 19, 1848; New York *Evening Post*, Feb. 19, 1848.
13. Albany *Atlas*, Feb. 21, 1848. Accounts of the convention are in ibid., Feb. 17, 18, 19, 1848; New York *Evening Post*, Feb. 19, 1848.
14. J. Van Buren to Van Buren, April 30, 1848, MVB-LC; see also Dix to Flagg, Feb. 3, 1848, ACF-CU.
15. Van Buren to J. Van Buren, May 3, 1848, MVB-LC; see also Van Buren to Blair, April 8, 1848, BFP-LC; Rayback, *Free Soil*, pp. 176-81; Rayback, "Martin Van Buren's Desire for Revenge in the Campaign of 1848," *MVHR* 40 (1954): 707-16.
16. Accounts of the convention are in Niles' *Weekly Register* 74 (Aug. 2, Nov. 22, 29, 1848): 69-88, 324-29, 348-49; also Rayback, *Free Soil*, ch. 11; Ferree, pp. 170-78.
17. See Rayback, *Free Soil*, ch. 11; Hamilton, *Taylor*, pp. 87-97.
18. Quoted in Wilson, *Slave Power*, 2:136.
19. McCormick, *Second American Party System*.
20. Stanton to Chase, June 6, 1848; S. Matthews to Chase, June 12, 1848, SPC-LC; Cincinnati *National Press*, June 28, 1848.
21. Albany *Atlas*, May 27, 1848; Flagg to M. Morton, June 19, 1848, ACF-CU.
22. Van Buren to Blair, June 22, 1848, BFP-LC; Van Buren to B. F. Butler et al., in *Proceedings of the Utica Convention . . . , June 22, 1848* (1848), pp. 9-14.
23. *National Era*, June 29, 1848; see also Ferree, pp. 200-207.
24. See Van Buren to Blair, July 26, 1848, BFP-LC; also Ferree, pp. 228-36.
25. An account of the convention is in Springfield *Republican*, June 29, 1848. See also Frank Otto Gatell's excellent "Conscience and Judgment: The Bolt of the Massachusetts Conscience Whigs," *The Historian* 20 (1959): 18-49.
26. Oliver Dyer, *Phonographic Report of the . . . National Free Soil Convention . . .* (1848), pp. 3-4. Other accounts are in Boston *Whig*, Aug. 12, 1848; Ashtabula *Sentinel*, Aug. 12, 1848; Henry B. Stanton, *Random Recollections* (3rd ed., 1887), pp. 162-64; Julian, *Political Recollections*, pp. 56-61. Good analyses are in Rayback, *Free Soil*, ch. 12; Frederick J. Blue, *The Free Soilers: Third Party Politics, 1848-1854* (1973), ch. 3; Sewell, *Ballots for Freedom*, ch. 7.
27. Sewell's analysis of this problem is quite good, and corrects Julian's (p. 58) assertion that the platform was drafted "without difficulty."
28. See Wilson, 2:150; Robert F. Lucid, ed., *The Journal of Richard Henry Dana, Jr.* (3 vols., 1968), 1:350-54.
29. *National Party Platforms*, pp. 13-14.
30. New York *Evening Post*, Sept. 21, Nov. 28, 1848. See also Albany *Atlas*, Oct. 3, 1848.

31.   Boston *Republican*, Aug. 24, 1848. See also Worcester *Massachusetts Spy*, Aug. 9, 16, 1848.
32.   Worcester *Massachusetts Spy*, Aug. 17, 1848. See also Chicago *Western Citizen*, Aug. 22, 1848.
33.   New York *Evening Post*, July 12, 1848; D. Wilmot, quoted in Going, *Wilmot*, pp. 174-75.
34.   See Sewell, *Ballots for Freedom*, pp. 176-85; Stewart, *Holy Warriors*, pp. 105, 119-20.
35.   See Blue, pp. 95-96.
36.   Dyer, pp. 31-32; *National Era*, June 29, 1848; see also Chase to McLean, Aug. 12, 1848, E. S. Hamlin to McLean, Aug. 17, 1848, McLean Papers, LC.
37.   See Dana, 1:352; Chase to J. W. Taylor, Aug. 15, 1848, Butler to Chase, Aug. 17, 1848, SPC-HSP; Wilson, 2:155-56.
38.   Dyer, pp. 27-28.
39.   Chicago *Western Citizen*, Aug. 29, 1848; Ashtabula *Sentinel*, Aug. 12, 1848.
40.   On organizational strategy, see Albany *Atlas*, Oct. 4, 1848. To compare this with the strategy of the Conscience Whigs, see Cleveland *True Democrat*, Aug. 22, 1848; Boston *Republican*, Sept. 21, 1848.
41.   See Albany *Atlas*, Sept. 15, 1848; New York *Evening Post*, Sept. 15, 16, 1848.
42.   See Boston *Republican*, Sept. 8, 1848; Gov. G. N. Briggs to Sumner, Sept. 1, 1848, CS-HL.
43.   S. Ford to Chase, July 29, 1848, SPC-LC. See also Cleveland *True Democrat*, Sept. 7, 1848; Ashtabula *Sentinel*, Sept. 23, Oct. 7, 1848.
44.   J. M. Niles to G. Welles, Oct. 29, 1848, Welles Papers, NYPL; see also Giddings to L. A. Giddings, June 20, 1848, GJP-LC; Rayback, *Free Soil*, pp. 277-78.
45.   See statistical appendix, below. See also Holman Hamilton, "The Election of 1848," in Arthur M. Schlesinger and Fred L. Israel, eds., *History of American Presidential Elections, 1789-1968* (4 vols., 1971), 2:865-920.
46.   King to Sumner, Dec. 25, 1848, CS-HL.

6. COALITIONS AND DIVISIONS

1.   Sumner to G. Sumner, July 31, 1848, in *Memoirs and Letters of Sumner*, 3:186.
2.   Giddings to B. Tappan, Nov. 17, 1848, B. Tappan Papers, LC.
3.   See the Columbus *Ohio Statesman*, Dec. 4, 1848, and the fully detailed description in Holt, "Party Politics in Ohio," 38:319-53.
4.   *National Era*, Jan. 18, 1849, provides a complete breakdown of Ohio Free Soilers and their past loyalties. See also J. C. Vaughn to Chase, Dec. 7, 1848, SPC-HSP.
5.   Giddings to T. Bolton, Nov. 14, 1848, JRG-OHS; also, Riddle to Giddings, Nov. 18, 1848, ibid.
6.   J. A. Briggs to Chase, Sept. 28, 1848, SPC-LC.
7.   See E. Nichols to Chase, Nov. 6, 1848, ibid.
8.   See N. Townshend to Chase, Dec. 5, 1848, SPC-HSP; *National Era*, Jan. 4, 1849.
9.   Ashtabula *Sentinel*, Jan. 13, 1849. See also *Ohio Statesman*, Dec. 8, 13, 1848; Chase to Mrs. Chase, Dec. 20, 1848, SPC-LC.
10.   Cleveland *True Democrat*, Dec. 6, 1848.
11.   See Nichols to Chase, Dec. 12, 13, 15, 18, 19, 1848, Chase to Mrs. Chase, Dec. 20, 1848, SPC-LC.
12.   *Ohio Statesman*, Dec. 21, 23, 1848; Ashtabula *Sentinel*, Dec. 23, 1848.
13.   See Holt, 38:357; Chase to Mrs. Chase, Dec. 30, 1848, SPC-LC. The platform is in Ashtabula *Sentinel*, Dec. 28, 1848.
14.   See Nichols to Chase, Dec. 21, 1848, SPC-LC; Hamlin to Chase, Jan. 18, 19, 20, 1849, SPC-HSP.

15. Cleveland *True Democrat*, Jan. 24, 1849; Riddle to Giddings, Jan. 15, 1849, JRG-OHS.
16. See Giddings to Chase, April 12, 1849, Hamlin to Chase, Jan. 17, 18, 1849, SPC-HSP.
17. Giddings to J. A. Giddings, Jan. 23, 1849, JRG-OHS; also Giddings diary, Jan. 2, 27, 1849, ibid.
18. See Matthews to Chase, Jan. 11, 1849, SPC-LC.
19. Cleveland *True Democrat*, Jan. 11, 1849.
20. *Ohio Statesman*, Jan. 22, 1849; Chase to Hamlin, Jan. 17, 1849, SPC-LC. Chase defended this course in a long letter to Giddings, Jan. 20, 1849, JRG-OHS.
21. Cleveland *True Democrat*, Feb. 1, 1849.
22. Giddings to J. A. Giddings, Feb. 4, 1849, JRG-OHS.
23. See Matthews to Chase, Jan 25, 1849, SPC-LC.
24. Cleveland *True Democrat*, Feb. 22, 1849. The revised Black Laws were summarized by the *National Era*, Feb. 22, 1849.
25. See Giddings to J. A. Giddings, Feb. 19, 1849, Giddings diary, Feb. 16, 1849, JRG-OHS.
26. *Ohio Statesman*, Feb. 23, March 1, 1849.
27. Giddings, diary, Feb. 23, 1849, JRG-OHS.
28. Riddle to Giddings, Feb. 21, 1849, ibid.
29. Cleveland *True Democrat*, Jan. 16, March 1, 1849. See also J. French to Riddle, March 6, 1849, Riddle Papers, WRHS.
30. Cleveland *True Democrat*, March 1, April 12, 1849.
31. Chase to Riddle, Feb. 24, 1849, Riddle Papers, WRHS.
32. Chase to Giddings, March 6, 1849, JRG-OHS.
33. Vaughan to Chase, Dec. 7, 1848, SPC-HSP.
34. See Ashtabula *Sentinel*, Dec. 2, 1849.
35. Cleveland *True Democrat*, June 27, 1849; Ashtabula *Sentinel*, March 24, 1849.
36. Townshend to Chase, May 3, 1849, SPC-HSP. Giddings tried hard to patch the split with Chase in the weeks following the election; see Giddings to Chase, March 14, 28, 1849, ibid.
37. See Chase to Giddings, April 28, 1849, JRG-OHS.
38. Giddings to Chase, April 12, March 14, 1849, SPC-HSP.
39. See Giddings to Chase, May 6, Aug. 10, 1849, J. Morse to Chase, Aug. 12, 1849, SPC-HSP.
40. See Holt, 38:376-83; Townshend to Chase, June 28, Oct. 16, 1849, SPC-HSP.
41. New York *Evening Post*, Nov. 8, 1848.
42. J. Van Buren speaking to the Utica convention, Sept. 14, 1849, reprinted in New York *Evening Post*, Sept. 15, 1849; ibid., Jan. 16, 1849.
43. See Ferree's detailed and excellent analysis, "New York Democracy," chs. 6 and 7.
44. See Albany *Atlas*, Jan. 1849; Albany *Argus*, Jan. 4, 5, 1849.
45. See Albany *Atlas*, Feb. 6, 1849; Albany *Argus*, Feb. 6, 7, 1849.
46. Albany *Atlas*, May 1, 1849; see also Albany *Argus*, April 18, 1849.
47. Albany *Argus*, May 17, 1849; See also Ferree, pp. 257-58.
48. Albany *Atlas*, June 5, 1849; Albany *Argus*, June 7, 1849.
49. Albany *Atlas*, June 3, 9, 1849. Pruyn's letter is in Albany *Argus*, May 17, 1849, and the official Barnburner reply is in New York *Evening Post*, July 5, 1849.
50. Albany *Argus*, June 18, 1849.
51. Albany *Argus*, Aug. 17, 18, 1849; Albany *Atlas*, Aug. 20, 1849; New York *Evening Post*, Aug. 17, 18, 1849. For the full report of the Rome convention, see *Proceedings of the Democratic and Free Democratic Conventions, Held at Rome on the 15th, 16th, and 17th Days of August, 1849* (1849).
52. See Spencer, *Victor and the Spoils*, pp. 188-89; Albany *Atlas*, Aug. 22, 1849.
53. See the reports in Albany *Argus*, Sept. 8, 1849; New York *Evening Post*, Sept. 7, 1849; Albany *Atlas*, Sept. 15, 17, 1849.

54. New York *Evening Post*, Sept. 15, 1849. See also Albany *Atlas*, Sept. 19, 1849; M. Van Buren to F. P. Blair, Sr., Oct. 9, 1849, BFP-LC.
55. Card in New York *Herald*, reprinted in Albany *Atlas*, Nov. 7, 1849; Van Buren to Blair, Dec. 11, 1849, BFP-LC. See also Ferree, pp. 299ff.
56. Sumner to Chase, Sept. 18, 1849; Chase to [Morse?], Oct. 26, 1849, Sumner to Chase, Sept. 25, 1849, SPC-LC.

7. COMPROMISE AND DISSENT

1. See Allan Nevins, *Ordeal of the Union* (2 vols., 1947), 1: ch. 7; Hamilton, *Taylor*, ch. 7; Hamilton, *Prologue to Conflict: The Crisis and Compromise of 1850* (1964).
2. See Robert W. Johannsen, *Stephen A. Douglas* (1973), chs. 11-13.
3. See Dalzell, *Webster*, ch. 5; Hamilton, *Prologue to Conflict*, ch. 3; Glyndon G. Van Deusen, *The Life of Henry Clay* (1937), ch. 14.
4. Edward Everett to Winthrop, Feb. 1, 1850, RCW-MHS.
5. See Blue, *Free Soilers*, ch. 7; Stewart, *Giddings*, pp. 179-88; Julian, *Political Recollections*, pp. 72-73.
6. See Hamilton, *Prologue to Conflict*, pp. 41-42; Blue, pp. 191-96; Winthrop to J. H. Clifford, Dec. 3, 1849, RCW-MHS.
7. *Congressional Globe*, 31 Cong., 1 Sess., part 1: 2 (Dec. 3, 1849).
8. Ibid., 19 (Dec. 12, 1849).
9. Ibid., 21 (Dec. 12, 1849).
10. Julian, *Political Recollections*, pp. 74-78.
11. *Congressional Globe*, 31 Cong., 1 Sess., part 1: 65-66 (Dec. 21, 1849).
12. Dalzell, ch. 5.
13. *Writings and Speeches of Daniel Webster*, 10:57-99.
14. Sumner to Jay, March 13, 1850, in *Memoirs and Letters of Sumner*, 3:213; Albany *Atlas*, March 9, 1850; New York *Evening Post*, March 11, 1850.
15. Boston *Atlas*, April 4, 1850; Winthrop to Clifford, March 10, 1850, RCW-MHS.
16. Julian, *Political Recollections*, p. 93; *Congressional Globe*, 31 Cong., 1 Sess., appendix: 105-07 (Feb. 15, 1850).
17. *Congressional Globe*, 31 Cong., 1 Sess., appendix: 1127 (Aug. 12, 1850).
18. Hamilton, *Taylor*, ch. 31; Hamilton, *Prologue to Conflict*, pp. 106-9; Dalzell, pp. 201-9.
19. Johannsen, pp. 294-98; Hamilton, *Prologue to Conflict*, chs. 8-9.
20. Adams to Julian, Sept. 14, 1850, GJC-LC.
21. Van Buren to Blair, Feb. 9, 1850, BFP-LC.
22. Albany *Atlas*, April 24, 1850; New York *Evening Post*, June 27, 1850; Albany *Atlas*, July 11, 15, 1850.
23. See Ferree, "New York Democracy," p. 327.
24. Quoted in Spencer, *Victor and the Spoils*, p. 190.
25. See Ferree, pp. 314ff.
26. See New York *Evening Post*, June 17, 20, 1850.
27. Albany *Argus*, June 20, 1850; New York *Evening Post*, Aug. 13, 1850.
28. Ferree, pp. 337-46; Albany *Atlas*, March 15, 1850; Albany *Argus*, March 28, 1850.
29. Albany *Atlas*, Sept. 14, 1850. Accounts of the convention are in ibid., and in New York *Evening Post*, Sept. 12, 13, 14, 16, 1850; Albany *Argus*, Sept. 16, 1850.
30. Albany *Atlas*, Sept. 14, 1850.
31. New York *Evening Post*, Sept. 14, 16, 1850; Albany *Atlas*, Oct. 1, 1850.
32. New York *Evening Post*, Oct. 5, 1850.
33. Sumner to Mann, Sept. 20, 1849, in *Memoirs and Letters of Sumner*, 3:183. For a general discussion of Massachusetts politics in this period, see W. G. Bean, "Party Transformation in Massachusetts, with Special Reference to the Antecedents of Republicanism, 1848-1860" (Ph.D. diss., Harvard University, 1922).

34.   See Gatell, *Palfrey*, ch. 12; E. R. Hoar to Palfrey, June 29, 1849, Sumner to Palfrey, Aug. 31, Sept. 13, 1849, Palfrey Papers, HL.
35.   Adams to Giddings, Jan. 27, 1850, JRG-OHS; Dana, *Journal*, 1:391 (Oct.. ?, 1849). See Duberman, *Adams*, pp. 158-62.
36.   See Boston *Republican*, Feb. 23, 24, June 23, 1849; McKay, *Wilson*, pp. 59-62.
37.   See Donald, *Sumner*, ch. 8.
38.   Sumner to Chase, Sept. 18, 1849, SPC-LC. On the election, see Boston *Atlas*, Nov. 15, 1849. See also Duberman, p. 162; McKay, pp. 60-62.
39.   Everett to Winthrop, March 14, 1850, Winthrop to Clifford, March 10, 1850, RCW-MHS.
40.   See David Van Tassel, "Gentlemen of Property and Standing: Compromise Sentiment in Boston, 1850," *New England Quarterly* 28 (1950): 307-19.
41.   Sumner to Wilson, Sept. 9, 1850, in *Memoirs and Letters of Sumner*, 3:223. See also Donald, pp. 186-87. Free Soilers in central and western Massachusetts were eager for a coalition (see Worcester *Massachusetts Spy*, Oct. 16, 1850).
42.   See Boston *Daily Advertiser*, Nov. 15, 1850; Boston *Atlas*, Nov. 14, 1850.
43.   See McKay, pp. 61-68.
44.   Mann to Sumner, Aug. 31, 1850, Sumner to Mann, Jan. 11, 1851, Mann Papers, MHS; Sumner to Palfrey, Oct. 15, 1850, Palfrey Papers, HL.
45.   Morton to F. Robinson, May 11, 1849, Morton Papers, MHS; Everett to Winthrop, Dec. 4, 1850, RCW-MHS. See also Sumner to Mann, Jan. 22, 1851, Mann Papers, MHS; Morton to B. French, Nov. 22, 1850, Morton Papers, MHS; and Morton's *Letter Addressed to the Free Soil and Democratic Member of the Legislature of Massachusetts* (Jan. 18, 1851).
46.   Adams, diary, Sept. 22, 1851, AFP-MHS; Howe to Palfrey, Feb. 13, 1851, Palfrey Papers, HL. Palfrey's circular is reprinted in Boston *Atlas*, Jan. 8, 1851. See also an anti-coalition card, signed by Hoar, Dana, et al., in Boston *Daily Advertiser*, Oct. 12, 1850.
47.   Adams, diary, Dec. 27, 1850, AFP-MHS. See McKay's excellent analysis, pp. 69-73.
48.   See Boston *Atlas*, April 23, 1851; Boston *Commonwealth*, April 25, 1851; Donald, pp. 189-204.
49.   Boston *Daily Advertiser*, April 25, 1851.
50.   See Duberman, pp. 176-77; Gatell, pp. 196-200.
51.   Morton to J. Van Buren, Feb. 17, 1852, Morton Papers, MHS.
52.   Adams to F. W. Bird, Oct. 9, 1851, Charles Sumner Bird Collection, HL.

8. "THE WORK IS TO BE DONE OVER"

1.   Chicago *Western Citizen*, April 24, 1849, March 11, 1851.
2.   Chase to G. Smith, Sept. 13, 1851, SPC-LC; Chase to Townshend, Aug. 2, 1851, SPC-HSP; Stanton to Chase, Sept. 23, 1850, SPC-LC.
3.   Chicago *Western Citizen*, April 8, 1851.
4.   Townshend to Chase, Sept. 23, 1850, SPC-HSP; see also Hamlin to Chase, Jan. 10, 28, Feb. 10, 1850, ibid.
5.   See Ashtabula *Sentinel*, April 13, 1850, April 26, 1851; Townshend to Chase, May 5, 1850, SPC-HSP.
6.   Cleveland *True Democrat*, May 8, 1850. See Stewart, *Giddings*, pp. 198-99.
7.   Chase to Giddings, Oct. 22, 1850, JRG-OHS. See Ashtabula *Sentinel*, Oct. 14, 1850.
8.   Giddings to J. A. Giddings, Dec. 16, 1850, JRG-OHS.
9.   Chase to [Townshend], Dec. 13, 1850, Hamlin to Chase, Dec. 6, 1850, SPC-HSP.
10.   See Hans L. Trefousse, *Benjamin Franklin Wade: Radical Republican from Ohio* (1963), ch. 5.

11. Ashtabula *Sentinel*, Mar. 22, Sept. 27, 1851. See also Trefousse, pp. 67-71.
12. Giddings to Chase, April 3, Aug. 12, 1851, SPC-HSP.
13. See Ashtabula *Sentinel*, July 5, 1851; Stewart, *Giddings*, pp. 200-201.
14. See L. W. Hall to Chase, May 7, 1851, Chase to [Leavitt?], Aug. 12, 1851, Taylor to Chase, April 22, 1851, SPC-LC.
15. See *National Era*, Sept. 11, 1851.
16. Vaughan to Chase, Sept. 16, 1851, Taylor to Chase, Sept. 5, 6, 1851, SPC-LC.
17. Chase to D. W. H. Brisbane, Sept. 15, 1851, SPC-HSP.
18. See Sumner to Giddings, Sept. 11, 1851, JRG-OHS; Ashtabula *Sentinel*, Sept. 27, Oct. 4, 1851; Wyatt-Brown, *Tappan*, p. 331; Stewart, *Giddings*, pp. 203-5.
19. New York *Evening Post*, Aug. 15, 1851; Albany *Atlas*, Oct. 9, 1851.
20. See Spencer, *Victor and the Spoils*, pp. 196-97.
21. See New York *Evening Post*, Sept. 11, 12, 13, 15, 1851; Albany *Argus*, Sept. 13, 1851; Ferree, "New York Democracy," pp. 391-400.
22. Sumner to J. Bigelow, Oct. 24, 1851, in *Memoirs and Letters of Sumner*, 3:255.
23. Sumner to Parker, April 19, 1851, in ibid., 3:246.
24. Dana, *Journal*, 2:412 (Feb. 15, 1851). See also Nevins, *Ordeal*, 1:385-90.
25. See Stanley W. Campbell, *The Slave Catchers: Enforcement of the Fugitive Slave Law, 1850-1860* (1968), ch. 3.
26. See Dalzell, *Webster*, ch. 8; Roy F. and Jeanette Nichols, "The Election of 1852," in Schlesinger and Israel, eds., *History of American Presidential Elections*, 2:919-1003.
27. Mann to Parker, Aug. 10, 1852, Mann Papers, MHS.
28. New York *Evening Post*, June 23, 1852; Van Buren to Blair, June 16, 1852, BFP-LC. See also King to Flagg, Sept. 30, 1852, ACF-CU; Ferree, "New York Democracy," pp. 448-62.
29. Chase to Hamlin, June 28, 1852, SPC-LC.
30. Tappan to Giddings, June 17, 1852, JRG-OHS.
31. Chase to Hamlin, July 19, 1852, SPC-LC; *National Era*, March 3, 1852.
32. On the Pittsburgh convention, see Stewart, *Giddings*, pp. 214-16; Blue, *Free Soilers*, pp. 239-48; Julian, *Political Recollections*, pp. 122-24.
33. See Chase to Hale, Aug. 7, 1852, Giddings to Wilson, Sept. 3, 1852, JPH-NHHS; Chicago *Western Citizen*, Feb. 3, 1852; Wyatt-Brown, pp. 331-32.
34. On Julian, see Patrick W. Riddleberger, *George Washington Julian, Radical Republican: A Study in Nineteenth-Century Politics and Reform* (1966), esp. pp. 85-87. See also his letter accepting the nomination (to Henry Wilson, n.d., Julian Papers, Indiana State Library [draft], which "repudiate [d] the separation of morals from politics."
35. See Blue, p. 243.
36. *National Party Platforms*, pp. 18-20; see also L. Tappan to Chase, June 23, 1852, SPC-LC.
37. Chase to Hamlin, Aug. 13, 1852, SPC-LC.
38. See Julian's entertaining account, pp. 124-28; Sewell, *Hale*, pp. 148-49.
39. See Wyatt-Brown, pp. 331-32; Riddleberger, pp. 86-88; McKay, *Wilson*, pp. 79-80; Stewart, *Giddings*, pp. 215-16; Blue, pp. 251-54.
40. See statistical appendix. Also, Nichols and Nichols, "The Election of 1852."
41. Ashtabula *Sentinel*, Aug. 7, 1852; *National Era*, Dec. 2, 1852.
42. McKay, pp. 80-81; Stewart, *Giddings*, pp. 222-23; New York *Evening Post*, Jan. 14, Mar. 31, 1853; Donald, pp. 238-49.

INDEX

Adams, Charles F., 36, 45, 50, 56, 154, 160, 161, 163, 165, 166, 180, 185, 189, *passim*
Albany Regency, 9, 10
Allen, Charles, 37, 159
Allen, William, 128, 129
Antislavery League, 86, 87
Appleton, Nathan, 38

Bailey, Gamaliel, 61, 67, 68, 179
Bird, Francis W., 160, 165
Birney, James G., 61, 66-69, 79
Black laws (Ohio), 132, 134-135, 139, 169
Blacks, Attitudes toward, 21, 46-48, 84, 116, 117
Blair, Francis P., Sr., 19, 124
Booth, William, 150
Bouck, William C., 27
Boutwell, George S., 162, 166
Briggs, James A., 130
Brinkerhoff, Jacob, 81, 124
Bryant, William C., 141, 155
Butler, Benjamin F., 10, 118

Calhoun, John C., 10, 20, 23
Cass, Lewis, 24, 94, 96, 107, 122, 123
Chaffee, Nathaniel, 133, 135, 140
Chase, Salmon P., 67-69, 72-76, 84, 86-91, 101, 102, 108, 112, 118, 129-141, 150, 168-173, 178-180, 183-185, 189, *passim*
Clay, Henry, 9, 24, 34, 149, 151
Clinton, DeWitt, 16

Cobb, Howell, 150, 151
Compromise of 1850, 149-155, 188
Constitution and slavery, 71-76
Corwin, Thomas, 92, 93
Crosswell, Edwin, 27, 143, 144
Cushing, Caleb, 163, 165

Dana, Richard H., Jr., 160, 175
Democratic Convention, (1844) 25, 26; (1848) 107; (1852) 176, 177
Dickinson, Daniel S., 27, 30, 143, 144, 146, 157
Dix, John A., 10, 30, 121, 142, 143
Douglas, Stephen, 148, 149, 154
Durkee, Charles, 150

Eastman, Zebina, 63, 88, 167, 168

Field, David D., 98
Fillmore, Millard, 154, 176, 177
Flagg, Azariah C., 10, 25, 97, 98, 142
Ford, Seabury, 121, 128
Free Soil Convention, (1848), 111-119; (1852) 179, 180
Fugitive slave act (1850) 149, 174, 175, 176

Garrison, William L., 3, 36, 60, 63, 64
Giddings, J. A., 47
Giddings, Joshua R., 39-41, 53-56, 93, 103, 104, 128-141, 149, 150, 153, 169-173, 178-181, 183, 185, 189, *passim*
Goodell, William, 70-72, 89, 173

Greeley, Horace, 3

Hale, John P., 77, 78, 88, 89, 102, 118, 119, 122, 150, 179, 181, 182
Hamilton County, Ohio, 128-141
Hammond, Jabez, 18, 24, 26, 30
Henshaw, David, 121
Hitchcock, Reuben, 133
Hoar, E. R., 37
Howe, J. W., 149
Howe, Samuel G., 37
Hunter, W. F., 150

Julian, George W., 4, 150, 151, 179

Keyes, E. L., 160, 165
King, Preston, 10, 33, 81, 97, 142, 149, 150, 177, 181

Lawrence, Abbott, 36, 94
Leavitt, Joshua, 89, 115, 116
Leggett, William, 14
Liberty League, 89

Mann, Horace, 44, 150, 162, 177, 181
Marcy, William L., 9, 27, 29, 143, 145, 146, 156, 157, 174
McLean, John, 92, 118, 135
Morse, John, 131-134, 137, 141
Morton, Marcus, 121, 124, 163, 165

Niles, John M., 122

O'Sullivan, John L., 14, 15, 17

Palfrey, John G., 36, 46, 50, 103, 160, 163, 165, 185, 186
People's Convention (1848), 102, 104, 108
Phillips, Stephen C., 37, 48, 49, 119, 121, 160
Pierce, A. N., 131
Pierce, Franklin, 176, 177, 181, 182
Polk, James K., 25, 29, 80, 81
Pugh, George, 131

Riddle, Albert G., 132-134, 136, 137
Root, Joseph, 149, 153
Runyan, George, 131

Scott, Winfield, 176, 177, 181, 182
Seymour, Horatio, 143, 145, 146, 157, 158, 174
Shannon, Wilson, 130
Smith, Gerrit, 61, 79, 89, 90, 173, 179-181
Spencer, O. M., 131
Sprague, William, 149
Stanton, Henry B., 89-91, 118, 168
Sumner, Charles, 37, 56-59, 103, 152, 160-164, 168, 175, 181, 183, 185, 189, passim

Tappan, Arthur, 61
Tappan, Lewis, 61, 63, 87, 90, 91, 173, 178, 181, 186
Taylor, Zachary, 91, 107, 122, 123, 148, 152, 153
Throop, Enos, 17, 18
Tilden, Samuel J., 10
Townshend, Norton S., 131-134, 137, 139, 141
Tuck, Amos, 77, 89, 150, 151
Tyler, John, 8, 20, 23

Van Buren, John, 10, 97, 98, 100, 106, 118, 143, 146, 156, 158
Van Buren, Martin, 9ff, 16, 24, 99, 106, 107, 109-111, 118, 119, 123, 155, 177, passim
Vanzandt case, 73-76, 113

Wade, Benjamin F., 170, 171
Webster, Daniel, 34, 85, 94, 151, 152, 154, 176, 177, passim
Whig Convention, (1848) 107; (1852) 176
Wilmot, David, 33, 81, 116, 150, 151, 181
Wilson, Henry, 37, 47, 48, 160, 161, 164, 165, 168, 179
Winthrop, Robert C., 38, 56, 57, 102, 103, 150-152, 163, 164
Worcester Convention (1848), 108, 111
Wright, Silas, 9, 23, 28, 30-32, 82, 95, 96